THE WESTERN FRONT

Irish Voices from the Great War

THE WESTERN FRONT

Irish Voices from the Great War

WILLIAM SHEEHAN ～

Gill & Macmillan

Gill & Macmillan
Hume Avenue, Park West, Dublin 12
with associated companies throughout the world
www.gillmacmillan.ie

© William Sheehan 2011
978 07171 4786 1

Index compiled by Cover to Cover
Typography design by Make Communication
Print origination by O'K Graphic Design, Dublin
Printed and bound in the UK by MPG Books Ltd, Cornwall

This book is typeset in 12/15pt Minion.

All photographs are supplied by courtesy of the Royal
Irish Fusiliers Museum

The paper used in this book comes from the wood pulp
of managed forests. For every tree felled, at least one
tree is planted, thereby renewing natural resources.

A CIP catalogue record for this book is available from the
British Library.

5 4 3 2 1

CONTENTS

To Ireland's patriot dead, 1914–1918
And to the Regimental associations who have worked
so hard to get their memory alive

ACKNOWLEDGEMENTS

This book would not have been possible without the vision of Fergal Tobin at Gill & Macmillan, who has supported the idea from its inception. I would also like to thank Deirdre Rennison Kunz and Jennifer Patton at Gill & Macmillan, both of whom have been a tremendous help. I must also thank my agents, Paul and Susan Feldstein of The Feldstein Agency, who have been a great help to me on this and other projects.

I would like to thank the ever professional staff at the Imperial War Museum Department of Documents and at the Imperial War Museum Photograph Archive. I also wish to thank the staff at the Special Collections Department, University of Leeds Library, for their help. Thank you to Amanda Moreno of the Royal Irish Fusiliers Museum for her invaluable assistance. All the photographs in this book appear courtesy of the Royal Irish Fusiliers Museum. This book would not have been possible without the assistance of these institutions.

Thank you to my partner, Rachel MagShamhráin, for her patience with me on this and indeed many other projects.

I want to thank the copyright holders of the following papers who have given permission for the personal papers and memoirs of their relatives to be included in this work: Brennan, Burgoyne, Crowe, Davies, Germain, McCarthy, McIlwain, Rixon and Trefusis. Every effort has been made to find the copyright holders of the other papers used.

William Sheehan
July 2011

AUTHOR'S NOTE

This book has sought to retain the original voices of the officers and soldiers whose personal papers and memoirs comprise the bulk of the book. Some of the accounts here were written during the events; others are recollections written long after the war. This means that tenses can vary, and later events can be mentioned side by side with a previous one, but it was felt that the texts reproduced should be preserved here as closely to the originals as possible. However, spellings, especially some placenames, and technical terms within the texts have been standardised so as not to distract or confuse the reader. Any additions or explanations made in the text are bracketed as follows: [ ].

The extracts have been arranged by year and in an order which I hope engages the reader. This has meant that not every event during the years in question is ordered chronologically, but is rather organised in themes, such as arrival in France, life behind the trenches, life in the trenches and the experience of combat. The intention is to allow readers a comparative framework in which to understand the experiences of Irish soldiers in France. Where an account touches on a major incident or battle, I have identified it, but I have left most as they were in the personal papers. (A glossary of battles is included for reference.) A list of abbreviations is provided at the start of the book to guide readers who may be unfamiliar with British military acronyms. Ranks and units have been changed for each officer and soldier as they were promoted or changed unit.

The stories in this book are drawn from the remaining accounts in British archives, and regrettably do not cover every regiment, but the London Irish and Tyneside Irish have been included. Some of the accounts are from non-Irishmen serving in the Irish regiments, yet their accounts also throw a light on the experiences of the Irish on the Western Front.

ABBREVIATIONS

AIF	Australian Imperial Force
ANZAC	Australian & New Zealand Army Corps
ASC	Army Service Corps
BATT	Battalion
BATTN	Battalion
BDE	Brigade
BEF	British Expeditionary Force
BN	Battalion
Capt	Captain
C GDS	Coldstream Guards
CO	Commanding Officer
COL	Colonel
COY	Company
CPL	Corporal
CQMS	Company Quartermaster Sergeant
CSM	Company Sergeant Major
DCM	Distinguished Conduct Medal
DIV	Division
DIVL	Divisional
DSM	Distinguished Service Medal
DSO	Distinguished Service Order
GDS	Guards
GG	Grenadier Guards
GHQ	General Headquarters
GIB	Gibraltar
GOC	General Officer Commanding
Gordons	Gordon Highlanders
GREN	Grenadier
GSO	General Staff Officer

Herts	Hertfordshire Regiment
HQ	Headquarters
LIR	London Irish Rifles
L&NW Railway	London and North Western Railway
Lt	Lieutenant
MC	Military Cross
MG	Machine Gun
MGC	Machine Gun Corps
MM	Military Medal
MO	Medical Officer
NCO	Non-Commissioned Officer
NZ Brigade	New Zealand Brigade
OC CO	Officer Commanding Company
OTC	Officers Training Camp
PS	Penal Servitude
PTE	Private
RA	Royal Artillery
RAF	Royal Air Force
RAM	Royal Artillery Museum
RAMC	Royal Army Medical Corps
RASC	Royal Army Service Corps
RE	Royal Engineers
RFA	Royal Field Artillery
RFC	Royal Flying Corps
RGA	Royal Garrison Artillery
RIF	Royal Irish Fusiliers
RIR	Royal Irish Regiment
RMC	Royal Military College
RSM	Regimental Sergeant Major
RSPCA	Royal Society for the Prevention of Cruelty to Animals
SA	South Africa
Sgt	Sergeant
SR	Special Reserve
SS	Shrapnel Shell
UVF	Ulster Volunteer Force
WAAC	Women's Auxiliary Army Corps
YCV	Young Citizens Volunteers
YMCA	Young Men's Christian Association

INTRODUCTION

For the first time in history we have today a huge Irish Army in the field. Its achievements have covered Ireland with glory before the world, and thrilled our hearts with pride. North and South have vied with each other in springing to arms, and please God, the sacrifice they have made side by side on the field of battle will form the surest bond of a united Irish nation in the future. We have kept our word. We have fulfilled our trust. We have definitely accepted the position and undertaken the obligations of a self-governed unit amongst the nations which make up the Empire.

JOHN REDMOND, Leader of the Irish Parliamentary Party

It is common now in Ireland to argue that those who fought in the First World War from Ireland did so out of some spirit of adventure or that they joined the British Army out of financial necessity. But there is a third reason, unspoken due to the substantial discomfort it would cause to the carefully crafted nationalist and republican mythologies of the Irish Free State and later of the Republic of Ireland. A profound sense of imperial patriotism led many to join. Redmond's call was answered by a generation steeped in the values of constitutional nationalism, a generation which sought something that should long have been granted, and indeed granted with far more generosity than the British establishment appeared willing to give—an Irish parliament. As a generation they fought for their country to become an independent self-governing nation—like Australia, Canada, New Zealand and South Africa—within the British Empire.

Irish commerce depended on the British Empire. Many in Ireland had close relatives throughout the Empire, especially in the Dominions, countries indeed to which many in the Ireland of the time still wished to emigrate and build their future. Imperial service created opportunities for Irishmen of all creeds and classes in its administration and defence. As with their Australian, Canadian, New Zealand and South African cousins, a sense of imperial identity in no way diminished or diluted each country's profound sense of its own national identity or destiny.

Yet in Ireland after 1922, this past had to be re-written. Indeed, one of the unique features of popular Irish history over much of the life of the Irish state has been the absence of popular or state interest in the First World War. This historical amnesia was carefully cultivated, and Ireland's involvement in the war the focus of an active forgetting. The idea of Irishmen gladly serving a 'British' Empire and dedicated to its cause was too subversive to be indulged by a state that needed to legitimate its own existence. Yet it remains a fact that never before or since have so many Irishmen served together in uniform or fought such a war.

Over the last few years, efforts have been made by many to redress this, and this book hopes to continue that tradition. This work has sought not to replicate the many fine works that have recently emerged and are listed in a bibliography at the end of the book; rather it has sought to free from archives in the United Kingdom the voices of officers and men who served in the Irish regiments, both Northern and Southern, in the First World War. The goal is to give readers an insight into the experiences, thoughts, hopes and fears of those who served. It seeks to take the reader back to the world of the Western Front from 1914 to 1918, and to allow them to understand, and hopefully empathise with, the men. It attempts to take the reader through the experience of enlistment and training, of life behind and in the trenches, and of the battles fought and losses mourned. This book is about the experiences of ordinary Irishmen in an extraordinary and terrible war. It is my hope that the stories herein will bring the reader closer to a generation who sacrificed a great deal for their country, and indeed some gave their all for Ireland.

Ar dheis Dé go raibh a n-anamacha dílse.

| 1914

On 4 August 1914, the German Empire invaded Belgium, and the British Government declared war on Germany. The German Army based their combat operations on the Schlieffen plan, and swept through Belgium and into Northern France. The British Expeditionary Force (BEF) had begun to arrive in France from early August and began to co-operate with the French Army in their efforts to protect Northern France. The force included many of the regular Irish battalions, such as the 4th (Royal Irish) Dragoon Guards, the 5th (Royal Irish) Lancers, the 2nd Royal Munster Fusiliers, the 1st Irish Guards, the 2nd Connaught Rangers, the 2nd Royal Irish Rifles and the 2nd Royal Irish Regiment, with the 2nd Royal Inniskilling Fusiliers arriving at the end of August. Many of the other Irish battalions were on imperial service. Indeed the first shot in anger by the BEF was fired by Corporal Edward Thomas of the 4th (Royal Irish) Dragoon Guards on 22 August outside Mons.

The Allied forces however could not hold back the German Army, and were forced to make a fighting retreat, which resulted in battles at Mons (24 August) and at Le Cateau (26 August). On 27 August, the 2nd Royal Munster Fusiliers arguably undertook the single greatest action by Irish arms in the twentieth century when they fought off far superior German numbers at Étreux to cover the retreat of the 1st Division. The action led to the loss of most of the battalion, a fate the 2nd Munster would experience several times during the War.

The tide turned for the Allied forces at the Marne (5–12 September) when the German advance was halted and pushed back, setting the stage for the trench warfare that would dominate the Western Front for the next five years.

Private David Starrett
9TH BATTALION, ROYAL IRISH RIFLES

> Yes, the lads of Ulster in 1914 were ready to fight. We were the Ulster Volunteer Force of Carson's Army. But little did we think we were drilling to fight not our own countrymen but the Germans.

Sergeant McIlwain
CONNAUGHT RANGERS

> The smell of the turf fire smoke as I got out of the station and the bustling and noisy crowds busy on market day. It was the same loveable old Galway.

Lieutenant C.A. Brett
3RD BATTALION, CONNAUGHT RANGERS

> My mother got me to write to the War Office seeking a commission in the Connaught Rangers, of which her friend Ford-Hutchinson was the Colonel of the 1st BN, and this I did, pointing out to it that I had served for almost four years in the Officers Training Corps at school (which I greatly enjoyed). I went to Dublin early in October and sat my exams (miraculously satisfactorily), staying in the Provost's House where Dr Traill was lying ill. He died before the end of the month. Immediately on my return I received my Commission by post, with orders to buy myself a uniform and necessary kit (including bed and bedding) and report to the 3rd BN, the Connaught Rangers at Kinsale, County Cork.

Private A.R. Read
'A' COMPANY, LONDON IRISH RIFLES

All along the roads people were making a great fuss of the troops. At one halting place a coster came along with a barrowload of fruit and tipped everything among us and asked a policeman to take his barrow and then he enlisted. Cigarettes, chocolates, beer, lemonade and tea was supplied by everyone and although it was gladly accepted it soon began to make us feel uncomfortable and several chaps fell out. We halted at Elstree and made ourselves comfortable in some fields. Being August it was very warm weather and sleeping under the stars was lovely. Next morning on the road again early. The sun came out and we soon began to sweat, and our Regimental Band (which was composed of mostly middle-aged men) got fed up with playing so some of them let the big drum roll down a hill and it got smashed up. This was reported to the Colonel who to punish them gave orders that they were to play, but the row they made was simply awful and after all the boys 'cut up rough' the so called music stopped. Besides this Band we had a 'Bag Pipe Band' (at this time I think the only Territorial Band of Irish Pipers).

Lieutenant C.A. Brett
3RD BATTALION, CONNAUGHT RANGERS

I got to know my companions and roommates and spent hours off duty discussing drink, sex, and other matters about which it became clear that many of them knew much more than I did. It would not have been hard. Many new recruits were coming in every day; more than 700 joined us from the Falls Road, Belfast, alone. The barracks were very overcrowded, few of the men had uniforms or rifles, and squads in civilian clothes drilled daily with us in the Square.

Private A.R. Read
'A' COMPANY, LONDON IRISH RIFLES

In all there were about 20,000 troops. Here we started training in earnest. Bayonet fighting, firing practices, night operations, drills, route marching (which by stages [got] to 25 miles every Saturday morning), also physical drills and running exercises, Sunday being reserved for church parades at St Alban's Cathedral or leave. Every man was medically examined and if unfit was sent away and others took their places, while we all had to sign forms agreeing to serve overseas.

Private David Starrett
9TH BATTALION, ROYAL IRISH RIFLES

Things were topsy-turvy, nothing good save the grub. 'Acting' Sergeants came round half a dozen times a day to ask your name. I doubt if some could spell their own. ...The first two–three days was Babel. My! It was a picnic. Others as well as myself did not know what they belonged [to], so roamed together in and about the camp.

Lieutenant J.H. Butler
5TH BATTALION, ROYAL IRISH RIFLES

When the war began I was called up at once and hurried off to Belfast. I was just a few days over 17 then. I was very young indeed and knew nothing of the Army. I had been in the OTC at Haileybury but that was all. Fortunately the 5th BATTN RIR was filled up with recruit officers like me, though I was the youngest. We did some concentrated training and gradually began to know something of what was expected of us. My first independent job was to be in charge of the guard on water works near Lisburn at Stonyford. I had bought a Douglas motorcycle and was retuning one night to my guard when I hit an unlighted cart and knocked myself out. I was in hospital for a few days and then went back to the Battalion.

Being so young I was left in Belfast while the other subalterns went off with draft to France. I was furiously jealous and thought I would never get out to the war.

Lieutenant C.A. Brett
3RD BATTALION, CONNAUGHT RANGERS

In the early days at Kinsale I learned much. A guest night was held in Mess every Thursday night, at which we drank the toast to the King (in port, marsala, or sherry at 7d a glass) when there was a certain amount of horseplay and quite a lot of drink drunk. There I learned how to behave and how to drink. I got very drunk once and was violently sick and was heartily ashamed of myself and decided it was not worth it, though I always gladly drank my drink in moderation. In this connection I remember Christmas Day 1914. Colonel Lewin had to go the rounds of the various men's and sergeant's Messes before lunch on Christmas morning. There were 22 in all; at each he had to drink half a tumbler or more of whiskey. In consequence he was quite unable to bite his little finger when half round, but he did the complete round and was then put to bed by his wife.

Private A.R. Read
'A' COMPANY, LONDON IRISH RIFLES

Besides ourselves there were another Brigade of Territorials composed of the 'North and South Staffords'; also 'Lincoln Regiments'. These chaps were mostly miners and used to go to their trench-digging by train, carrying nothing except an overcoat and haversack. This they used to remind us of, and as a further taunt started a stunt of pinching cap badges. Then the fun started. Free fights were all over the town every night and it was quite the thing to walk out with an entrenching tool handle (a stick about 14 inches long) tucked up a sleeve, and soon the Guard Room was full up, also the Hospital, but I think that we let them see that 'Cockneys' could do their share when it came to a scrap, and nearly all of us had a cap badge of theirs as a memento of the 'Battle of Braintree'.

Private David Starrett
9TH BATTALION, ROYAL IRISH RIFLES

We did not fare badly with our officers, though they had their faults, but whilst detecting the faults of their men, those like Captains Gafficken, Membry and Crozier hid their own.

Lieutenant C.A. Brett
3RD BATTALION, CONNAUGHT RANGERS

I was shortly sent to Dollymount, Dublin on a month's course of machine gunnery, which pleased me very much. But it had its problems. Dollymount golf course had been converted into Ireland's first School of Musketry, and this was the first course to be held. We lived and messed in the golf club house, and the club secretary was in charge of catering for which he charged 5/6d a day. Fair enough, but my pay was 5/3d a day. I was told that after the course I could claim ration allowance, but in the meantime I had to find the money to pay my Mess bills, and money was so short that for a time I was unable to afford to take a train into Dublin. However, I greatly enjoyed the course and passed out as a first class instructor of Maxim and Vickers guns. When I got back to Kinsale I was told I had been appointed Battalion machine gun officer and I was given an excellent reservist sergeant (Sgt Mulrooney) and about 30 hand-picked men. This was a splendid job, as no-one but me knew anything whatever of machine guns, and I had to teach my men from scratch.

Private David Starrett
9TH BATTALION, ROYAL IRISH RIFLES

Ballykinlar was a dismal hole, nothing but sandhills hemmed in by Dundrum bay ... But it was in that dismal hole our boys were really trained to be one of the best fighting brigades in France.

Private J.L. Stewart Moore
12TH BATTALION, ROYAL IRISH RIFLES

We had a tremendous send-off from Ballymoney Station—half the countryside seemed to have gathered on the platform to say goodbye. There was great emotion and loud cheers as the train pulled out. There was a sort of feeling in the air that Clandeboye was only the first stage and perhaps we would be in Berlin by Christmas; the war could not last longer and we were all keen to get into it before it was over.

Arriving in Belfast we marched across from the Northern

Counties to the County Down station and thence to Bangor. When we got to Clandeboye we found everything ready, the tents had been pitched and adequate preparation made, no shortage of essential food, water or blankets and no confusion, a great achievement on the part of those responsible especially when one remembers that there were four battalions in the camp, comprising in all about four thousand men. These battalions were the 11th Rifles from South Antrim, the 12th Rifles from North Antrim, the 13th Rifles from County Down and the Royal Irish Fusiliers from County Armagh. Together they formed the 108th Brigade. Our company was drawn from the Ballymoney, Portrush, Bushmills, Ballycastle area, was commanded by Sidney Lyle of Ballycastle, Miss Boyd's estate agent. The majority were working class lads who had left school at the age of twelve and had never been away from home before, never slept out of the family bed.

Lieutenant C.A. Brett
3RD BATTALION, CONNAUGHT RANGERS

I fear I did not attend Church [Kinsale] often. The Battalion was 99% Roman Catholic, and the Church of Ireland Church parade, which I took a few times, was not stronger than 9 or 10 men and 3 or 4 officers. It was a strict regimental custom that the entire Battalion of all denominations should attend Mass in state, band playing and colours flying, on St Patrick's Day, and I of course went and enjoyed myself. Later in the summer of 1915 there was a mission in Kinsale Chapel run by a Jesuit which I and several others attended every night for a week and found it very good.

Private David Starrett
9TH BATTALION, ROYAL IRISH RIFLES

The woman question occurred only on Sundays, hundreds flocking from Belfast, some good wives, some not so good, and the others. The cooks had orders to well feed the visitors. My! The roast joints. The crowding and the fun in the dining tents. After a good tuck-in away to the sandhills—many a tale those dunes could tell if they could only speak. Some of the females had not quite got over their ruffling when tea was ready.

Private J.L. Stewart Moore
12TH BATTALION, ROYAL IRISH RIFLES

Our training in the UVF before the war stood us in good stead. We were not raw recruits but men who knew how to drill and march. We also had the help of a number of non-commissioned officers called up from the Reserve who had been sent over from England by the War Office to assist in our training and provide the stiffening which the War Office thought necessary. We had a particularly nice man from a London suburb called Sergeant Golding; he had served in the South African War. We had another advantage over the other Divisions of Kitchener's Army then being formed—the stores accumulated in Belfast by the UVF were immediately made available so that we received uniforms and equipment straight away without the long delays experienced by other Divisions.

Private David Starrett
9TH BATTALION, ROYAL IRISH RIFLES

I remember the Scotland Road district for one thing particularly, that started unpleasantly. It is one of the Catholic quarters of Liverpool, like Falls Road in Belfast, and there's no love loss between the faiths. A crowd of men, young and old, at the corner commented on my badge, one shouting, 'the bloody hand of Carson'. They pressed around and I wondered, being alone, what was best to be doing. But no hand was laid on me, though for a bit I thought there would be. From shouting we fell to talking and presently some of them accompanied me to the office, saying up to now no one told them we recruited Catholics as well as Protestants. So that was that, and afterwards we had many Scotland Road men.

Private J.L. Stewart Moore
12TH BATTALION, ROYAL IRISH RIFLES

During my years in Trinity I had enjoyed many arguments and debates on politics and religion as well as other topics including of course the burning question of Home Rule. Now at Clandeboye I found myself in a camp of four thousand men where no such debates were possible because everyone thought exactly alike;

patriotic and Protestant fervour was at its height. All had signed the Ulster Covenant and all were out to win the war. Even the non-commissioned officers sent over from the Reserve in England were invited to sign and I think most of them did so. The tents were decorated, many of them with Union Jacks and Orange emblems and at night the overflowing enthusiasm of the men found its outlet in song. For the first week or so I went to sleep every night to the strains of Orange ditties such as:

'Come back to Ireland those who are over the sea,
Come back to Ireland and fight for her liberty,
They are flying the flag, the harp without a crown,
So come back to Ireland and keep popery down.'

Captain Gerald Burgoyne
4TH BATTALION, ROYAL IRISH RIFLES

At dinner a man rushed in to say a soldier had just cut his throat on the fo'c's'le—I was in command on board so I rushed out. Found the starboard side of the fo'c's'le running with blood and a man of the Northumberland Fusiliers lying in it. Amid cries of 'He's gone!' 'No he ain't,' 'Ah! Poor fellow, 'es dying' and other cheery remarks. I forced my way into the crush around him. Had a horrid jag in his throat, in which I could see his windpipe, but that wasn't severed. The drizzling rain eventually brought him round and he was carried off the ship crying for his mother. Did it with a Government Jack Knife. Probably have succeeded if he'd used a steel blade! Jolly start for active service, and on a Friday too!

Captain John Trefusis
1ST BATTALION, IRISH GUARDS

It is a perfectly glorious day today, and this morning I saw what I think a wonderful sight. The Germans were shelling a French aeroplane high up in the air. The sun was brilliant, the sky dark blue, and the burst of shrapnel from six guns one after the other; at first you saw one small puff of white, then another, then heard the explosions of the first as the puff gradually got bigger and whiter, and so till all six had burst, leaving great thick white puffs gradually getting larger, while the aeroplane sailed away as if nothing had happened. It was a wonderful sight, and an artist might make a very striking picture of it.

Captain Gerald Burgoyne
4TH BATTALION, ROYAL IRISH RIFLES

Mud everywhere, and ankle deep near camp, and our camp wasn't fit to walk in with gum boots. Put our men 14 to 15 in a tent. Calverly and I got a tent to ourselves, and found a rough bunk there, for which we were charged two francs a day, robbery, as we were only in a Government Hospital tent, ate off a rough deal table, with the commonest of cutlery, and not enough of that either, and put up with rations. Someone was making a bit.

Private William Barry
AUSTRALIAN IMPERIAL FORCE

Spud Murphy and a few of his comrades crept onto a farm house one day unseen and hearing a woman screaming, crept in and up the stairs, only to find four Germans and a young girl in a room. When the Germans found out the British soldiers were in the house, they held up their hands and said, 'Mercy, Comrades.' Spud said, 'Sure we gave them mercy and drove our bayonets through the lot of them.' These were only a few of the tales that the heroes of the Retreat from Mons had to tell.

Captain John Trefusis
1ST BATTALION, IRISH GUARDS

Orders to be prepared to move at an hour's notice came just after breakfast, about 8 am. One of the mails we have missed came in today, and got boots from Peal, puttees, watch, etc, and a parcel from Fortnum and Mason. There was an open air service at 10.30, but I could not go, as I was on a Court Martial. A good many French soldiers passed through here last night. All Territorials and fine looking, medium aged men. Their officers all look like bank clerks, and it is the lack of them that the French Army is suffering from. We expect to be off soon, but in what direction we can't say. The people in this town speak a mixture of French and Flemish, very difficult to understand. They have also very harsh voices.

Second Lieutenant Neville Woodroffe
1ST BATTALION, IRISH GUARDS

We continue to hold this position, the other side of the Aisne, and have been entrenched now for over sixteen days. One is beginning to feel the reaction after all our previous marching and we are longing to be on the march again. This is really the first time we have been in the same position for more than one day. It is in some way a rest after our previous excursions but we are shelled all day long and have occasional fusillades at night. We take turns to relieve one another, and one day we are in the trenches, and the other day are in reserve.

There has been more fighting and more loss of life, crowded into seven weeks, than there was in the whole of South Africa. It is awful what the Brigade of Guards have lost, and being like one big regiment one knows everyone and feels it all the more.

Captain Gerald Burgoyne
4TH BATTALION, ROYAL IRISH RIFLES

Heard some of our troops had been looting a bit on the Aisne, but that is put down with an iron hand, and six men of a certain Corps, caught looting and 'other things' at the Base, have been shot. At Harve some English troops broke open a lot of cases lying on the quay, Xmas gifts for the troops and looted eighty plum puddings.

Captain John Trefusis
1ST BATTALION, IRISH GUARDS

Up at 4 am and our march orders came at 4.45 while we were having breakfast. They were, that we were to march to Ypres, and drive in the enemy wherever met. We left B [Bethune] at 6.35 am, a cold misty morning, but good for marching in. One of the signs of winter approaching was that some of the cows had sacks on their backs to keep them warm. Sounds of firing became ever more distinct. Between Vlamertibbe and Ypres an ever increasing stream of refugees passed us. Men, women, and children of all kinds and description. All the women had terribly haunted expressions on their faces, and that perhaps more than anything else I have seen made one realise the horrors of war. We halted at Ypres for about five hours, and then moved into billets at St J. about two miles out. We are now quite close to the fighting and 3 Battalions of the Brigade have gone out, and we alone remain in reserve and expect to go out at any moment. Many French troops passed us today, nearly all Territorials and for the most part away from the fighting. There is a certainty of fight tomorrow. One hears of the Germans advancing and burning everything as they come.

Captain Gerald Burgoyne
4TH BATTALION, ROYAL IRISH RIFLES

Arrived at Bailleul where we detrained; a guide met us who seemed uncertain about the way. Over awful cobble stones we marched 6 miles to Locre; there I heard the 2nd Battalion were in the trenches, and I was sent a further 2½ miles to some huts at West Outre. Arrived there in the dusk, fagged out all of us. My NCOs not of great use, except one Sergeant whose name I forget; harangued them in discipline; told them I could not be bother with petty crime; they must make their men obey them, how I did not care; and that I would back them up in all they did. Ten minutes later a miserable corporal runs up to me, 'Please Sir, Rifleman X has his rifle loaded and he won't unload it, and all the men's afraid of him.' I went back to Rifleman X, and without a word punched him twice under the jaw, told him luridly to unload his rifle, and the thing was done.

Captain John Trefusis
1ST BATTALION, IRISH GUARDS

Started this morning from Densil, and rode to Soupin where Headquarters, 4th Brigade, are. On the way we had coffee at 2nd Division Headquarters. We were told to be careful on the way as if the Germans saw many horses together they would be certain to shell us. Unfortunately a batch of remounts caught us up and we had three or four shells amongst us in less than no time, and all the horses stampeded. Francis Scott was knocked off his horse, but not much hurt. Having arrived at Headquarters about 10 we were taken up to the Battalion which was holding a line of trenches, on top of a flat topped hill just outside a wood. One or two German were sniping at us and one of our men was wounded this morning. I found all in the best of spirits and delighted to see us, in spite of the fact that Guernsey, Arthur Hay and Bernes had all been killed on Monday. The first two by Germans up trees. They did not live long afterwards I am glad to say. Guthries and Hugo Gough were both wounded the same day, and the latter lost an arm.

Captain John Trefusis
1ST BATTALION, IRISH GUARDS

The high explosive shells are most terrifying, but if one keeps well in a trench they do not do much harm. They went on firing these shells till 8 pm sometimes singly and sometimes the universal, which has three bursts. Many fell within a few yards of us but did no harm. In the afternoon the CO and I walked all round our trenches and up to those of the Light Infantry on our left. We walked right out in front and passed David Bingham's grave. There were many dead Germans lying out in front, and it is difficult to see when they will get buried.

When we got the hill we are on at present the Germans tried a sort of counter attack and drove cattle in front of them and the whole place is littered with dead cows and smells most unpleasantly.

Second Lieutenant Neville Woodroffe
1ST BATTALION, IRISH GUARDS

We had a small patrol out in front of our trenches yesterday and it was awful to see the massacres and refuse which a wood to our left disclosed. Dead Germans and a few of the Wiltshire regiment, which had been there fully a fortnight ago, unburied and in terrible conditions—legs, stuck in boots, lay out in the open and corpses shattered from shell fire lay at short intervals. Kits and rifles, ammunition, helmets, boots, etc, all lay in heaps. The stench was awful. We buried what we could, but most one could not touch.

Captain John Trefusis
1ST BATTALION, IRISH GUARDS

When I got back to my Headquarters I found a letter from the Brigade Major saying that as our billets in the town had been left in such a dirty state the General had ordered us to stay in the trenches another night, i.e. three nights altogether. The Coldstreams had complained about it; we don't complain about them as we have every reason to do, but simply set to work and clean up their mess. One would have thought this sort of thing would not have gone on on active service. However, we shall know in the future. The men will never forget it and it will make for bad feeling I fear.

Sergeant McIlwain
CONNAUGHT RANGERS

At sunrise, to our disgust, ordered to retire from our beautiful trenches. Retiring all day. Dropping from the want of sleep. I had been away from the Army; that I held the rank of sorting clerk and telegraphist in the Post Office; that only twenty days before I was working in Newcastle; whereas now, I reflected, looking down at my dirty and sun-burned hands, it was as if I had never been away from the service, this kind of manoeuvring and in the company of these Irish lads I had known so long.

Captain John Trefusis
1ST BATTALION, IRISH GUARDS

I cannot describe my feelings at having no friends here, when only a few days ago, there were 25 of us, and all such a happy family. It is too sad. I sincerely hope we shall be relieved from the trenches tonight. We have been in them day and night for 15 days and it is a very great strain on the officers and men.

Captain Gerald Burgoyne
C COMPANY, 4TH BATTALION, ROYAL IRISH RIFLES

From 3.30 to 4.15 pm the French and our artillery bombarded Wyschaete and the German lines round them. In the growing gloom the gunfire burst out below us and about a mile or rather less to our front; over Wyschaete and all along the ridge to the south of it, there is a cloud of little white puff balls, each burst heralded by a flare like the spark which comes from the top of an electric tram arm occasionally.

Captain John Trefusis
1ST BATTALION, IRISH GUARDS

The best night I have spent, I think, as I did not get up till 7. Then we began to hear the bands of the Germans in our front playing. The tune was 'God save the King', also some hymn tunes, so I suppose they were having a church parade.

After breakfast we received an order to advance and to send out patrols to clear up the situation. As far as per immediate front is concerned we know the situation perfectly, as the moment anyone puts his head over his trench he not only gets fired on by rifle fire, but generally gets three or four rounds of shrapnel as well. About 11.30 am heavy firing began, both rifle and shrapnel, the cause of it being the Leinsters on our right trying to send out some patrols covered by the fire of our right company. They could not make much headway and we were forced to lie down.

Captain Gerald Burgoyne
C COMPANY, 4TH BATTALION, ROYAL IRISH RIFLES

Forty of my men are in immediate support of the trenches in dug-outs; things so filthy in muck and mud that no farmer, however callous, would sty a pig in any of them. I slept with the remainder of my men in the loft, some in a filthy cellar, the rest divided among half a dozen tiny rooms and cupboards and in the kitchen and tap-room (for the farm was also an estaminet) where I lay down amongst them on some barely clean straw. I had no blankets and got but little sleep. My feet, mud up to my knees, and my puttees caked as in a plaster cast, just froze, and I lay and prayed for the dawn. The fields around here are a sea of slimy clayey mud, smothered with shell holes, some half as big as our 'pond', full of water, into which, if you are not careful, you slide, and generally stick, till some man lifts you out again.

Captain John Trefusis
1ST BATTALION, IRISH GUARDS

Up at 1.45 am and marched off to relieve the 2nd Gren Guards in the trenches. We went round the position and all got into their trenches by 5 am, and then a certain amount of sniping began and a few shells came over. The whole place is very dirty, the weather wet, and one is simply covered in mud with nothing to change in. I can't complain as I have only just come out. The Battalion has been here a week.

Second Lieutenant Neville Woodroffe
1ST BATTALION, IRISH GUARDS

We were in action the day before yesterday. We got in a wood with the Coldstreams and were surrounded by Germans. The wood was very thick and the enemy was no less than a hundred yards off at times. We lost considerably. Of the nine officers, three of whom only can be accounted for, the CO was wounded but through no one had heard where. The 2nd in command was killed. Six others are missing.

Captain John Trefusis
1ST BATTALION, IRISH GUARDS

The Gunners have been making some very good shooting today and driven the enemy out of several trenches. It is most interesting to watch our shells bursting over their trenches. And to see the Germans run out of them, so I hope they are getting a real good doing. But in spite of this, their trenches are getting nearer.

Captain Gerald Burgoyne
C COMPANY, 4TH BATTALION, ROYAL IRISH RIFLES

I am told that one company of this battalion on the Aisne was surrounded and were all shot down. The last to go was a Sergeant who put up his hands to surrender, but though he was hit in three places, the brutes bayoneted him. A body of some 400 Germans tried to surrender in a body about this time, and some regiment turned a machine gun on them; the next day they had to tell a fatigue party to bury their bag, so we got a bit of our own back.

Captain John Trefusis
1ST BATTALION, IRISH GUARDS

From 2 pm onwards we have been under a very heavy fire from big German guns, and they have been pitching shells on top of the cave and all around. It has been a most unpleasant experience and very nerve-wracking although it has not done any very material damage as far as I can tell. The Germans are certainly wonderful gunners. An aeroplane came over this morning, and they got the range here in a very short time. A furious fusillade started at 9 pm which lasted till 10 pm. The Germans lit us up with star shells and searchlights.

Captain Gerald Burgoyne
C COMPANY, 4TH BATTALION, ROYAL IRISH RIFLES

At dawn this morning two unwounded Gordons hopped into our trenches. These two men and two others badly wounded had crept into an old French fire trench, some seventy yards in front of our line, and lain there since Monday morning (14th) not daring to come out, as they had lost all sense of direction and did not know where our trenches lay. Starving and drenched the two unwounded men, thinking they heard Irish voices, chanced it and came over. Four of my men very pluckily at once jumped over the parapet and went to the two badly wounded men, taking them some hot tea and food, but the Jocks refused to allow themselves to be brought in then, preferring to wait another day in the cold until nightfall. Our fellows brought in two other wounded who were lying in front of them.

Captain John Trefusis
1ST BATTALION, IRISH GUARDS

Stepney, my CO, went out at 7 am and I heard at 1 pm that it was thought he had been shot. He had been very much depressed for the last two or three days, and told me that without relief he could not stand it much longer. He also felt responsible for some of our losses, which really had nothing whatever to do with him. I send out to see if he could be found after dark, and they found him between the regiment on our left and the enemy, quite dead, with bullet wounds in his head and chest.

Private Frank Germain

ROYAL IRISH FUSILIERS

Lots of our boys got killed outright. It was then we knew we were fighting. We got it hot and heavy all day and night. Next was, the front line of the Germans had to be taken. Then [nothing] for it, we pulled together. Started on a dark morning, up and over the top, right into the enemy line, sticking as we went, firing shot and shell till we landed in the German line.

Captain John Trefusis

1ST BATTALION, IRISH GUARDS

Bullets were coming into the town and the enemy were bursting shrapnel in the town. I went to the Brigade Office after turning out the Battalion, for orders. Companies were sent to various points, and all was carried out in perfect order. The firing by this time had become furious and when I had taken two companies down a road and given them orders I went back to Brigade Office under the cover of a wall. The Brigadier was standing outside quite calm, bullets flying about from enemy machine guns, and shrapnel. He, Brigade Major and I stood together. I did not like it a bit, but in half an hour's time, the firing slackened and at 9 am, my Battalion was told to return to its billets and the attack was repulsed.

Private Frank Germain

ROYAL IRISH FUSILIERS

St Eloi. Well, this battle started on the 13th of Feb at 3.30 in the afternoon. It was raining heavy. The Germans started to shell us, and he shelled the village. The 1st BN Leinsters were all in the line at the time. They got it heavy and lost a lot of chaps, and they could not stick the fire as it was too much, and they retired back to another trench. Then the Germans came over and took our line. The Leinsters lost 3 trenches.

Captain John Trefusis
1ST BATTALION, IRISH GUARDS

Our line was fairly dug in, and at 7 am the enemy began the most terrific bombardment with guns of every calibre. Not a house within a range of three of four miles was left untouched, and the incessant roar went on all day, shells dropping within a very few yards of our dug-out. We had many casualties amongst them. Coke killed, Francis Scott, Kingston, and Fergusson wounded. About 4 pm, the Battalion on our left gave way, and with considerable difficulty we bent back the left of our line and got a fairly good one. Eventually we regained our original line. Shelling went on till 11 pm and as it was a very bright moonlight night, only the reserve companies could get teas, although we managed to get supplies to all. I think this was one of the worst days I ever spent, both with anxiety as to what was going to happen, and the great strain on one's nerves to say nothing of want of food. The Grenadiers were relieved by the French during the night, but we had to remain in our trenches. No one in the front line could put their heads up over their trenches, without a bullet coming at it. Casualties, I think about 40 officers and 50 to 60 men.

Major E.H.E. Daniell
2ND BATTALION, ROYAL IRISH REGIMENT

For ten days I was unable to wash and take off my clothes or get a complete wash, and I had to keep on the same wet boots for 5 days. My bullet wound in the leg has not quite healed up as it should have done. We had no doctor with us, and probably a little bit of dirt went into it with the bullet; it is now being taken in hand and will be well in a day or two.

Captain John Trefusis
1ST BATTALION, IRISH GUARDS

We began an attack at that hour [5.30 am], but could not get very far as the enemy were prepared in their trenches. We got rifle fire from every direction, and a man had his leg broken within two yards of me by a bullet. The enemy was very active all day and so were we, but we could not advance although it was attempted by two brigades. We suffered considerably, losing our Medical Officer, a very fine man killed, and about 70 or 80 killed and wounded, including those killed by one shell the day before. I hope we did as much if not more damage. We got many orders today, once to resist a desperate counter attack, supposed to be about to be commenced by the enemy, then to be prepared to assist another brigade who were going to advance, and then to hold our ground. We had been digging all day, no sleep or food for at least 36 hours, so we were rather fatigued.

Captain John Trefusis

1ST BATTALION, IRISH GUARDS

Every day much as another, very heavy shelling all day with the enemy occasionally seen in front. They are trying desperately to break through our lines, and we are desperately trying to prevent it.

Captain John Trefusis

1ST BATTALION, IRISH GUARDS

All was quiet till 1 pm when a terrific bombardment began, which lasted for an hour. Shells of every description burst on our support trenches, where I was, and within a few yards of us, and the effect on one was awful. About 2.15 we got a message to say that the French on our immediate right were retiring. This meant that our right flank would be in the air. We pushed up some supports, and I was sent to report to the Brigadier. By this time a hail of bullets were also coming over from hostile maxims, and my walk was anything but pleasant. The Brigadier told me some cavalry would be immediately sent to our support. I made my way back to my Battalion and saw the French running in all directions, and learnt that the enemy had got on to our right flank and turned it. I ran back with the news to the Brigadier, and then began to try and get back to my Battalion. I was met by streams of men coming back and with the help of a colour sergeant managed to form a firing line in the edge of the wood, someway behind our firing line. The 1st and 2nd Life Guards and Blues and Royals came up and made a very fine advance through the wood. Our men, about 100 of them on their left under Norman Orr Ewing, helped and drove the enemy back, killing a good many with the bayonet.

Captain Gerald Burgoyne
C COMPANY, 4tH BATTALION, ROYAL IRISH RIFLES

Last night the Germans were doing a great deal of funk firing, and both sides, using blue flares freely, were wasting a great deal of ammunition. Our windows are fairly rattling with the salvos of fire our howitzers and the French artillery are directing on the Middlestede and Wyschaete trenches. The 'funk' firing at night is very catching, as new troops think there is something up, or imagine they see movement in the darkness, and one man's firing will set off the whole line.

Major E.H.E. Daniell
2ND BATTALION, ROYAL IRISH RIFLES

We have not had a day's repose since we started the campaign; previous to this, it has been march, fight, hell-fire from shells continuously. A few days away from action will work wonders for us.

Major E.H.E. Daniell
2ND BATTALION, ROYAL IRISH REGIMENT

Five of our nights in the trenches we spent in the pelting rain. Most of the men had no great coats and, as the cold was intense, I do not know how they get their health, but they have done so, as there is next to no sickness. We have been sitting in the trenches exposed to shellfire, and where our artillery has been unable to reply or give us any assistance, during the day we have kept very few in position; the rest have been underground. Every man had to dig a hole in the bank and completely disappear like a rabbit.

Captain Gerald Burgoyne
C COMPANY, 4TH BATTALION, ROYAL IRISH RIFLES

A moment ago word was given up to me that there was a wounded Gordon in front crying for help. I ran up the line, stripped off my overcoat and had a look: and sure enough saw the poor devil's face about fifty yards in front of us, just beyond our wire entanglements, peering over the top of a shell hole. At my call all the men volunteered to fetch him in. I took two and went out to him. We found the poor fellow, shot in the groin, lying in the muddy water of a shell hole and had been there since Monday! My two men picked him up, and wound or no wound, ran him smartly into our trenches, where he stood a moment and stoutly cursed the Gordon Highlanders for leaving him there. He was so grateful to us. I just stayed outside a minute, as I thought I heard another cry and called out to see if any among the bodies lying thick around were but wounded, but no answer, and I was very glad to skip back again, as the enemy was not averse to firing at men rescuing the wounded. I learnt later that away to our left was a wounded officer. For two days he was heard crying for help. At last two stretcher bearers went out, by day, carrying a stretcher. One man was at once killed. The other put the stretcher down, and had his arms round the officer to lift him on to it, when a bullet hit him through the head. The officer had to be left there, and his cries became weaker and weaker and then stopped. But if Irish Riflemen had been there, I am sure the poor fellow would have been brought in.

Captain Gerald Burgoyne
C COMPANY, 4TH BATTALION, ROYAL IRISH RIFLES

I have been digging out rifle pits in front of my trenches, a preliminary to making a new trench by connecting these pits, but we got down to water after digging a couple of feet. No fun either, digging in the dark, out in the open, within 200 yards of the Huns. We buried 5 Gordons whom we found lying there. Three of them we just rolled into water-filled shell holes which we afterwards filled up. Seemed very sacrilegious, but we had no time for more, and out here after all, the dead are but carrion. We did our best to mark their graves by sticking their rifle muzzles down into them. No means of identifying them though, as we cannot get at their identity discs. Poor fellows.

Sapper J. Davey
2ND FIELD COMPANY, ROYAL ENGINEERS

I entered the trenches of the 1st BN Royal Irish Rifles, of the 25th Infantry Brigade, 8th Division, just about 8.00 pm on Christmas Eve 1914. Whilst making our way to a selected point in the trenches to commence sapping towards the German line, somewhere in the Neuve Chappelle area, a succession of fancy lights started coming over from the enemy lines to ours. As I remember it these were *not* Verey lights. At the same time German voices were constantly calling out to this effect, 'Don't fire, it's Christmas; if you don't we won't; come over and talk.'

After a while I saw a private of the R. Irish Rifles go over (it was quite dark except for the lights being sent up) and I saw him come back with a box of cigars. In a short while numbers of our men were meeting the Germans in No-Man's Land, chatting, walking about together and exchanging what they could in the form of smokes and food.

I saw a number of Irish, English and German soldiers chasing a rabbit or hare in No-Man's Land, throwing clods of frozen soil at it. I don't know whether it was caught.

Captain Gerald Burgoyne
C COMPANY, 4TH BATTALION, ROYAL IRISH RIFLES

Rarely do the men write of their life out here; too illiterate; most of the letters are confined to remarks on their own health; questions as to the welfare of those at home, and prayers, so very often, prayers to God to care for those they have left behind them. From 90% of the letters you would never discover the men were on active service. A very strong religious strain runs through most of the letters, and I rather admire my old shell-backs for it.

Chapter 2 ∾

| 1915

1915 saw the stalemate of the Western Front intensify as both sides became locked in trench warfare. The advantage rested with the German Army who occupied large areas of France and Belgium and could therefore assume a defensive posture, forcing the cost of offensive operations onto the Allies. Two of the Irish divisions of Kitchener's New Army were now in the line in France, the 16th (Irish) Division and the 36th (Ulster) Division. The 16th (Irish) Division contained the names of many of the most famous Irish regiments, the Leinster Regiment, the Connaught Rangers, the Royal Dublin Fusiliers, the Royal Irish Regiment, the Royal Munster Fusiliers, all represented by newly formed service battalions drawn from the flood of volunteers in Ireland in 1914. The 36th (Ulster) Division contained its share of famous names, the Royal Irish Rifles, the Royal Irish Fusiliers and the Royal Inniskilling Fusiliers.

The two divisions were largely composed of volunteers who had little or no military experience, although many had been members of either the Ulster Volunteers or the Irish Volunteers. Many of the officers and rank-and-file had perhaps anticipated fighting each other, but now found themselves in France facing a German Army side by side. Battles were fought on the Western Front in 1915, namely at Neuve Chapple (10–23 March) and at Loos (23 September–14 October). Both the 1st Irish Guards and the 2nd Royal Munsters, now re-formed, fought at Loos, the Guards also having fought at Festubert (15–25 May). The London Irish Rifles gained international fame as 'the footballers of Loos' as they dribbled a football across No-Man's Land during their attack on the German trenches.

Despite the efforts of all sides and the considerable loss of life, 1915 ended in stalemate, and with little or no changes in the geography of the campaign.

Company Sergeant Major Arthur 'Jimmy' Rixon
'A' COMPANY, LONDON IRISH RIFLES

It appears at last we are bound somewhere outside England, by the preparations being carried out. In case it is so, I have decided to make the long proposed will and forward same to Jimmy with note. Sent ring home to dear old May [his wife]. So sorry shall not be able to see them again, before leaving, perhaps never. Who knows? Decide to put away such thoughts.

Second Lieutenant J.L. Stewart Moore
15TH BATTALION, ROYAL IRISH RIFLES

After landing at Boulagne at midnight on the 3rd of October 1915 we marched through the cobbled streets to a rest camp on a hill overlooking the town. The rest camp was not attractive and not particularly restful. After a boring day doing nothing we marched down into town at dusk and entrained at the Gare Maritime. The train was made up of covered wagons marked 'Hommes 40 Chevaux en long 8'—for the officers there was an empty first class carriage with rounded doors and windows reminiscent of an eighteenth-century mail coach. The speed at which French troop trains moved was rather less than the speed of an eighteenth-century mail coach and it was well into the next morning before we arrived at a large railway junction which must have been Amiens, though we had no means of knowing at the time. Here we saw a French ambulance train and one of our young officers named Hogg who was an incorrigible practical joker and had a very lively imagination. Hogg tried to make our flesh creep by telling us that he saw bandaged limbs with blood dripping. Of course we did not believe him, but all the same.

Sergeant F. de Margry
2ND BATTALION, ROYAL IRISH REGIMENT

I can't remember much of my journey from Dublin to Southampton, except I was very disappointed when our train stopped only a few minutes in Birmingham—thereby robbing me of a last chance of seeing my girlfriend before going to the Front (no Embarkation leave having been granted me prior to being drafted overseas). The crossing from Southampton to Rouen was quite a pleasant and restful change, especially the more leisurely trip up the river to Rouen, with cheering and waving French people watching us sail past from the river banks. Once temporarily installed in our Transit Camp there we had a final kit and medical inspection, and were issued with various extra items of equipment, such as field dressing, entrenching tool, steel helmet, groundsheet, some rations, etc, till we felt quite loaded up, somewhat like pack mules. We finally entrained for the Front and after a very slow and tedious journey, broken only by frequent stops to enable us to jump out of the horse truck we travelled in and marked '8 chevaux—40 hommes' and stretch our legs as well as cadge sufficient hot water in an enamel mug from the engine driver to brew some concoction vaguely like tea, before moving slowly on to the next stop. Eventually we reached Poperinghe where we all gladly disentrained to assemble outside the station.

Second Lieutenant T.H. Witherow
17TH BATTALION, ROYAL IRISH RIFLES

On the 4th of February 1915 a telegram arrived at the 'digs' where my cousin Alick Witherow and I were living in Londonderry at 10 p.m. It conveyed to us the welcome news that we had both been given commissions in the 17th BATT Royal Irish Rifles and we were ordered to report immediately at the School of Instruction at Queens University, Belfast. So we had been launched on our military career, knowing not what the future held in store for us, but with a firm conviction that we had done the right thing.

After a month spent in strenuous training we were attached to the 14th Royal Irish Rifles (The Young Citizens Volunteers) who were encamped at Randlestown. There a further period of training was gone through and about May I was ordered to be attached to the 36th Divisional Cyclist COY who were then stationed at Enniskillen. Here I had a very enjoyable time and had many opportunities of seeing the sights and scenery for which this district is justly famous.

Captain Gerald Burgoyne
C COMPANY, 4TH BATTALION, ROYAL IRISH RIFLES

The late German Ambassador in London, Lichnowsky, has I heard, enlisted as a private in the German Army, and all the old German diplomats have gone to 1000 to 3 with the Emperor and his leaders. The Ambassador, some time before the War was ever thought of, met Walter Long at a private dinner party and asked him about the state of Ireland. Long said he thought there was certain to be civil war there. Lichnowsky repeated this to the Emperor. My RE friend happened to be in the House seated close to the Ambassador when Redmond made his famous speech saying we could leave the defence of Ireland to the Irish. He told me the Ambassador turned white, and leaving immediately, had to be supported to his carriage, the shock of this news had so great a physical effect on him.

Lieutenant J.L. Stewart Moore
15TH BATTALION, ROYAL IRISH RIFLES

On the crossing from Southampton to Harve I had the misfortune to be appointed for guard duty along with two other officers and guards men with rifles. The idea was that if a submarine appeared we were to fire at it with the rifles. It was one of those schemes which looked nice in paper but was unworkable in practice. The ammunition to be used was said to be in a store somewhere on the ship but I could not find out where. Anyhow it was unlikely that rifle bullets would be of much use against a submarine even if we could hit it in the dark. My tour of duty was from midnight until 3 a.m. I had difficulty in assembling the men assigned to me, some of whom I found asleep on the floor of the saloon. The sea was rough, and long before 3 a.m. I was wishing that a submarine would come along and put an end to my misery. I expect the men felt likewise.

Lieutenant C.A. Brett

3RD BATTALION, CONNAUGHT RANGERS

Early in 1915, Colonel Lewin left us on promotion to Brigadier General and Colonel Deignan took his place. It was then becoming obvious that trench warfare was the order of the day, and so a trench was dug at Prehane rifle range, about three miles away on top of the cliffs, shooting out to sea. It was not a very good trench, nor was it like the real thing, being much too wide, but we thought it was alright. One day there was to be a demonstration of an elementary catapult for throwing bombs from one trench to another, and I and my machine gunners were ordered to attend, together with the Colonel and many others. The catapult was a wooden affair with strong elastic and a pouch into which the bomb was placed. Fred Lewin, a good friend of mine, had been made bombing officer at the same time I was made machine gun officer, and he was in charge of the demonstration. It was necessary to wind back the catapult, then place the bomb in the pouch, then light the fuse of the bomb with a match, pull the trigger and let it go. This time, things went wrong. I was about five yards away on top of the trench and saw it all.

Fred Lewin lit the match and made to light the fuse which apparently did not light; he fumbled for another match when the thing went off. He was bending over it and took the full blast and was seriously damaged and the catapult reduced to matchwood. There were of course no first aid arrangements, but Fred's Talbot car was standing nearby, and I offered to drive him back to hospital at Kinsale, so he was lifted into the passenger seat of the open car and I drove him back over very rough roads, just the two of us. But he was dead when we got to hospital.

Private B.W. Page

C COMPANY, LONDON IRISH RIFLES

Paraded at 4.30 am and after standing for four hours entrained at the Midland Railway Station, reached Southampton about 3 o'clock. Waited in the big wharf sheds till 6 pm, then embarked on a small pleasure boat formerly in the Clyde service. There were about one thousand aboard and accommodation very limited. No water for washing and no room to sleep properly.

Private A.R. Brennan
2ND BATTALION, ROYAL IRISH REGIMENT

As we marched through the streets preceded by our regimental band, it seemed as if all Dublin had turned out to give us a send off. The streets were thronged with cheering people, and the windows mostly of girls waving all kinds of flags, cheering, and wishing us 'God speed'. It made all of us feel very proud and heroic, except perhaps the few old soldiers. However, the average age of the draft could hardly have been more than 20, and we were fully conscious of the emotional nature of the send-off. Crowds of men and women followed us right up to the gates of the North Wall Pier, from where the boat was due to depart. Here, except for a favoured few, we left them, and there were one or two painful scenes of wives and mothers bidding 'goodbyes' to husbands and sons. As our band moved off, the band (who were not accompanying us), determined to get the last ounce of emotional effect out of the situation, played 'Come back to Erin'. Many of us who then watched the shores of Ireland receding from view were doing so for the last time.

Lieutenant C.A. Brett
3RD BATTALION, CONNAUGHT RANGERS

The *Lusitania* was sunk by a submarine off the Old Head of Kinsale, about 15 miles away. We knew she had been torpedoed before she actually sunk, and I remember well seeing every craft in Kinsale Harbour, steam and sail, setting out to sea as fast as they could go. That evening a procession of farm carts came up from the Harbour to the military hospital, each piled high with corpses, many of them women in light dresses, giving me a bitter dislike for all Germans and a desire to kill as many as possible.

Second Lieutenant T.H. Witherow

8TH BATTALION, ROYAL IRISH RIFLES

I sailed from Southampton on the 24th December, arriving in Havre on Xmas Day. So on the great day when Christ came into the world to preach the doctrine of 'peace and goodwill among men', I landed in France to do my part in the great war to uphold the doctrine of 'right over might'.

The millions of tons of war material which crowded the Havre docks conveyed a good idea of the enormous scope of the war and the enormous amount of material required in its execution. Havre is not a place which impresses one and its dirty appearance rather tends to give one a poor idea of France. I reported at the 36th Division Base Camp which was commanded by Major Long, a brother of Mr Walter Long, and there saw several old acquaintances including Andy McCay who was acting as an instructor at the Camp. I was told that I had been posted to the 8th Royal Irish Rifles (East Belfast Volunteers) and needless to say this was most pleasant news as I would be with Ballymacarret men.

I left Havre for the front about 30th Dec, travelling luxuriously in an ordinary goods wagon. As you approach the battle zone everything bears the hallmark of war. Training areas with their huts and the great general hospitals and above all huge dumps of all kinds of material from foodstuffs to barbed wire. It was towards evening on the 1st January that I approached the actual battle line and as darkness came on the first sign of war was distinctly seen, namely the Verey lights which illuminate the whole line of the Belgian Coast to the Swiss Border. These brilliant lights as they ascend and descend can be seen a great many miles off, especially the German variety which like many other things used in the war were vastly superior to our own.

About 8 p.m. I arrived at the railhead of our Division, Steenwerck, a station on the Bailleul–Lille line, and was met by a limber, the small square carts used in the war area, and along with my valise set out for the Battalion who fortunately were in billets in the Belgian village of Nieuve Eglise. It was an awkward hour and date in which to arrive as naturally the New Year was being celebrated, but I received a very hearty welcome to the Regiment.

Private S.E. Speed
LONDON IRISH RIFLES

Embarked at Southampton for Harve, entrained at Cassal 42 miles distant. This took 22 hours. We were penned in cattle trucks lined with straw—could not lie down and could hardly turn around. From there went on to La Tempe near Winnezelle, 3 miles from the Belgian Frontier.

Private B.W. Page
C COMPANY, LONDON IRISH RIFLES

Reached Harve at 5 am and stayed aboard till eight, afterwards marching to camp 3 or 4 miles out of the town. The camp was a large affair, occupied every day by troops on their way to the front. It contained also a large military hospital. Occupied day making up deficiencies in clothing, etc. Retired about 11 o'clock and slept indifferent well—14 men in a tent.

Private A.R. Brennan
2ND BATTALION, ROYAL IRISH REGIMENT

After a terrible night of sea sickness in a boat in which we were packed like sardines, awoke and went on deck. We were steaming briskly up the Seine to Rouen. It was a lovely morning, and in happier circumstances one would be able to get the maximum enjoyment out of it. As far as I was concerned, however, the 'heroism' and exaltation that animate one in the streets of Dublin had vanished with the sea sickness of the previous evening, and given half a chance, I would cheerfully have responded to the call of 'Come back to Erin'. Rouen was reached about noon. On stepping ashore for the first time in France I was commissioned by a young officer to take his kit up to Base Camp. This was my first sample of the endless 'fatigues' which beset the path of the 'young' as opposed to the 'old' soldier, because of his inability, through lack of experience, to sense trouble a long way off. Eventually we reached our section of the vast Base Camp, and I was able to dump the officer's kit. I never saw him again. The Camp was a tremendous affair. Thousands of tents as far as the eye could see. Tents of all shapes and sizes from the humble 'bell' variety to the aristocratic 'Marquee'. Each regiment had its own section of tents, which was usually indicated by a huge appropriate cap badge in chalk and many-coloured flowers. As is the way of the Army each regiment tried to outshine all the others in the magnificence of the ornamentation to its particular regimental symbol. We spent the day seeing the sights of the place, and writing letters in the YMCA hut.

Private David Starrett
9TH BATTALION, ROYAL IRISH RIFLES

French cattle trains, with the brats running alongside shouting 'Bully-Beef!' took us slowly down the coast to the Front. Starting and stopping all the time. Engine driver getting down for drinks, crowds every now and then cheering.

Second Lieutenant J.L. Stewart Moore
15TH BATTALION, ROYAL IRISH RIFLES

In due course we arrived at Medauville a few miles north of Albert and there we were billeted in an outhouse in the yards of the chateau. A day or two later we relieved a battalion of the Somerset Light Infantry in the trenches in front of the village of Mensil. Going up to the trenches at dusk for the first time was still a nervy business but all went well and we spent a quiet night. Next morning working parties were told to fill sandbags and carry out repairs. The trenches were in good order but there was always room for improvement and we were keen to show what we could do. It was a fine sunny morning, not a sound to be heard and the Germans were four hundred yards away, so some of the working party from 'B' company climbed out of the trench and started walking about at the back, the better to perform their task; and Captain Ryall the Company Commander saw no reason why he should restrain them, all was so calm and peaceful. Then there was the crack of a bullet and a man was hit by a German sniper. It was our first casualty. We were told afterwards that the wound in itself was not mortal but the man died of shock. It was all so unexpected.

Private B.W. Page
C COMPANY, ROYAL IRISH RIFLES

Parade 7.30, marched 3 miles and boarded motor buses to Hauzelbrooke St Vermot where we disembarked. Marched through town to billet in barn about 3 miles away. 6.30 walked into town for grub. Omelette and potatoes. Walked back nearly losing way in the dark. On arriving at billet was told to go back and draw rations. Hunted for rations in dark and came away disgusted without them. To bed without blankets.

Private A.R. Read
'A' COMPANY, LONDON IRISH RIFLES

Each man was given 120 rounds of ammunition besides cold meal tickets (round discs with name, number and religion stamped on); these were attached to a piece of string and worn round the neck. Field dressings had to be put in little pockets provided in the tunic. Paybooks in which we had to make our will (very cheerful) and other odds and ends to increase the load. This took 3 or 4 hours and finally we marched to the station and entrained for Southampton, where we arrived at 2.30, having passed through Hendon, Finchley, Acton, Richmond, St Margaret's, Staines, Winchester etc. Southampton is the dreariest place possible—nothing but docks and railways lines with huge sheds, not a civilian to give a cheer, nowhere to get a cup of tea, and being the merry month of March (1915) it was bitter cold. We embarked at 7pm on the troopship *Queen Alexandra*, in detachments from different regiments. The idea was to form a convoy of troopships with an escort of destroyers in case of submarine attack. Each man had a life belt which had to be worn. Just before sailing (10pm) our pipers played 'Auld Lang Syne'; also a favourite tune 'The Dear Little Shamrocks of Ireland'.

Private A.R. Read
'A' COMPANY, LONDON IRISH RIFLES

Marching through 'Harve' we had a good welcome from the French civvies, but noticed that they were very different from our own people, not smart or refined. The kids kept on saying 'Souvenier, anglais', which meant cap badges, buttons or anything for nothing. The town itself was a dirty hole and some of the sanitary arrangement in the streets made us feel disgusted. At last we arrived at our rest camp. Here we had tents, with 20 men in each, which didn't give us much room. The remainder of the day was spent in drawing more kit. French gloves, mittens, scarves, woollen caps, gas respirators and sheepskin coats (Teddy Bears), and these caused great fun when some of the comics started getting on hands and knees and calling 'Ba Ba' like sheep.

Private B.W. Page
C COMPANY, LONDON IRISH RIFLES

Bethune. Billeted in large disused orphanage or hospital with nearly all the windows broken. The London Scottish GG 6th City of London Inniskillings and many other regiments had been here before us and left their signatures on the walls. Went into the town about 6 o'clock. Spent last two francs on tea and pastries, the first I had obtained since leaving St Albans.

Captain Gerald Burgoyne
C COMPANY, 4TH BATTALION, ROYAL IRISH RIFLES

A gunner officer has just told me that some three months ago, long before there was any mention of operations in the Dardenelles, a lady told him (in the Albert Hall at a concert of all places) that there would be land operations there and they would have at least 300,000 men engaged. I suppose some shining light at Headquarters told his wife the secret. The Convent of the Black Sisters at Ypres has been burnt, also the Convent of Les Dames Anglaises, where hung the standards of the Irish Brigade which fought so well in the service of Louis xv at Fontenoy, as they did in the days of his father at Malpaquet when the Royal Irish Regiment with Marlborough beat them.

Captain Gerald Burgoyne
C COMPANY, 4TH BATTALION, ROYAL IRISH RIFLES

I have just heard one of the finest things that have happened during the War. Young Pike, a son of the Pike's near Ballincollig, has for years been paralysed from his legs down. Unable to do anything but motor, he has joined the flying corps. He is helped into and out of his plane, and though a cripple is able to do 'his bit'. Rather a fine example of spirit, I think.

Private A.R. Read
'A' COMPANY, LONDON IRISH RIFLES

Wennezellee is a dead-and-alive hole. The people are Flemish and speak half French and half German. Our billet was an old barn with pigs on one side and cows on the other and a filthy muck pond in front. On this barn I had my first guard, and as the nights were pitch black, we often came near to shooting our own chaps.

Corporal Norman James
LONDON IRISH RIFLES

It was quite unforgettable—the landscape, the trees blasted and then in the summer of 1915 I will never forget the whiteness of the trenches. It was a very chalky area and the poppies, scarlet and white, I well remember. And life seemed to be good actually in the sunny days. Later I did some drawings. Occasionally I drew a portrait of some of my men in a quiet 20 minutes in the front line.

Private David Starrett
9TH BATTALION, ROYAL IRISH RIFLES

We went to the Fourth Division at Hamel, singing along to the line, in the best of spirits—some of them from the estaminets of Vignacourt. The well known songs were sung and slogans shouted. We were off to knock spots off the Germans, marching through peaceful and lovely fields, accompanied by kissing and hugging French girls.

Halting, we were divided, half of the Battalion going up to the line with the Rifle Brigade. The Major had this half, and so I got my first impression of this one bit of the big battlefield. Shell holes in plenty and broken trees, and bursts front and back.

Lieutenant William Carden Roe

1ST BATTALION, ROYAL IRISH FUSILIERS

This battle Mess was shared by the officers of two companies and there we partook of our evening meal and often a cup of tea before morning 'Stand to'. In those days the resources of France as regards the catering for an officers' Mess had not yet been fully exploited, so we lived almost entirely on rations; but these I am glad to say were supplemented by many a parcel from home, and last, but not least, a stock of champagne procured (tell it not in Gath) from the ruins of an adjacent Chateau. The floor of the cellar could never be kept really dry—it was below the level of the well of the farm, and the brazier with which we maintained a little warmth would have choked anyone but a hardened trench warrior. If a howitzer shell had landed on the roof, the latter would have crumpled like an eggshell—yet even so I shall always look back on this spot as a miniature paradise.

Private Frank Germain

ROYAL IRISH FUSILIERS

Well, after we left Le Harve we took a train up the line, and landed near the front line. The 1st place we went to was a place called Dickey Bush. That was 12 Jan 1915 and I mind us chaps going up the road with shot and shell hopping all round us. There we walked over fields of mud and water, there we reached a trench the French soldiers left. The French soldiers dead was buried in the walls of the trench and all round us was dead Frenchmen. In front of our trench was a long line of dead Frenchmen, all who were killed at Xmas 1914. They were trying to take the German line in front of a big wood but failed.

Private A.R. Brennan

2ND BATTALION, ROYAL IRISH REGIMENT

Up early and to Mass. Medical inspection, followed by a gas-test of our helmets. After dinner fell in and marched to the railway station, where we entrained for the journey to our 2nd Battalion. Evidently, the Battalion was badly in need of reinforcements as it had been decimated in the first 'gas attack' of the 24th May, and the base authorities were losing no time in making good the losses sustained. We had a long tiresome journey of about twenty-four hours' duration; halting for a number of hours during the night outside (I think) Amiens. Here again, my inexperience resulted in my being 'bagged' for two hours on sentry duty. Hearing a movement from carriage to carriage along the train and finally the door of my carriage being opened, I foolishly opened my eyes and looked up just in time to catch the eye of the Orderly Sergeant, who promptly detailed me for duty.

Private David Starrett
9TH BATTALION, ROYAL IRISH RIFLES

Returning from Headquarters Mess one evening I found the old woman in our billet smashing everything with a large stick, windows, furniture, pictures, and cursing the English guns. Poor dame, they had banged her few wits away. Glaring at me she yelled evermore loudly and took a couple of swipes at me with the stick. Just as I wondered what was the best tackle to put her out of action she fell down in a faint, and I hauled her back to her room just as the Major appeared.

Acting Lieutenant Colonel John Trefusis
1ST BATTALION, IRISH GUARDS

A perfectly beastly day, ruining with a thick mist. I had intended to go into Bethune to get my hair cut, but I shall postpone it till a finer day. The men spent the day cleaning themselves and their clothes as best they could, and 120 were able to get hot baths at a brewery near here. There are big barrels put in a large room and filled with hot water. Two men get in each barrel. They are provided with soap. When they have taken off their clothes, they are tied in bundles and sent upstairs where there are many women employed to iron them with hot irons. This I am told, kills anything there may be in them which is living! The men are allowed ten minutes in the tube, and then another lot come in. If a man has any article of clothing in a very bad state, he is given a new one. The whole thing is a splendid arrangement, and it is a pity that all the men in the Brigade cannot each get a bath during the time they have here. I think just over half will be washed by the time we leave.

Private A.R. Read
'A' COMPANY, LONDON IRISH RIFLES

Things are very dear out here and we had a payday 5 francs (4s 2d), the first since leaving England. Beer is like dirty water, while vin blanc (white wine) and vin rouge (red wine) is 2 francs (1s 8d) a bottle. The French soldiers only get 5 centimes a day (2½d) so everyone thinks that the Tommy is a millionaire.

Lieutenant William Carden Roe
1ST BATTALION, ROYAL IRISH FUSILIERS

As a rule I hate that expression so often and loosely used by Englishmen, 'He is a real Irishman.' But in this case I might almost make use of the phrase, for George Bull, though not Irish by name, was typical of all that is best in the Irish race. Cultivating a strong North of Ireland accent when telling a story or addressing the men, he would raise a shriek of delight in the trench as he shook his fist at the spot where a sniper's bullet had just cracked above his head, exclaiming with much expression, 'Yer dirty divil!' Above all things he was possessed of the soul of humour, and an hour in his company was an hour of laughter and great comradeship. He was fortunate in possessing a sense of intuition which made him more than ready for a fresh situation, and inspired in his officers and men a complete confidence in his leadership. He was a man who would have gone far in his profession on his merits as a real sound soldier, but alas! he fell in his prime, a few days only after being appointed to the command of a brigade.

Acting Lieutenant Colonel John Trefusis
1ST BATTALION, IRISH GUARDS

The evening turned out fine, after a rather cold wet day. I walked round the bivouacs and found the men very cheery, playing games and singing. I had previously sent into Bethune for wood for them to make fires with, so that they might get themselves dry, and this arrived about the time I was going round. I had allowed no fires, as the only wood to burn was tobacco drying poles, and hedges, and as the former are valuable to the inhabitants of the farms, I thought it best to allow no fires. It certainly saved unpleasantness with the inhabitants which is always a good thing to avoid. The men sang songs till past 11 pm. They are in the best of spirits and ready for anything.

Private A.R. Brennan
2ND BATTALION, ROYAL IRISH REGIMENT

On the way to Acheux we heard the sounds of guns for the first time and we were immensely thrilled. Up to this time we of the 'Cadet' Corps had been kept as a separate unit. In barracks in Dublin we had occupied quarters apart from the other companies and we had an idea that this practice would be followed even in France. On arrival at Acheux, however, our Company was broken up and we were drafted to different companies. I suppose this was inevitable, but we were new to the Army then and some of us thought that it was a breach of faith. I was sent to 'A' Company, and remained with it for the whole of my two years in France. Others who came with me were Frank Waldron and Dick Breen, both of whom were eventually to be killed in France. We three were allocated to NO 14 Platoon. We had some difficulty in finding sleeping quarters and had a length to sleep in an out-house, which smelt suspiciously like a pig-sty. I spent the night keeping off rats with an entrenching tool handle.

Acting Lieutenant Colonel John Trefusis
1ST BATTALION, IRISH GUARDS

During dinner I got a note from the lady of the house where we had our dinner party the other night, saying that she had intended to come up and pay me a visit this afternoon, but had been to the country and came back too late, so I sent a note asking if I could come up and see them after dinner, which she answered by saying she would be delighted to see some of us. So I took Father Knapp up with me, and found them all, i.e. the owner, her two daughters and one son, and her mother all dressed in their best. They were very nice, and quite sorry we were going as they said some people who were billeted on them never take any notice of them at all, and that they had never known English before we came, properly. They hope if we come back here we would be put up at their house again. I think it is such a mistake not to be friendly with these people in Bethune, if one is even from a purely selfish point of view, they will do anything for one, and I think it only right that we should treat them civilly, and take a little trouble to look after their property which we use. So many don't, and that is why the British soldier and officer has not got a very good name here. If one talks to the French people about their behaviour they shrug their shoulders, and say 'Mais, c'est la guerre', which is full of meaning.

However, I hope as this may possibly be the rest place of troops of the 1st Corps for some time, we may undo the harm that has been done here by other troops in the last three months.

Private A.R. Read
'A' COMPANY, LONDON IRISH RIFLES

Bethune is a big town well within range of the enemies' guns. Next day April 8th we were ordered up to the Trenches. Proceeding along the 'La Basse' road we received our baptism of fire. German shells began dropping on the road, and although we all dropped flat two men of B Company were wounded. These were our first casualties, and their names were Valentine and Richardson (both Riflemen). Continuing on our way we noticed that all the houses were smashed up, also big shell holes everywhere, with a dead horse at very short intervals. Mud was over a foot deep.

Company Sergeant Major Arthur 'Jimmy' Rixon
'A' COMPANY, LONDON IRISH RIFLES

Heard from Jimmy and Dad. By all accounts the poor girlie takes my leaving pretty badly. So sorry as I had no business to sign for foreign service; wouldn't have done so if I thought we were to be sent here. The CO led us to believe it would be Gib or Malta.

Private A.R. Read
'A' COMPANY, LONDON IRISH RIFLES

Just behind our support line was a graveyard and it made us feel very downhearted to see so many wooden crosses of our own countrymen. That morning we moved up to the front line. Here we found the 1st Kings Royal Rifles and were attached to them for instruction. They were very good chaps and were very keen to help us, and as one of their officers said, it was fine to see the Territorials willing to give a hand with the Regulars.

Private William Barry
AUSTRALIAN IMPERIAL FORCE

There were with us a number of British soldiers who were taken prisoners of war in the dark days of 1914 and 1915 and to hear them tell of the way they had been treated was something awful. Six of these chaps were men from the 88th Connaught Rangers, Dublin Fusiliers and the Munster Regiment. Private John Murphy, better known as 'Spud' of the Dublin Fusiliers, and I soon became friends and he told me that when he was first captured along with his pals, they were starved into submission and the boys were compelled to rake out the pig tubs for something to eat and he once received seven days in prison for having in his pocket some pieces of potato peeling and a few fish bones which he had found in the pig tub, and his plea was that he intended to make soup with them. In those days it was an unwritten law among the British prisoners that no man was allowed to have more than three pieces of potato peel in the fire at one time; if he did, his mate was quite justified in taking the other. Spud also told me how the Germans tried to get the Irish soldiers to turn traitors. It was just before the Casement rebellion in Ireland, that all the Irish prisoners were sent to a camp called Limburg and for seven days these poor wretches received hardly anything to eat, and at the end of that time they were all taken to a large room where there was a banquet spread before them. On the table was roast beef, turkey, bottled beer and the best of everything. On each man's plate was five sovereigns. Sitting at the head of the table was a man who was decorated with green and yellow ribbons, who turned out to be Casement's agent. Bailey was his name and as these starving men had to stand against the wall gazing at the good feed on the table, he told them that Ireland was in a terrible way. There had been a great naval battle. The British navy had been defeated. The Germans had landed in London and were marching on to set Ireland free. A Regiment of Loyal Irishmen was being formed in Germany to help Ireland to fight for her freedom and if you men joined up, you would get a free pardon out of Germany and enjoy the Banquet. Out of all of those starving men, only three volunteered to join and the rest of them were put in a room where the steam pipes were turned on; they suffered a Turkish bath, and were then sent out into the cold. Several of these men were suffering from consumption and other chest complaints. Several of these Irishmen, through the brutal treatment they received, their minds were affected and it was terrible to see such big men behaving like they were.

Lieutenant William Carden Roe

1ST BATTALION, ROYAL IRISH FUSILIERS

Under the circumstances there were few opportunities for training. Nevertheless a certain amount of time was devoted to ceremonial and physical drill. The latter was a splendid antidote to rheumatism and other ills brought on by trench warfare. Charles England was particularly keen on making the men run up and down the road (the water-logged fields were quite impossible) for ten minutes or more at a time. This was rather a strain on men of a certain age who had in many cases taken little exercise in the years which had elapsed since the completion of their colour service.

One morning we had been for our usual run and on its completion the panting company were dismissed in the yard of the farm where we were billeted. Both officers and men had their billets there, the officers in a room downstairs which served as both Mess and sleeping room, the men in a large loft up above and in the barns and outhouses. As we, the officers, passed through the hall which was covered with a faded wallpaper depicting children playing by the seaside, the platoon, whose quarters were in the loft, followed close at our heels, led by a solid-looking old soldier, whose very audible pants showed that the exercise had told hard on his frame. Between his gasps his eyes lit on the wallpaper. 'Buckets and spades (pant) in the sand! (pant)' he exclaimed. 'Oh Jesus, yon were the days!'

Private A.R. Read
HQ, 141ST INFANTRY BRIGADE

'South-Maroc', a village just behind our lines which was full of civilians, was found to be infested with spies and they were ordered to take what belongings they required and clear out. Every house was left full of furniture, also the gardens full of fruit and vegetables to say nothing of chickens. At the communication trench was an estaminet and the boys used to leave the front line (in daytime) and skip down the trench and buy wine and beer, until they was found out. Well, each house in the village was ransacked. The 17th Band got a bass drum, the 19th had half a dozen new bikes, while the different officers were walking along the streets dressed in female attire. The chickens, vegetables, and fruit soon disappeared.

Private A.R. Read
HQ, 141ST INFANTRY BRIGADE

Vermilles, a large town, was just on our right so I took a walk to have a look at it. The houses had been badly knocked about and [it] was empty of civilians. On entering the main street the first thing that caught my eye made me smile. A pole was stuck out of an upper window. Fastened to it was a pair of woman's drawers, with the word 'welcome' painted across them. Even our officers had to grin when they passed and whoever thought of the idea must have been a bit of a wag. The place was very desolate and one of our artillerymen told me that the French and Germans had 55 days hand to hand fighting in the streets.

Company Sergeant Major Arthur 'Jimmy' Rixon
'A' COMPANY, LONDON IRISH RIFLES

Pipers inflict torture on inhabitants with pipes; can't think what the people have done to deserve it. Hooray! A letter at last from my old darling. She appears to be bearing up as I asked, but I bet she is in a state. Still I wish I could have dodged coming here, more for her sake than my own. I don't mind a bit personally as I am only one, but it would be rotten for her if anything happened to me. Can't bear to think of not seeing the old boy and hearing from him again. The baby is too young to know. Must buck up as I am not dead yet, far from it, but it is so rotten having to leave them. Guns booming all day near. We leave tomorrow. I wonder what and where for? Another supper. Old lady upset because we are leaving. Rum issue! Bed 10.30. Not the St Patrick's day I'm used to.

Private B.W. Page
C COMPANY, LONDON IRISH RIFLES

No parades for platoon. Went to the fields twice and played footer, and wrote letters. Letters and parcel from home. Letter containing another ten francs, very acceptable. Sgt Hirst came into our room in his usual bullying manner, demanded four orderlies and was 'given the bird' by whole room.

Captain Gerald Burgoyne
C COMPANY, 4TH BATTALION, ROYAL IRISH RIFLES

The way we are all fed here is wonderful. Packets of pea soup and cubes of Oxo are issued as rations. Machonocie tinned meat and vegetables. 'Home & Colonial' margarine and very good too, and so much jam, cheese, bacon, and bully beef that any amount is wasted. Tea and sugar is of course issued, but I can't understand why they don't issue compressed tea. We had an excellent dinner in our dug-out—pea soup, hot stew, bread, butter and jam, which all things considered is not too rough.

Company Sergeant Major Arthur 'Jimmy' Rixon
'A' COMPANY, LONDON IRISH RIFLES

Some soft soap today. Was inspected by Gen French and he told the usual tale of us being some of the best troops he had ever seen! Help! The old boy looks very well and is evidently pleased with our appearance. Hope he doesn't thrust us out for anything too big just yet. In case anything happened to me so early it would be too much of a shock for the kiddie. Don't care personally but others must be thought of.

Private B.W. Page
C COMPANY, LONDON IRISH RIFLES

Reville [sic] 6.30, moved off at 8 back to bivouac. Spent day building tent and doing nothing in particular. A battery of 4.5 guns in same field. One gunner said that there were many spies among the peasants. An officer of theirs found telephone in estaminet with pretty girl who supplied fried spuds and things to the troops. They shot the inhabitants of the house.

Company Sergeant Major Arthur 'Jimmy' Rixon
'A' COMPANY, LONDON IRISH RIFLES

Nothing much doing still. Received papers from England. Glad as news is a bit scarce here and papers much appreciated. Second trench party left tonight. Wonder when I am for it. Somehow have developed the habit of thinking of May and babies every night before going to sleep. Hope nothing wrong.

Private A.R. Brennan
2ND BATTALION, ROYAL IRISH REGIMENT

We were up early and on parade to make the acquaintance of the Captain (Taylor) and the Sergeant-Major (Thornton). The latter had just returned from a spell of sick leave, and was apparently not very popular with the Captain, who on this occasion bullied him unmercifully before the whole Company. I felt rather sorry for the Sergeant-Major, as he was one of the quiet type of NCO, and did not appear to merit such treatment. I found out later that the Captain was something of an 'eccentric', which probably lessened the severity of the 'strafing' for the Sergeant-Major. Found a certain amount of hostility towards us prevailing amongst the other members of the Platoon. This was due to the fact that we had come from the 'Cadet' Company, about which they had all sorts of funny ideas. To them we were 'swells' of a kind, and for a good many months we had to put up with various forms of 'pin-pricks' and many unjust and unmerited 'fatigues' because of this erroneous idea.

Captain Gerald Burgoyne
C COMPANY, 4TH BATTALION, ROYAL IRISH RIFLES

Three scoundrels were sentenced last week to Field Imprisonment NO 1, 28 days, which means tying them up an hour at a time, for two hours a day and giving them, of course, every dirty and unpleasant jobs you can think of. So far, they've done nothing, but I'm tying them up today, hands behind their back, and then tied on to a loop or ring or anything to prevent movement. In SA we used to tie them up to the seat rail of a wagon; this pulled their arms (tied behind their back) up and forced them to bend their bodies forward. An hour of this was perfect torture, but there were many natures to which this is the only appeal, and really flogging would be quite a good thing with some men, as there are natures so low that nothing but actual physical pain can appeal to them.

Company Sergeant Major Arthur 'Jimmy' Rixon
'A' COMPANY, LONDON IRISH RIFLES

The evacuation of village has started. The gendarmes were round last night warning them to be out in 12 hours which expires at 9 pm tonight. Every means of transport is being pressed into service. Wagons minus the necessary horse (which is unattainable) to perambulators and homemade barrows. If it wasn't so tragic it would be funny. We give them a hand where they are in difficulties, as they are at times. During the afternoon a shell exploding near a house where a girl about 10 was alone, her mother engaged in moving household effects. Poor little beggar was paralysed with fright so carried her down to the dug-outs and gave her tea and cake. She was alright in about an hour when her mother came back, but seemed to be glad to get away. Appeared somehow to think we were to blame.

Private William Barry
AUSTRALIAN IMPERIAL FORCE

That evening Murphy announced at supper that a band was going to be formed and any gentleman who could play any old music was invited to join. Twelve chaps were enrolled and the rest were kicked out of the room by the band conductor, PTE John Halissey, as the band's movements were to be kept secret. Halissay was dressed in a white pyjama suit with a sash made of green wallpaper, two tablespoons were stuck through it, to represent medals, and a mask over his face to make him appear like a goat and needless to say he acted like one. For a baton he used a walking stick which was bound around with green and yellow paper. The band consisted of nine players and the instruments, if they could be called such, were a triangle, mouth organ, a deluce mour, a few pieces of comb covered with paper and two small boxes to act as drums. After the conductor had given the band advice on how to play, he announced they would try 'Tipperary' and to the amusement of all present he said the piano was to be very loud and the fiddles soft and low, and by the way he spoke one would have thought that he was a born musician instead of a lunatic. When he had handed around several pieces of paper to be used as music, he tapped the floor with his stick and said, 'At the rose quick march.' The drummers banged the boxes five beats and the band started, and of all the unearthly noises you ever heard this was one. The German staff, hearing the row, came down to the ward and seeing the cause touched their forehead[s] and said, 'Englander feld cronk,' meaning the Englishmen were mad. That was what the Irish chaps wanted, for I honestly think they were only insane when the Germans were watching them.

Company Sergeant Major Arthur 'Jimmy' Rixon
'A' COMPANY, LONDON IRISH RIFLES

Two more pigeons this morning, but nothing important on them. Orders for all stray dogs to be destroyed. Scout corporal of 17th on the job; 18 shot this morning and still plenty around. The French very unlike the English as regards animals. Plenty of scope for an

RSPCA out here at all times. I have seen horses worked which should have been destroyed long ago, and no regard for their condition.

Captain Gerald Burgoyne
C COMPANY, 4TH BATTALION, ROYAL IRISH RIFLES

The wastage in rations is terrible. Going round the place this morning, I saw enough good tins of Bully thrown away, or simply left in their boxes, to feed a Battalion. The men really get too much, far more than they can eat, and extra rations like tinned salmon are counted extra and the same amount of it is issued to the men. The same with biscuits. Men prefer to buy bread, and tins and tins of biscuits are lying about everywhere, while the wastage in ammunition is remarkable. Every man is supposed to have 150 rounds in his pouches and going up to the trenches he carries an extra 100 rounds in two bandoliers. These bandoliers he has to leave behind him, either in the trenches or in the Support Farm, etc, and so, since so far, few of our men fire more than a few rounds a day, the trenches are full of cartridges and clips of cartridges; broken bandoliers, etc, half stuck in the mud or frozen to the parapets and every farm used for Supports is almost paved with them. However, I suppose the country can afford the waste.

Private A.R. Brennan
2ND BATTALION, ROYAL IRISH REGIMENT

Most of the Waterford chaps in the Platoon were old soldiers in the sense that it was not safe to leave anything lying about. I myself had every reason to suspect that a parcel of butterscotch sent out to me had been received by the Lance Corporal who use to collect the post at Battalion Headquarters. In all the six weeks spent away from the Battalion we had just one bath, and we had to walk fifteen miles to get it. We looked like ghosts, or tramps, perhaps, would be more appropriate. Our uniforms were white with the chalk of the dug-outs and the mine, and our faces were no less white.

Private A.R. Read
HQ, 141ST INFANTRY BRIGADE

We were billeted with some Indians. These belonged to the Indian corps, Lahore and Meerut Divisions, and were composed of all different classes, such as Pathans, Rajputs, Bengals, Ghurkhas, besides having mountain guns (pom-poms) which were carried on the backs of mules. The amusing part was to see a herd of goats which followed each Transport Section. These supplied the milk used for the Indian soldiers who were very strict over their food. Although being fine soldiers, they didn't care for trench warfare owing to the mud and water.

Captain Gerald Burgoyne
C COMPANY, 4TH BATTALION, ROYAL IRISH RIFLES

Davey [a fellow officer] was brought down to our dressing station last night. He was shot bang through the head from front to rear. We buried him at 9 a.m. this morning. All of us here attended, and some dozen men too. I had to read the service, or part of it. A most heart breaking job as far as I am concerned, and it affected me as much as if it were a relative of mine. I hate funerals, but no one else would take it on, and of course it was my job.

Acting Lieutenant Colonel John Trefusis
1ST BATTALION, IRISH GUARDS

The training that we have to do in Corps Reserve is that most calculated to improve the smartness of the Brigade. This is very necessary, as men seem to think that on active service they can do as they please in this respect, but in reality nothing is more liable to create indiscipline and slackness sooner than the lack of supervision in small details. We already do a good deal of drill whenever possible, and this combined with frequent kit inspections will make a vast difference to the appearance of the Brigade in five days, making of course every allowance for the existing condition of things.

Private David Starrett
HQ, 119TH BRIGADE

Titch and McCann and Hunt went with me one day to see what Arras was like, on the way passing Father O'Flioghtry [sic] bringing the boys cigarettes and games and writing paper. He waved a parcel at us and shouted 'More love-letters, buoys.' He certainly was a good specimen of his cloth.

Acting Lieutenant Colonel John Trefusis
1ST BATTALION, IRISH GUARDS

Cardinal Bourne paid the Battalion a visit in the afternoon quite unexpectedly, and I paraded all the Roman Catholics for him to see. He made an address and then walked down the ranks. The last time he had seen the Battalion was when it went to Westminster Cathedral just after the war broke out.

Captain Gerald Burgoyne
C COMPANY, 4TH BATTALION, ROYAL IRISH RIFLES

Our Padre (RC) came in to see us this afternoon and told us of some executions at which he had been present. Two men were shot last Monday for 'absence from the trenches', and the other time one of the men shot was a lad of eighteen years of age; his battalion was very upset at his execution. It seems his father, an old Reservist in the Gordons, had just been killed, and the lad got very unhappy at hearing this and hooked it one night when his Battalion was for the trenches. Stupidly and inadvisably he pleaded 'Guilty' and never brought this fact, which might have been considered 'extenuating', forward. One poor chap required three volleys, as the firing party were very nervous, although the Padre adjured them to shoot straight as the kindest thing to do. The men, on the whole, he said, met their death very pluckily.

Private A.R. Read
HQ, 141ST INFANTRY BRIGADE

I rode along 'Queens Road' and came across a little graveyard with a white painted wooden gate. The paths were made of bricks taken from the ruined houses and each grave had a wooden cross erected on which the man's name and regiment was either stamped or in pencil, and the whole effect was one of neatness with the wild flowers (mostly red poppies) making a pretty spectacle. Standing there I wondered how many of our lads would be lying here before it was all over and whether I should be one of them, and altogether I felt very downhearted as I turned away.

Captain Gerald Burgoyne
C COMPANY, 4TH BATTALION, ROYAL IRISH RIFLES

Rifleman Drennan, one of the two heroes which every halfpenny paper in England and Ireland made such a fuss of recounting their story of their 'intrepid flight through the German line' and their escape to England, has just returned to us as a deserter. To give him his due he is a very brave man and behaved well all through, but being put in the Guard Room for some little crime or other, he escaped and fled to England, no mean feat, by the way. He has just been tried by Court Martial for desertion, but the evidence of his bravery will undoubtedly get him off the death penalty.

Acting Lieutenant Colonel John Trefusis
1ST BATTALION, IRISH GUARDS

Shamrock was sent to us by Queen Alexandra, and I gave it out to Company Commanders to distribute to their companies. The men had an early service in the morning, and then the whole battalion went by companies to have baths in Bethune, which was about the most profitable way the day could have been spent. I arranged that each man who wanted it, had beer with his dinner, which is their height of bliss provided it is free.

Captain Gerald Burgoyne
C COMPANY, 4TH BATTALION, ROYAL IRISH RIFLES

There is a very general impression that our lines are full of spies who report all movement of our troops to the Germans who thus are able to get their guns on them. Our interpreter, a French NCO one Bertrand, suspected an interpreter (also a French NCO attached to some artillery); he reported this man who was tried by Court Martial, Bertrand himself giving evidence, and evidence was provided which convicted the fellow of being a traitor, and he was shot. This happened in this district and within the last 5 days.

Acting Lieutenant Colonel John Trefusis
1ST BATTALION, IRISH GUARDS

I rode out in the woods with Desmond Fitzgerald to see the companies drilling. I found only one of them, but the woods were glorious and quite big enough to lose one's way, which is what I imagine the other companies did, as they were not where they said they would be. However, the exercise is what they want chiefly, which they all got. On my return I found a message to say we were to be prepared to move at a half an hour's notice.

Captain Gerald Burgoyne
C COMPANY, 4TH BATTALION, ROYAL IRISH RIFLES

A beautiful sunny morning to cheer us all up. On arriving at Headquarters on St Patrick's night, the platoon I sent there found half a jar of rum left behind by the men they had relieved and the Sergeant and Corporals polished the lot off getting beastly drunk. But I'll have it in for 'em, the swines. What disgusts me most is the hoggish selfishness which made them drink it among three or four, instead of giving each man in the platoon a tot. But the selfish spirit, this want of 'pal-ship', is an extraordinary trait among Irishmen, at any rate among those in our Special Reserve. We've had so many cases of men only thinking for themselves, where food, and especially drink is concerned.

Private David Starrett
9TH BATTALION, ROYAL IRISH RIFLES

Going back one night I saw staggering through the village a big fellow I'd known well at home. 'Here, Alec,' I shouted. 'You are going the wrong way.' He said something back about knowing where he was going and passed on. Next morning there he was frozen stiff on the road to the trenches. He'd got a feed of rum from somewhere and the frost had done the rest. Pity. A good soldier and well liked. Just weak about the drink.

Acting Lieutenant Colonel John Trefusis
1ST BATTALION, IRISH GUARDS

Another lovely day, and I sat in the garden most of it. I went round and inspected all the billets. The men have plenty of room, and seem very comfortable, though some of the places where they are, are very hot. In the evening, Straker, my machine gun officer, who has hired a small motor, took me for a drive. The country is perfectly lovely, so different to the flat country we have been in, so long, and it is a real joy to see such things as hills and woods again. We went through several villages, all packed with French troops. The view from the tops of some of the hills is magnificent. We heard today that this is the first day of Italy's mobilisation.

Second Lieutenant J.L. Stewart Moore
15TH BATTALION, ROYAL IRISH RIFLES

One day when we were halted at a crossroads we saw a large French Army transport column go by. It was a weird and wonderful sight for it consisted of requisitioned civilian vehicles of all sorts and sizes; probably it was little different from the transport columns which served the armies of Louis XIV and Napoleon.

Captain Gerald Burgoyne
C COMPANY, 4TH BATTALION, ROYAL IRISH RIFLES

We paraded on the 5th at Kemmel (the farmhouse) at 5.45 p.m. pitch black. The men in their khaki coats quite invisible and one ran into them, and was very lucky to escape a rifle muzzle in the eye. We stumbled out of the farmhouse across a slushy field clattering over a causeway of old jam and meat tins, and into Kemmel where we almost literally bumped into our own ration carts. Then we had to collect rations for two complete companies, our own and one other. Wooden cases 18" by 18" [by] 12", each containing 2 jars of rum; square unwieldy weighty tins of Army biscuits; cases of jam; sacks of charcoal (1 per company for cooking purposes), bags of tea and sugar mixed with a good deal of dirt and, failing spare sacks, the cheese and the bacon carried in the same sack as the tea.

The Quarter Master Sergeant with an electric torch divides the rations into two companies, and the CQMS sub-divides these as best he can into platoons. Pitch dark, only the tiny circle of the flash lamp and withal, a most persistent damnable drizzle. And the mud, the heavy filthy mud under foot. The rations are served out to the platoons of my company for further sub-division, by daylight in the trenches, and the rations of the other company are apportioned out, in their huge cases to men unwilling to add to their already heavy kit of 180 rounds, pack, entrenching tools, full water bottle, rifle and rainsodden clay-caked overcoats. Then commences a veritable 'March of the Damned' which I lead. At first a mile of road, 'Mind the hole', I slip and slither and save myself, and the rest in single file, a line of scarcely visible shadows, curve round the big ss hole, whose waters had caught, just in time, the reflection of the starlights which were bursting dimly in the haze a thousand yards away.

'Bang,' 'Who the Hell has dropped that tin?' I go back: fall over a tin of biscuits no one owns to carrying. 'Here, you,' and I touch a bent shadow with my stick, 'pick it up and carry it.' And so we shuffle on at about a mile an hour, halting every 100 yards or so to readjust our burdens! And ever round us and over us sing those blessed bullets, now striking from somewhere in the mud alongside, now whistling sparks overhead, sometimes with a wicked 'phit' burying themselves viciously at our feet. For our track lies right along that zone of fire, when unaimed bullets from the German fire trenches to our right hit the ground. 'Come on, follow me boys, and God's sake keep up and buck up.' We turned off the road, and sink in over our boot tops, sliding and slipping forward across a field, over a long greasy bank (heavy casualties here to jam and biscuit tins) on to a plough. Heavy 'funk' firing breaks out on our right; bullets come our way more frequently; a pyrotechnic display in the distance gives form to my shadow line and silhouettes the trees on which I am directing my march. How we curse the men in the trenches for firing and irritating the Germans to fire back. Neither hurts each other. It is we poor devils 1,000 yards behind who get it all. We slosh on our way, my men sullen, patient, spiritless, I cursing, urging, imploring, threatening, exhorting, in every endeavour to get my poor sheep safely and quickly across 300 yards of high open, shell pitted, slippery, waterlogged clay plough into which 'strays' are thudding, most unpleasantly and frequently. I fall full length over a telephone wire and my leading men, missing me, at once go astray. Get them right once more, the dug-outs at last, mud deeper than ever.

Acting Lieutenant Colonel John Trefusis
1ST BATTALION, IRISH GUARDS

I went round all the billets in the afternoon and found the men quite comfortably established in the barns with plenty of straw and braziers. I forgot whether I ever mentioned the fact that during our latter turn of duty in the wet trenches, our medical officer, Capt McCarthy, who is a civilian doctor in Grosvenor Street, tried the experiment of mixing some mustard with the lard, before the men put it on their legs, in order to try and stimulate circulation. Anyhow this was done, with the result that not a single man suffered from swollen feet during the last 72 hours they were in the trenches, whereas for the first 48 hours about 40 had to be sent sick with bad feet.

Private A.R. Brennan
2ND BATTALION, ROYAL IRISH REGIMENT

At night time the ration party would set out for Auchonvilliers, a ruined village about a mile in our rear. Our transport wagon came up every night after dark, as did the transports of the other companies, and it was a busy and surely a unique scene at the cross-roads every night when the Quarter-master Sergeants started the job of dishing up the rations for each platoon. To get to the village from our trenches one had to cross about three or four hundred yards of open space—I believe there was a communication trench, but it was so full of mud and water that we preferred to risk a stray bullet and remain dry. Once or twice we did have the unpleasant feeling of the close 'swish' of a bullet, but I don't remember that anybody was ever hit. Later, when the weather broke, and this much traversed pathway became muddy and slippery, it was a way of tribulation for many an overburdened ration carrier, and many the heartfelt curse went up to Heaven from the lips of an exasperated 'Tommy' as he measured his length on the slushy earth, or slid headlong towards the ubiquitous shell-hole. Given a large four-cornered box of biscuits; a couple of sand-bags loaded with anything from tins of 'Bully' to bricks for the Captain's dug-out, and slung around one's neck a rifle and two bandoliers of ammunition, and the things that could happen to one's person and one's temper on that three hundred yards of slippery, uneven footpath on a dark night were enough to try the patience of the meekest 'Tommies'. I myself once finished one such exasperating journey by sliding down into our six-foot communication trench on my back, much to the amusement of our only DCM Sergeant. He consoled me, I remember, by telling me not to worry, and that I would be a long time dead.

Captain Gerald Burgoyne
C COMPANY, 4TH BATTALION, ROYAL IRISH RIFLES

Our battalion is the 'bad boy' of the Division, and tomorrow the Divisional General (Haldane) is to inspect us, and I suppose, give us Hell. We are a lot of rapscallions, I confess, that's the fault of our GOC's precious brother who ruined the SR to build up his 'Terriers'. All of us are deploring the state of the Battalion, and we trust we may not be asked to attack, before we have an opportunity of weeding out the men and instructing those who are left. It's disgraceful that we out here should have to do the work which should have been done at home.

Second Lieutenant J.L. Stewart Moore
15TH BATTALION, ROYAL IRISH RIFLES

After the trenches at Fonquevilers the next event was a review by King George V and President Poincare, not a formal ceremonial review but rather a drive past. The Battalion paraded after breakfast and no doubt there was an inspection to ensure that every man was smartly turned out. As riflemen we had black buttons which did not need to be polished but an occasion like this called for the highest standard. We set out from our village about nine or ten o'clock and proceeded over rough farm tracks until we reached our rendez-vous about noon. Here we came to one of those long straight French roads, *route nationale* as they are called, and we joined with the rest of the Division in lining it on either side. It was a raw October day with a bitter wind and we stood there for nearly three hours waiting for something to happen and chilled to the bone. If we had had overcoats it would not have been so bad but General Nugent our Divisional Commander has issued an order to the effect that General Officers and their staffs could wear overcoats and gloves but others could not. It must have been nearly three o'clock when at last the King and the President drove slowly past in an open car. When they had gone we re-formed and started home again to our village. The rough farm track made marching difficult but we stumbled on, halting for a rest every hour. I had some liquor brandy in my flask and with its aid I just made it. I would emphasise that King George and President Poincare drove in an open car and it is to their credit that they did so on such a cold day.

Sergeant F. de Margry
2ND BATTALION, ROYAL IRISH REGIMENT

Our draft joined the few survivors of the 2nd BN, Royal Irish Regiment, in the Ypres Salient rear positions and were told as we were still not up to Battalion strength and, therefore, unable to occupy a front line section of the trenches, we would be employed on night fatigues mostly. That same night [the day he joined the Battalion] I was given some wooden stakes and a couple of reels of barbed wire to carry to the front line, so after joining the others similarly loaded up, we moved off in the dark, taking a 'B' line to our destination across some very rough ground, pitted with shell-holes, half-full of stinking water and intermittently lighted up by bright aerial flares fired from the trenches. We hadn't gone very far in this slow and laborious fashion when we tripped more and more over dead bodies (most of them belonging to Princess Pat's Canadian Infantry who'd been gassed) and their long rifles scattered round them. I had already slipped down a couple of fair size shell-holes and got somewhat wet and muddy in my efforts to scramble out without losing my cumbersome load, but not long afterwards we came under cross-fire from enemy machine guns and several of our group fell on the spot while the topmost reel I was carrying was hit causing some of the barbed wire to drop in coils round me and tripping me up every few steps as well as scratching me and tearing my uniform. At this stage the Officer i/c our party, noting my predicament, enquired 'Have you been hit?'—to which I replied 'It's only the barbed wire broken loose that's causing me to trip more and more, Sir.' He then advised me to dump the offending reel there and then—and to get a move on before worse befell me.

Captain John Trefusis
1ST BATTALION, IRISH GUARDS

This morning, hearing that the wood in our immediate front was clear of the enemy, I went through it to see what was on the other side. The whole wood is strewn with dead Germans, and a few English. A horrible sight. I had 30 Germans buried and 5 English. There are many other Germans probably, 100 all dead for about 10 days, partially buried. Some are blown to pieces by our guns. There was a fight in this wood about 10 days ago. I also collected a lot of rifles and ammunition and other German equipment. Unfortunately one of our men, PTE O'Shaughnessy, NO 1 COY, was killed by a sniper while looking out at the end of the wood, just after I left. The Germans belonged to the 64th, 56th, 89th and 49th REGTS. But we could not get anything off them, as they had been dead too long.

Lieutenant William Carden Roe
1ST BATTALION, ROYAL IRISH FUSILIERS

They were a splendid regiment to work with, the Seaforth Highlanders, and with a thoroughly good understanding the progress of work on our trenches was most satisfactory. The greeting of the men on relief nights showed at once the excellent feeling that prevailed. Many a time since, I have seen a relief carried out in dumb silence, but with them it was a continual succession of 'Good-night, Jack,' 'Good-night, Pat,' and so on.

Sergeant F. de Margry

2ND BATTALION, ROYAL IRISH REGIMENT

A striking example, one might say, of learning the hard way to gain the experience that pays in the long run—if one survives to benefit from it. Not many days later I was detailed to report to a certain newly joined officer at Bogey-Bogey sap in our front line at some specified time for special duty, which I must say did not altogether surprise me even if it did not convey much to me at the time. On reporting later, as instructed, I was informed that our objective was to locate and destroy a certain advanced enemy machine-gun post which was causing us quite a bit of trouble. We then proceeded to make our way through this sap which led into No-Man's Land and out by our own barbed wire when, owing to my bulk, I suddenly found myself stuck and unable to move either forward or backward, and finally had to be pushed and pulled by the others till I could crawl out unaided. The night was so dark that the Officer in Charge of our small party felt his way gingerly with the aid of an unsheathed sword-stick, thereby creating quite a noise as the metal blade struck some of the many empty bully tins littering the ground. As he was obviously quite unaware of the danger of announcing our presence in this fashion, I took it upon myself to warn him, for which he thanked me as he sheathed his sword-stick. After which I more or less took the lead as we crawled on our bellies towards our objectives. As a matter of fact, I was soon right by it, and before I had realised it myself, for almost the next moment the German machine-gun opened fire immediately in front of me, only barely missing my head which was slightly raised at the time. Somewhat annoyed about this I promptly prepared a Mills hand grenade for action and at the first opportunity threw it through the wide fan-wise opening and quickly followed this up by throwing another one the same way. We then lost no time wrecking the gun and its emplacement, and suddenly hearing the sound of fast approaching Germans rushing along the adjoining slit trench, we quickly dispersed to make our own way back to the trenches independently and under a regular shower of flares, bullets, stick-bombs, etc. The cost of this little operation was unfortunately pretty high as we lost two killed, three wounded, one missing and the rest badly shaken, out of our small party.

Private B.W. Page
C COMPANY, LONDON IRISH RIFLES

Saw my first shell of shrapnel. Shell burst first 100 yards behind and then about 75 yards in front of my platoon. Two men hit in B COY. One in arm and other in thigh.

Acting Lieutenant Colonel John Trefusis
1ST BATTALION, IRISH GUARDS

As a set off to our bomb-throwing of last night, my Headquarters was bombarded for half an hour just as I had finished breakfast. I did not take much notice of the first few sent, but when one pitched quite near, I went out to see what was going on, and then advised everyone to get into a dug-out. I stood in the orchard just behind our house, and watched the bombs coming over. They must have been sent from at least 700 yards off. One couldn't hear the discharge, only the whistling through the air. When they came over the house you could see them coming; they looked about the size of a cricket ball, but were probably larger really. One burst within 30 yards of me, and another within 15, and the only effect was a big hole in the ground, about 3 ft deep and 4 ft across and a lot of mud thrown up in the air. It was a novel and interesting experience for a short time. They exploded with a fearful noise. In all about 20 were sent over, only one of which hit the corner of the house and did no damage.

Sergeant F. de Margry
2ND BATTALION, ROYAL IRISH REGIMENT

The first time we went into the trenches as a fighting unit (cheered on our way by ironical shouts of 'You're going the wrong way, Chum!' from other troops watching us—as if we didn't know!) we occupied support trenches immediately behind the front line for a period of a week, after which we relieved the Battalion holding the front line in front of us for a week. After being relieved in our turn a week later we moved back of our 'rest camp' where for another week we were sent up and down the line, daily or nightly, engaged on various arduous fatigues ranging from ration parties to trench maintenance, or latrine digging to hauling heavy ammunition boxes to the front line, or laying barbed wire entanglements in No-Man's Land to building timber tracks for heavy vehicles—in fact quite a variety of back-breaking jobs, especially on bully and biscuits which was more or less our staple daily ration. Water was so scare that one had to save half one's morning mug of tea for shaving purposes and wait for rain for a wash of sorts. Once in a blue moon one had a quick shower at the Divisional Baths (generally miles away) and a clean change of underwear, so it's no wonder we were almost permanently lousy. Our drinking water (rationed) was so heavily chlorinated as to be almost undrinkable, and more often than not our tea was greasy and onion flavoured due to the dixies being used for soups or stews serving as receptacles afterwards for tea-making—without any sort of cleaning for want of facilities. In fact, many a time we had good cause to exclaim 'If only our Mum (or Wife, etc) could see the b.... mess we're in!' knowing full well it was beyond description.

Private B.W. Page
C COMPANY, LONDON IRISH RIFLES

Marching through the multitudinous twists and turns of the communication trenches, every section of which is named Harley St, Morhpia St, Mile End Road, Conduct St, etc. Arrived finally at the firing line (80 yards from the German trenches) and were mingled with South Staffords who turned out to be very decent fellows. Found life in the trenches not half bad except that I got very dirty and had very little sleep. Many dead bodies of Germans lying between the lines; had been there for weeks. Looked for hours through periscope but could not see a single German. Plenty of shelling all day, but none came near our trenches, except bombs thrown from trench mortars. One man hit by one of these. Our own trench mortars do a great deal of execution; one was just behind my section.

Acting Lieutenant Colonel John Trefusis

1ST BATTALION, IRISH GUARDS

I went round to see what companies were doing this morning, by way of training. I had been to 1 and 2 and had just finished with 4 when I heard an explosion and saw some smoke, and men running and shouting in all directions about 300 yards away. I went over to see what had happened, and found that Keating, one of my best officers, had been showing some men how to throw bombs, and he had held one too long after having lighted it and it had exploded. He himself was lying in the ground quite dead, blown to pieces, a truly horrible sight and 13 men had been wounded. It is a terrible calamity and I would not have had it happen for worlds. It was purely an accident. Keating seems to have cut off too much fuse, and having lit it, it went off sooner than he expected.

Private David Starrett

9TH BATTALION, ROYAL IRISH RIFLES

I was actually climbing over the top to get a near view when I was stopped by a warning that that way I'd get my blinking head shot off! There was no reason, I soon knew, to go out of my way to view craters. The Bosch provided them carefully quite close to wherever one happened to be.

The man who warned me, a rifleman, was friendly and I got to telling him about myself and the regiment. 'Blimey, mate,' he said, 'I don't understand you Irish. Before the war you were all for fighting each other and now you're all pally like and contented.'

Private B.W. Page

C COMPANY, LONDON IRISH RIFLES

Spend large part of day fighting vermin with paraffin; nearly every man in the regiment is like the proverbial cuckoo. Working party 8–12. More rumours of presence of some of Kitchener's mythical millions.

Acting Lieutenant Colonel John Trefusis
1ST BATTALION, IRISH GUARDS

In the afternoon I tried the experiment of shooting through two loose blankets, folded two, four, six and eight times and hung on a string about six inches apart. It was supposed to stop a bullet, but it did not; the bullet going through the six and eight folds turned sideways and went into the target in this position. The blankets were dry and the range about 30 yards.

Acting Lieutenant Colonel John Trefusis
1ST BATTALION, IRISH GUARDS

I went back to my dug-out and tried to find out what officers I had left. I found Gutherie and Fox had been killed, and the following wounded: Rosse badly in the head, Young Ralli who came to my forward headquarters with a nasty wound in his thigh, Alexander, Greer, R. Paget, Persse, Boyse, Tallents, and Campbell, while Billy Reid had been knocked unconscious by a shell; I saw him in a dug-out. A truly awful list and this left me with twelve officers. Very few of the remainder of them who were present at the action escaped without some slight scratch, for of the twelve left, five were right behind with transport according to orders. MacCarthy got hit on the head by a bit of shell, Desmond Fitzgerald a bruised back, and I got a piece of shrapnel through the peak of my cap which made a very slight scratch just above my eye, so that only left two untouched.

Company Sergeant Major Arthur 'Jimmy' Rixon
'A' COMPANY, LONDON IRISH RIFLES

I got hung up in some old German trenches and was spotted from their lines. Made for the road and a maxim was turned on me but luckily they were too high. A house I was making for was smashed by two shells immediately after. I went back into the trench, and every time I moved a sniper had a go at me. Decided to wait until dark before moving again when rescued by PTE Riding, SW Borders. Never more pleased to see anybody in my life. A hot time getting back to Port Arthur, as maxim and sniper was keen on bagging us both. Reached there eventually running and crawling. Found party had left so was told to wait and go with SW Borders. Retired to an old cellar with signallers of the Gloucesters, heard a fine mouth organ solo over the wire, but interest waned when discovered the audience were all 'cooty'. Can't be helped. Suppose I shall be the same one day. Went out by the boundary corner as Hell it was too hot. Three men hit in half an hour. An awful 1½ miles; doubled over like a pocket knife. Reached the corner, then had to go along a road for about a mile under fire all the time. One man hit in the leg; almost wish it had been me, if this is the usual thing. Pegged in with the SBS of the Gloucester REGT. Fagged out.

Acting Lieutenant Colonel John Trefusis
1ST BATTALION, IRISH GUARDS

Burke is much worse than I thought, and both he and Rosse were operated on today. I cannot say too much in praise of the officers and men and how magnificently they all behaved in very trying circumstances during the attack on the 18th and held on to the ground they had gained, so it is no use trying to do so. I deplore the casualties, but it is no use thinking too much about them as they are bound to occur.

Lieutenant J.L. Stewart Moore
15TH BATTALION, ROYAL IRISH RIFLES

I had vivid recollection of going up into the front line and taking over in a steady downpour of rain. Next morning there was water and mud everywhere and the sides of trenches had begun to fall in. I got a working party together to clean up the mess in our section of the trench but they made little headway. Had they been farmers before they joined up they would probably have done better for they would have known something about cleaning out ditches. As it was, they were all from the backstreets of Belfast, tradesmen whose lives had been spent working in the shipyards and linen mills so they were unskilled in handling spades and shovels. Throwing sticky mud up out of a trench is no easy task, especially when you have to keep your head down for fear of German snipers. We were on the extreme left of the battalion front and next to us was a battalion of the Royal Irish Regiment from Wexford and the South-East of Ireland. Suddenly our Brigadier-General turned up and took in the situation at a glance. 'Come on now,' he said. 'Stick it, Ulster. Don't be disheartened. There's a southern Irish regiment just round the corner. They're watching you. Don't let them see Ulster giving way.'

Acting Lieutenant Colonel John Trefusis

1ST BATTALION, IRISH GUARDS

I heard last night that George Nugent had been killed. It is very sad —several old Irish Guardsmen have lost their lives. He apparently was talking on the brick path leading to the Givenchy trenches, up which I have so often gone, and a stray bullet came and hit him in the spine. Funnily enough it was within 200 yards of where his boy was hit in March.

Acting Lieutenant Colonel John Trefusis

1ST BATTALION, IRISH GUARDS

I went up to the top of my much dilapidated house in which my Headquarters are situated, to watch our heavy artillery shelling a certain place in the German line. From this observation post, one can get a good view of the whole position and apparently the enemy got a good view of me, as three shots hit the wall, and one came right through, where there is no wall. So I went below for a bit, but returned as soon as I heard our heavy guns begin to shoot. They made perfect practice and were followed after each shot by shrapnel, to hit off any of the enemy who might be running back from the effect of the heavy artillery. I watched this for some time, and then the Germans began to shell all the houses, so I retired below to the cellar. Two or three shells took more off the roof of this house, so it was probably lucky for me that I had gone below.

Private B.W. Page
C COMPANY, LONDON IRISH RIFLES

Marched 5 mls to Cambrian and Guinchy [sic] which is at the end of communication trenches, walked with full pack through 2½ mls of communication trench to pave some of them with bricks. Had to lay low every two minutes to avoid shrapnel shells. On arriving at destination, it was found to be too hot to work in, so returned. One man hit in the hand. Started 12 am digging reserve trenches, with shells from our own guns whistling over head. The enemy were shelling one of our machine guns in a churchyard about 500 yards to our front. They dropped 63 shells in that neighbourhood and set a house on fire.

Private Frank Germain
ROYAL IRISH FUSILIERS

While we were in the front line we all got the wind up, what with the heavy shells coming over our trench with mud and water and a line of dead Frenchmen in front.

Lieutenant William Carden Roe
1ST BATTALION, ROYAL IRISH FUSILIERS

It was quite dark when we reached the line, and unaccustomed as I was to these new conditions of warfare, I had many a stumble into shell-hole or barbed-wire fence before, after passing into the ruins of a small farm, I saw a glimpse of light shining up from the farm cellar beneath my feet. Feeling my way down the steps and pushing aside the blanket which guarded the entrance, I stood blinking in the comparative brilliancy of the cellar, temporarily blinded. My appearance was the signal for a shout of laughter, through which the voice of George Bull rang out, 'Well, I'm damned, it's "Tip". What on earth have you come out here again for? You know it's dangerous sometimes.' I was amongst the men who really mattered once more.

Private B.W. Page
C COMPANY, LONDON IRISH RIFLES

Marched to Guinchy [sic]. Spent time bricking reserve trenches and carrying sandbags. Returned 1 o'clock; 5 o'clock several shells dropped within 30 yards of the billet, but nobody was hurt. Two French soldiers came into house to take shelter. One of them was anxious to learn 'Tipperary' which we did our best to teach him.

Acting Lieutenant Colonel John Trefusis
1ST BATTALION, IRISH GUARDS

A quiet, but wet night, and I found the trenches very bad in some places, but the men are in excellent spirits because they said they had been shooting a lot of Germans. There is no doubt that the enemy's snipers are much less active since we established properly protected places for our sharpshooters to shoot them, i.e. loopholes made of steel through which the German bullet will not penetrate.

Lieutenant William Carden Roe
1ST BATTALION, ROYAL IRISH FUSILIERS

At 'Stand to' the next morning I was able to make myself better acquainted with my surroundings, and very soon got to know every inch of the trench. The trenches that winter in the vicinity of Ploegsteert Wood, where my regiment held the line, were all very much of the following type. Our line consisted of one firing trench, with in a few places a services trench running about twenty yards in the rear and containing the shelters of officers and men, similar in appearance to my own abode. The actual firing line became a breastwork in those places where, on digging, water was found close to the surface. In spite of this, even in the finest weather, our Company line from end to end contained water varying in depth from a few inches to the height of 'Gum boots thigh'. In No-Man's Land a strong belt of wire had already been erected and this was increased nightly. A few cows with their toes turned heavenward supplied the 'Bruce Bairnsfather' atmosphere in more senses of the word than one. The enemy trenches, no doubt resemblant on every way to ours, were roughly two hundred yards distant.

Company Sergeant Major Arthur 'Jimmy' Rixon
'A' COMPANY, LONDON IRISH RIFLES

Dead Cow Farm. Bullets whistling over all night, rather surprised this morning to see two sparrows very complacently building in a tree [of] which not much left. I wonder how long it will be before their domestic serenity will be disturbed. Wrote to old love and Aunt Pollie. Nothing much doing, try to do a bit of sniping but no targets so have a sleep until dinner.

Acting Lieutenant Colonel John Trefusis
1ST BATTALION, IRISH GUARDS

The Brigadier gave us some information as to the trenches we had to take over. They are rather wet, and the part this Battalion has to take over is only about 50 yards from the enemy. The present Brigade is suffering from 'Trenchitis', i.e. they sit still in their trenches, and go on the principle Live and let live. This will not win a war.

Private B.W. Page
C COMPANY, LONDON IRISH RIFLES

Trench very soon a quagmire and soon we were covered in mud from head to foot. Too dark to see and shovelled down each others' necks and sleeves. Barely finished rampart when order came to stand by. Felt rotten. Was wet to the skin and had but 2 hrs sleep in 36 hours.

Lieutenant William Carden Roe
1ST BATTALION, ROYAL IRISH FUSILIERS

Life in the trenches at that time was arduous. We had no general issue of gum boots, no duck boards, no pumps—in fact, none of the little things which later in the war helped to make trench life bearable. Our very shelters even we could not keep dry, and night after night we snatched our brief hours of sleep between hours of duty in the line, lying in pools of ice-cold water. The saving factor was that the enemy shelling was never severe and our casualties were correspondingly light. It was pleasant to march out of the trenches each time we went back to billets with practically the same body of officers and men. In this way I got to know intimately the men under my command, and the best of understanding sprang up.

Private A.R. Read
HQ, 141ST INFANTRY BRIGADE

Companies were told off for working parties and used to go up to the Trenches to repair barbed wire and put in order any damage made during the day. To see a working party start off was a strange sight. Each man was loaded up like a pack mule. Trench boards, sandbags, barbed wire, stakes, picks and shovels besides rifles and a canvas bandolier of ammunition. It was usual to work under the supervision of the Royal Engineers and the Infantry used to swear like mad over this.

Acting Lieutenant Colonel John Trefusis
1ST BATTALION, IRISH GUARDS

The trenches were bad, both from the point of view of comfort and also from the military point of view, i.e. too many loopholes, and in many places the men could not see to fire over the top of the parapet, which of course is essential to repulse an attack, or look out over at night. The water in most places varied from 50–200 yards away. They have got in many places 'chevaux de frises' and would have to come through a great deal of surface water to attack us. The relief took a long time to complete owing to the narrowness of the communication trenches, and the depth of the mud in them. Seven men were stuck in the mud, and had to be dug out. One was in for six hours. I saw him next morning, and asked him how he was, and he said he was alright except for a little rheumatism!

Private A.R. Brennan
2ND BATTALION, ROYAL IRISH REGIMENT

I had to crawl along to the end of the lowest 'sap' and lie in a cramped area of about three-feet square, 'listening' for sounds of the enemy, who were supposed to be 'mining' in our direction. The technical part of the work, including the 'timbering', had been done by Welsh miners, and I may owe my continued existence in part, at least, to the excellence of their work. I never heard any sign of the Germans during my long vigils, but the engineers, who had special 'listening' apparatus, declared that they could hear them very well. When the 'saps' were finished and everything was ready, the engineers brought down their explosives and placed them in position. We then packed the 'saps' with sand-bags of the displaced chalk on our side to prevent any 'throw-back' from the explosion, whenever it came, and our work on the Mine was finished.

Acting Lieutenant Colonel John Trefusis
1ST BATTALION, IRISH GUARDS

I hear there is rather a peculiar situation up the line. Some Saxons insist on sitting on the top of their trenches, and apparently our men do not like to shoot at them. An ultimatum was sent to say that at noon if they sat there they would be fired at. They were still sitting there, and some shots were fired over their heads, and all they did was to wave the papers they were reading! It is also said that they pointed further up and shouted: 'There are the damned Prussians up there, who would shoot as soon as look at you!' I have not since heard what happened since.

Private A.R. Brennan
2ND BATTALION, ROYAL IRISH REGIMENT

Over the entrance to the Mine some pessimist had inscribed the fateful 'Abandon hope all ye who enter here!' We all felt pretty miserable, but few, I imagine, could have quite abandoned all hope. We used to sit about during our 'shift' discussing the probable duration of the War, and even the most hot-blooded of us would vote the conflict over by the following Christmas. It was a case of the 'wish' and the 'thought'. Alas, there were to be three more Christmases, and a good many of my comrades of those days were not fated to see them. By the time we finished working on the Mine our constant contact with the chalky soil had made us white in body and countenance, if not in soul. What with working for eight hours underground and sleeping in an overheated and poorly ventilated dug-out for the greater part of the rest of the day—we had to keep under cover during the day-time because of enemy observation balloons—we looked a thoroughly unhealthy lot of rascals. We had not a decent wash, much less a bath, during that time, and we were, of course, completely 'lousy'. Most of us hoped that we should now be returned to our battalion.

Private A.R. Brennan
2ND BATTALION, ROYAL IRISH REGIMENT

We were taken into a dug-out, and wet though we were, sleep soon claimed us. After a couple of hours, had to leave the dug-out and proceed to the front line (what a thrill!) where we were told to mix with the men of the East Lancashires, who were already 'standing to'. I was with a party of six men occupying an old railway signal-box. The railway line ran by our 'box' and straight to the German lines, so that from where we were we looked down the line and knew that at the end the enemy was watching us. That night we sent a patrol along and remember waiting with a thrill to hear the first sounds of conflict; not realising, as I was to later, that 'patrols' had always a healthy respect for each other, and except where it was necessary to procure a prisoner for the benefit of the 'Intelligence' branch of the Army, gave each other a wide berth. I did a spell of sentry that night with a sixteen-year-old boy, who had been out in France with the East Lancashires for several months and was quite the hardened veteran.

Acting Lieutenant Colonel John Trefusis
1ST BATTALION, IRISH GUARDS

We heard this morning we had to take over a new line of trenches between Givenchy and Guinchy [sic], I mean new to us. I wish we could be put back into ones we know, as the casualties are always much larger when we first go into new trenches; and by the time we know the surrounding country, and the various devices of the enemy, we are taken out, and can do no really good service as one might do if one went back to ground one knew.

Private A.R. Brennan
2ND BATTALION, ROYAL IRISH REGIMENT

At that hour precisely our party marched off for a destination unknown and on a task of the nature of which we were completely ignorant. After proceeding through miles of trenches—or so it seemed—and walking along 'duck-boards', through narrow communication trenches—all the time drawing nearer to the front line, as we could tell from the nearness of the Verey lights—we reached, at last, what turned out to be the forward trench, although we did not know it at the time. Somebody drew aside a macintosh sheet and exposed the door to what appeared to be a dug-out, but in reality was the entrance to the Mine upon which for the next three weeks we were busily engaged. The engineer in charge lost no time in starting us on our various tasks. Mine at the beginning was that of hauling up sand-bags of chalky soil to the trench from the sloping 'sap' which led from the door in the trench to a long gallery sunk probably about ten feet or so under our side of No-Man's Land. From this gallery five or six 'shafts' were sunk perpendicularly to a depth of twelve or fifteen feet, and from this depth 'saps' ran out towards the Germans. This was the famous Gommecourt Mine, which was blown up in the spring of 1917, when the Canadians (I think) went over the top. We used to find it very difficult to get rid of the chalky contents of the sand-bags, without attracting the attention of the enemy. Here at this Mine we worked for about three long weeks. We had, in addition to the eight hours spent in the actual work, to spend another hour wending our way to and from our dug-out, and the end of each shift left us very tired and weary.

Acting Lieutenant Colonel John Trefusis
1ST BATTALION, IRISH GUARDS

I went round the trenches soon afterwards and found them very muddy, but gradually being dug out so as to get them down to dry ground again. Eric Greer was trying an experiment of shooting rifle grenades point blank out of a rifle, instead of up in the air, and dropping on to the required spot, as this gave the enemy time to see them coming. There are one or two snipers about 70 yards off who have been giving trouble, and I hope we may get at them by this means.

Private A.R. Brennan
2ND BATTALION, ROYAL IRISH REGIMENT

We were put to work making big dug-outs capable of holding about thirty men each. It was only a short walk from our own dug-outs, and we always worked at night. Every night when we arrived at our place of work we used to find the floors of the dug-outs completely covered by frogs. They seemed to like the chalky soil. We usually started work about nine, and judged the time for knocking off by the position of the North Star. Dick Breen, Frank Waldron, and a chap named O'Connor had made themselves a small dug-out apart from the rest of the Platoon. The other fellows did not like it and thought it was just a bit of a Cadet Corps 'standoffishness', but since they benefitted by the extra room thus permissible in the big dug-out, they contented themselves with a grumble or two. As I had more in common with Breen and Waldron, especially as they were Kilkenny men, than any of my other Platoon comrades, I asked the former to let me join them and they consented. From that time onwards we were as inseparable as the circumstances of the War would permit.

Acting Lieutenant Colonel John Trefusis
1ST BATTALION, IRISH GUARDS

The new method of firing the rifle grenades has been a success and the snipers have been completely silenced, and their loop holes blown in, and one of their dug-outs set on fire, so I hope they will change their position, unless they are killed.

Acting Lieutenant Colonel John Trefusis
1ST BATTALION, IRISH GUARDS

I went round the Herts trenches with their CO. I never realised what a good position they had got. They completely overlook the German line, and in some places can fire right into the backs of the enemy trenches where they bend back. They are also building a series of small forts which will eventually be connected with the trenches.

Private A.R. Brennan
2ND BATTALION, ROYAL IRISH REGIMENT

Within forty-eight hours of our return we were heading for the trenches again. Our new line, which we were taking over from the French, faced a wood that afterwards became very well known— Gommecourt Wood. The German trenches were six hundred yards away from ours, and life was so easy during the French occupation that the War to all intents and purposes ceased to be. The British, however, with their policy of the 'offensive spirit' were soon to change all that. The weather, when we moved in, was very mild and pleasant for mid-September. The French had buttressed their trenches with a kind of basket work, and although it was not as neat as the sand-bags, piled in brick wall fashion, by which we replaced it, I'm sure that it could hardly have been as ineffective as the said sand-bags proved to be. During the fine weather we sat about in the trenches and lazed and 'deloused' in our spare moments. Of course, our officers and NCOs saw that our hands were not 'idle' long. It was not an uncommon sight to see some 'Tommy' aroused from a 'furtive' forty winks in order to busy himself in the useful art of picking straws from the otherwise spotless duck-boards. At night time, after 'stand-down', those who were not on sentry duty were detailed either as ration party or for other fatigues, such as sand-bag filling, or strengthening the barbed wire out in front. There would also be a party for patrol duty, but this duty was usually assigned to old soldiers, or men who had been in France for some time. I should perhaps explain that it was the unfailing custom in the trenches throughout the War for all arms to assemble in the front-line and reserve trenches at dawn and sunset. These were thought to be the most likely times for the enemy to attack. They were called 'Stand-to' times, and usually lasted from a half to three quarters of an hour. At the end of this time the word 'Stand-down' would be passed along from the senior officer in the trench. The 'Stand-to' periods were also utilised for occasional rum issues in the summer months, and regular ones in the winter.

Acting Lieutenant Colonel John Trefusis
1ST BATTALION, IRISH GUARDS

The Battalion started off to relieve the Grenadiers about 4.30 pm and I rode up about 5.30. The enemy aeroplanes were very active and flew over us, but very high and fired at by our guns. I do not think they were paying the least attention to us, but trying to destroy some of our heavy guns which had caused them some annoyance and damage in the morning. We got the relief over all right about 7 and I went around all the trenches. The Germans certainly have more wire up in front of all of them, especially in their second-line trenches, and they were very musical, singing and making much noise, but otherwise they did not worry us except for an occasional bomb, which did no harm.

Acting Lieutenant Colonel John Trefusis
1ST BATTALION, IRISH GUARDS

I sat up in the dug-out all night and at 5.30 am, Desmond Fitzgerald and I went round to examine the place near the White House where the mine was supposed to have exploded. I could not see much trace of an explosion and later on the mining expert decided it was only a shell, so the White House mine has still to be exploded. After breakfast I went around again, and saw the two men who voluntarily went down the mine after the explosion to find the officer. It was a gallant deed and I have recommended them for the DCM. I can hear of no other mines so far. I had men listening at many points but not one of them heard anything. I have urged a definite mining policy for this area should immediately be adopted. We are truly sitting on a volcano without apparently taking any defensive action, and to me the mine danger is very real and I have written somewhat strongly on the subject.

We have all been issued out with an antidote to the latest German villainy, i.e. that of asphyxiating gases. They become more devilish every day, and it does not seem fair to men to fight them with clean weapons.

Private A.R. Read
HQ, 141ST INFANTRY BRIGADE

Our Brigadier General while inspecting the forward positions was killed by a sniper at 'Sidbury Mound'. Strange to say but I myself had passed this spot a good many times, and it must have been the General's red hat band that caused his death. His body was brought back to the Headquarters and each of us in turn was allowed to have a last look at him. We went out and picked some wild flowers and the Pioneers made a wooden cross. He was taken back to Bethune and buried in the civilian graveyard. His name was Brigadier General Nugent, late Colonel 1st Irish Guards, a good soldier well liked by all ranks. The staff officers were greatly upset. Next morning Col Godding of 17th Londons came as Temporary Brigadier. After this our boys were out for revenge.

Acting Lieutenant Colonel John Trefusis
1ST BATTALION, IRISH GUARDS

A very peaceful night, and the best I have had for some time. One of our big howitzers began shelling a German redoubt at 8.30 am which is only a few hundred yards on our left. I went into the Grenadier lines to watch it, and saw wood and earth flying in all directions; nothing could have lived in it, but I expect at the first shot the Germans went to ground somewhere near.

Acting Lieutenant Colonel John Trefusis
1ST BATTALION, IRISH GUARDS

We heard in the night that some more trenches have been taken by Territorials and also some 50 prisoners. The smells in this farm and the noises of all the various animals which inhabit this farm are awful. I cannot imagine how the family, of which there are many, can possibly live in this sort of atmosphere, but they seem to thrive on it.

I went round all companies in the morning. Some new sort of masks have been issued, all ready prepared with solution to counteract the effect of gas, and they seem very good. The men are being practised in putting them on quickly. The mask is a most necessary weapon now, as without it whole companies and more can be disposed of by the gas. We have not had it used against us as yet, but any moment it might be.

Sergeant F. de Margry
2ND BATTALION, ROYAL IRISH REGIMENT

Another somewhat similar occasion I can remember occurred during 'Stand-to' at dawn when I foolishly started on the cleaning of my loaded rifle with a ragged oily cloth, and it so happened that I accidentally pulled the trigger and in so doing the bullet from my rifle all but grazed the right side of my face and the flash from the barrel nearly singed my eyebrow. This certainly taught me a useful lesson, as when attempted one day to outwit a certain German sniper who turned out to be too smart for me (or better armed, perhaps, with the advantage of a telescopic sight in his favour), and whose last shot at me proved so dangerously close to my head that I there and then stopped fancying myself, or my chances, as a sniper.

Acting Lieutenant Colonel John Trefusis
1ST BATTALION, IRISH GUARDS

We relieved a Battalion of the 6th Brigade in the trenches about 3 pm and I immediately went round all the line. It is heartbreaking to see the state the trenches have been left in. It looks as if no-one had touched them since we left them at the end of February last, and it will take endless labour to get them anything like good and safe again. In some places too, the Germans have been allowed to come very close. In one place they have a post as near as 20 yards. I do not in the least wonder now, why in some parts of the lines the Germans are able to take our trenches; and I hear the trenches we left in May are even in a worse state than these.

Acting Lieutenant Colonel John Trefusis
1ST BATTALION, IRISH GUARDS

Up at 3.30 am and breakfast at 4. About this time an allied aeroplane flying very low was brought down, but luckily just behind our lines, and the men were unhurt. The battle began at 4.45 am and soon there was intense gunfire, about two miles north of us. One cannot describe it except by saying that it was one continuous roar of guns, occasionally relieved by a deep scrunching sound denoting one of our big howitzers had burst its shell somewhere. The whole horizon was thick with smoke, and occasionally one saw the flashes of the bursting shrapnel. It seems as if nothing could live in the area of this bombardment.

Captain Gerald Burgoyne
C COMPANY, 4TH BATTALION, ROYAL IRISH RIFLES

The Huns apparently have a big (11 inch) howitzer (the Jack Johnson) here now, as they put one slap into H3, making such a hole (22 inches wide, and 9–10 feet deep) that we were most of last night building fresh trenches and parapet around it. The enemy also scared the life out of the men in the dug-outs by placing a dozen or so shells round them, but only one went really close, and we suggest turning the hole it has made into a dug-out—it would hold comfortably fifteen men. Our guns will have to destroy the monster. Two men were killed yesterday when the shell burst in H3. They were blown out of a trench, and, if not killed outright, possibly got up and ran, half stunned, into the open where they were shot down and the Germans opened rapid fire on them.

Second Lieutenant J.L. Stewart Moore
15TH BATTALION, ROYAL IRISH RIFLES

At night in the trenches sentries were posted in every traverse and relieved at intervals of two or three hours. The Platoon Commanders took it in turn to patrol the company front from dusk to 9 p.m., from 9 p.m. to midnight, from midnight to 3, and from 3 to dawn. The officer on duty carried a very light pistol and fired it off occasionally so as to illuminate No-Man's Land. It gave one an eerie feeling to get on the firing step and talk in some whispers to the sentry while he stood there with his rifle at the ready, peering into the darkness through our barbed wire entanglement. Once I found a sentry asleep. It was an offence punishable by death but I did not report it, hoping that the man would be so scared that he would never do it again. At dawn everybody turned out and lined the firing step for stand-to in case of a dawn attack. After an interval we stood down again and each platoon officer accompanied by his sergeant distributed tots of rum to the men. At the end of our first four days in the Mesnil trenches we were relieved by the Somersets and returned to Medauville.

Captain Gerald Burgoyne
C COMPANY, 4TH BATTALION, ROYAL IRISH RIFLES

A man in another company, coming off parade, deliberately, it is said, put a bullet through his instep, in order to get sent home wounded. There's a good deal of self mutilation out here; but it is after all a very old military crime, and a very despicable one. However, this man will probably be court-martialled. Sentences are heavy here. I read out on parade today a sentence of 10 years PS on a private in a Scottish regiment for 'striking a superior officer' (a lance corporal) and several others; three years hard labour for drunkenness, assaulting a gendarme, etc. Gives our men something to think about. If only I could get rid of about 25 useless old wasters, get two or three real good NCOs, and have a month in which to train my Company I'd get them quite all right.

Acting Lieutenant Colonel John Trefusis
1ST BATTALION, IRISH GUARDS

[Monty Gore Langton] rang me on the telephone and told me the result of the reconnaissance. He went out across one crater with an orderly and a bomber, and found another deep crater between himself and the enemy's line. Here, while waiting for the lights to be sent up from behind to examine the German trenches, and he was now within a very short distance of them, a German came up to within eight yards of him, but he was seen by his orderly, who had two shots at him, the second killing him, and he fell back into the crater nearest the German line. Having now discovered what he wanted he came back. This was a very daring piece of reconnaissance work and well carried out. Later on he went out again to put some wire out, but fell in with a German bombing party, and only with difficulty got back to his trenches, being knocked down three times by the explosion of bombs near him. The men with him got back alright too.

Captain Gerald Burgoyne
C COMPANY, 4TH BATTALION, ROYAL IRISH RIFLES

Blowing up for another wet night. All around grey and God-forsaken. Little villages attract the eye, but on examining them through glasses they are only gaunt, blackened skeletons of houses; wherever we point our glasses, and look, nothing but the most complete ruins can be seen. Even Ypres, standing out so fair against the grey horizon, on inspection holds out roofless buildings and broken spires. I noticed near that town what I took to be the smoke of a factory; an hour later, huge flames betrayed its mystery. The wood, and trees, and even fences have suffered, and hold out to High Heaven blasted limbs, showing white where the shells have shattered them, the tops a mass of interlaced broken boughs. Huge stumps stand out prominently, their upper part slivered into firewood. A blasted country, damned and cursed in every meaning of these words.

Captain Gerald Burgoyne
C COMPANY, 4TH BATTALION, ROYAL IRISH RIFLES

My company, all told, is just 209 strong, with three soldiers, or, in other words, I can put some 155 in the firing line. During the last month I have had over 100 men, new drafts sent to me; but still the company keep the same strength, so it shows the tremendous wastage of war, even with an action. Since December 24th, doing merely outpost work, we have lost six killed, and five wounded in action and three accidentally, and the remainder going sick, bad feet mostly. Now we have to make the men rub their feet with fish oil before going into the trenches.

Second Lieutenant J.L. Stewart Moore
15TH BATTALION, ROYAL IRISH RIFLES

At sunset we moved up into the trenches in front of Fonquevilers.

The line there was held by a territorial battalion of the Warwickshire Regiment, the 7th Warwicks if I remember right. We did not take the trenches over from them but went in as their pupils and guests. They gave us a warm welcome and spent the next two days instructing us in trench life and routine.

Private A.R. Brennan
2ND BATTALION, ROYAL IRISH REGIMENT

At a later date, bad feet became so prevalent in the trenches that for the purposes of greasing the 'Tommies' feet, platoons were divided into two-men sections, each man of the section being responsible for another man's feet. As far as I was concerned, the MO treated me well. He excused me, with two other men, from the trenches indefinitely, and we spent the time, when the Battalion was in the front-line, doing all kinds of silly 'fatigues' in and around Englebelmer. I soon tired of the monotonous life away from the Platoon, and as well I missed my friends and found separation from them irksome. My two companions were not much to my liking either, so in the end I asked to be allowed to rejoin my Platoon after a lapse of only four days. My request was granted.

Sergeant F. de Margry
2ND BATTALION, ROYAL IRISH REGIMENT

I can well remember flopping down one evening dead tired, just inside a dug-out I shared with a few others, only to be hauled out a few minutes later by some NCO who was making up a fatigue party for some digging work or other to be carried out urgently in some communication trench nearby. Fuming inwardly I joined the others waiting outside and then our party marched off in more or less orderly fashion. Some few seconds later there was a blinding flash and a terrific explosion, and as we automatically turned round to see what had happened we were horrified to find that some heavy shell had completely obliterated the dug-out I'd only just left, and that all that could be seen of it was a huge crater about which some of the smoke and dust from the explosion could still be seen, but of the poor chaps I'd left sleeping there no sign of them could be seen anywhere.

Captain Gerald Burgoyne

C COMPANY, 4TH BATTALION, ROYAL IRISH RIFLES

One of our fellows, while a German flare lit up his trench as it shot over it, saw half a dozen of our raw Irishmen on their knees, praying to the Virgin as if their last hour had come. I don't think it's a bad thing for men to pray at any time, but when they are in the trenches a man should pray standing up, with his rifle ready. I think such a man's prayers are more efficient.

Private A.R. Brennan

2ND BATTALION, ROYAL IRISH REGIMENT

Every six days we were relieved from the trenches and went back to billets in Englebelmer. As we approached the village one of our fellows, Old 'Jock' Whitney, would start singing 'Here we are again' and we would all join in feelingly, especially if our time in the trenches had been a rough one. Going back to the billets was the nearest we could get to going to 'Blighty', and we were always glad to find a roof over our heads, and a nice warm, dry floor to sleep on. We had very comfortable quarters in a farm-house in Englebelmer. We had our own particular corners to sleep in and there was a fine old fireplace with an open chimney. There was even a kitchen cupboard where we kept our big round of cheese—there was always plenty of cheese—and tins of Tickler's jam of all shapes and varieties. Yes! There were many happy memories of good times spent in billets in Englebelmer—we were there for eight months— and of good comrades, too, most of whom were killed or wounded in the Somme offensive of the summer of 1916. We had got to know each other better before we left Englebelmer, and although a good many of them would steal the cross off an ass's back, they were just as willing to share their last crust with a comrade who needed it. Indeed, after six months of common hardships and common dangers we were just like one big family. Casualties in the winter months were few, so for the most part we were a happy family.

Sergeant F. de Margry
2ND BATTALION, ROYAL IRISH REGIMENT

A rather gruesome find was made during our final attempt [to locate some wounded] as one of our fellows came upon an officer's trench boots sticking out right by the German wire, and in trying to drag the officer clear by tugging at these boots, he suddenly found the decomposed legs inside these boots parting company from the officer's body which must have been lying there for quite a time. As the fellow concerned brought these foul and macabre boots back with him to our own trench after we had located and carried our wounded officer to safety, we were able to examine them more closely and found that they were obviously of French pattern and origin, from which we concluded that the officer must have been killed in the early days when French troops were holding this sector. To complete the gruesome story, the finder insisted on wearing these boots which he thought still serviceable enough to be well worth the unsavoury trouble of cleaning for further wear.

Captain Gerald Burgoyne
C COMPANY, 4TH BATTALION, ROYAL IRISH RIFLES

We found two Germans of, by the Loin on the buttons, a Bavarian regiment I believe (uniform; grey with red pipings and red facings), and two or three more Frenchmen. We buried all of them. Horrible sights, they'd been there at least five months. Some of my men went through their pockets and got some fancy souvenirs for their disagreeable job! I collared a little cheap locket, found in a German's pocket containing evidently the photographs of his children, a little girl and a little boy. Poor fellow, sad that he should lose his life in such a rotten cause.

Private A.R. Brennan
2ND BATTALION, ROYAL IRISH REGIMENT

Many a beautiful curse went up from our mud-filled dykes in Northern France during that awful winter of 1915. On one occasion I had to go on 'listening post' duty with another man and a lance corporal. The 'post' was in No-Man's Land just in front of our barbed wire. Our job, to look out for enemy patrols. What we should have done had we seen or met any I do not know. In any case the Germans had more sense than to spend their nights at this particular time of the year wallowing in the mud of No-Man's Land. They knew quite well that we, like themselves, were 'mud-bound'. Apparently their General-Staff had a better knowledge of conditions in the front-line than ours. The 'listening post' was an old shell-hole containing four inches of water in which we had to lie and 'listen'. We should have been relieved after two hours, but it was nearer to five before our 'relief' turned up. In the meantime the water froze and so did we. To add to our woes, on the way back to our dug-out we found the communication trench—a very deep one—completely blocked by a barbed wire obstruction hurdle, and had to make a long detour which put an end to any hopes we had of a few minutes sleep before 'Stand-to'.

Captain Gerald Burgoyne
C COMPANY, 4TH BATTALION, ROYAL IRISH RIFLES

I was talking to our Belgian interpreter today and he was telling me about the German atrocities. He keeps a note of three regiments of Bavarians who are responsible for the atrocities in Dinant and he told me he would give no mercy to any man of those regiments who fell into his hands. He knows of one case of a Belgian officer who was captured by the Germans close to his (the officer's home). His wife and their six or seven children went to the German Major and begged for the father's life, and the wife pointed to all her children. 'You have too many', said the Major, and then and there before the mother and father he had two or three kiddies shot. If one did not know such stories to be authenticated, one would almost feel sorry for the Germans, when the French and Belgian troops get into German territory.

Sergeant F. de Margry
2ND BATTALION, ROYAL IRISH REGIMENT

After carrying out a big and successful raid on the enemy trenches, we returned to our original starting point (the ruins of a large farm) a mile or so behind our lines where, by way of reward or celebration, we were all treated to a tumble-full of strong Army rum. As a result of this potent and generous libation on empty tummies our lads soon became fighting mad and to such an extent that, afterwards, it was remarked with a certain degree of truth that there had been almost as much fighting going on after as during the actual raid itself.

Captain Gerald Burgoyne
C COMPANY, 4TH BATTALION, ROYAL IRISH RIFLES

My company took over their trenches [near Elzenwalle] last night by 10 p.m. and we got in with no difficulties. The enemy appear to be peacefully inclined opposite us and if we don't annoy them they won't annoy us. Just as well as, if there was any volume of fire, the relief of the trenches would have been impossible. 'A' Company caught the Germans relieving their trenches and let them have it, and naturally if they caught us doing the same we would deserve all we got. We were working up to 4 a.m. filling sandbags and building parapets: digging communication trenches; putting out wire— though owing to the full moon it was impossible to put the wire out in front of our advanced trench where it was most wanted.

Private A.R. Read
'A' COMPANY, LONDON IRISH RIFLES

Of course we had to keep our heads down because there were snipers who were very good shots. These were hidden somewhere between the lines. A good number of dead bodies were lying between the trenches and were mostly Germans, who had been killed round about Christmas 1914, and were decomposed. Here was the Brickfields where Mick O'Leary of the Irish Guards had won the Victoria Cross just previously. Pat Weathers and myself were detailed to dig a sap jutting out towards the Germans. As luck would have it a dead Bosche was lying right across where we had to sap. After about two hours we must have been spotted, because whizz bangs began to pop near and one being extra close made me duck, when suddenly something hit me a whack on the back of the neck. It was the leg of the dead Jerry. The weight of the boot had caused it to part from the body. Well, when I discovered what had happened I simply bolted to the back of the trench and all the boys (except me) had a good laugh.

Company Sergeant Major Arthur 'Jimmy' Rixon
'A' COMPANY, LONDON IRISH RIFLES

About 8 am we have our first experience of what shells can really do. Guinchy [sic] church smashed to blazes with the exception of a crucifix which stands up through it all, and almost untouched. This is the third time I have seen the same—the church may be smashed but the crucifix seems to miss it. Wave and Gotobed [sic] buried in trench during bombardment and came in very white around the gills. Personally I must admit was glad when it was over.

Company Sergeant Major Arthur 'Jimmy' Rixon
'A' COMPANY, LONDON IRISH RIFLES

About 1 am sniper got particularly annoying, so after a lot of manoeuvring we managed to locate him, so to make no mistake brought gun along, and waited for his next flash to make certain of his position. Got it, and gave him about 15 rounds. He yelped and squealed a bit but we had no more trouble that night. The chances are his sniping days finished there.

Private A.R. Read
HQ, 141ST INFANTRY BRIGADE [BATTLE OF LOOS]

My next job was to go and find Captain Franks of the 19th somewhere out in front. Well this was just what I wanted and over the top I got. After clambering through our barbed wire, I walked half-right, and came upon the old German front line which had only been captured a couple of hours and it had cost us something. The sights were horrible, everywhere dead and wounded. British and German were mixed up and one could see that some hand-to-hand fights must have been terrible. The 15th Division had gone over determined on one thing (no quarter) and they used the bayonet whenever they got close enough. In one trench alone it was full of German dead for about 40 yards, so it was no wonder that the Jocks were known as the 'women from hell'. Honestly speaking there were 6 German dead to every Tommy, the cause of this being that Fritzy was down in deep dug-outs when our boys arrived as a good number were trapped. I came across where the London Irish had charged. There had been a tough scrap and I knew a good many of those who lay there. Passing on to the second line it was even worse. I found Capt Frank and he pointed out a cemetery at the corner of Loos village. Here the 19th were scrapping with Fritzy and we could see them firing at one another from behind the tombstones. I got hold of a German bayonet, cartridges, etc, and made my way back to Headquarters. I suppose that my nerves had given way at the sights I had seen, because on reaching the signal office down I went in a heap.

Private A.R. Read
HQ, 141ST INFANTRY BRIGADE

A prisoner was taken and brought down to Headquarters. He was immediately taken before the Brigadier and cross-questioned. First he said his age was 20, but afterwards confessed that he was only 18. He belonged to a Bavarian Regiment and had been on active service 12 months, having been at Ostend, Ypres, Hulloch, and Loos. As he was so boyish looking we did our best to cheer him up. It turned out that he was an officer's servant, and while going out to get a pail of water (and being very misty), had lost his way and stumbled into our trench.

Acting Lieutenant Colonel John Trefusis
1ST BATTALION, IRISH GUARDS

I got a message at 1.30 am to say there was a mist rising from the German trenches, and that gas was thought to be about. I got up and went round the trenches. So far as the mist was concerned it was a genuine one, but at least in two places I smelt or thought I smelt a strong smell of ether. I was out for some time, and found everyone alert who should be, and each man I asked knew exactly what to do in case of emergency. It may have been imagination what I smelt, but it also may have been that the enemy has ether ready in his trenches, and some of it may have been leaking. On the previous night some men of the Battalion on my right were overcome while digging, and there is evidence to show that some sort of sulphuric vapours were about that night. So whatever happens we are ready with masks and anti-gas mixtures and unless some new form of poison is tried of which we do not know, I think we can cope with anything that may happen.

Private A.R. Read
HQ, 141ST INFANTRY BRIGADE

The 1st Division went over and when they reached the German wire found that it was uncut. The Artillery had failed. Four times we attacked and each time were repulsed. The Camerons managed to gain the first trench, but the Germans who had retired to the second line pumped water into it which made the 'Jocks' evacuate and as they came out were mown down by machine gun fire. Those taken prisoner were stripped of their kilts and told to get back to our lines. As soon as they got over the parapets they were wiped out. As if this was not enough the 'fiends' threw petrol bombs at the dead and wounded and this of course burnt them.

Sergeant Major Thomas Davies
11TH FIELD AMBULANCE, 47TH IRISH BRIGADE, 16TH DIVISION

We received the gas attack, when hundreds of Irish and Jocks died a lingering death fighting for breath. It took us a whole week to clear all the casualties of this gas attack.

As last we relieved the Welsh Division (38th Division) in Mametze Wood and advanced to Guinchy [sic], Guillmount [sic]. This was real slaughter and some of the regiments lost over eight hundred men in those three days and nights. One Battalion had only fifty left out of 900. Here in the mud, shells, machine bullets, gas shells we poor stretcher bearers lived in Hell trying to save the wounded. Day and night it was real Hell everywhere and we were glad when we saw the Guards Division coming in to relieve the Irish Brigade.

Company Sergeant Major Arthur 'Jimmy' Rixon
'A' COMPANY, LONDON IRISH RIFLES [BATTLE OF LOOS]

I remember seeing A CO. as they swore they would, kicking their football on the way over and personally being more or less guilty of inanely and with parrot-like frequency exhorting the boys to keep their 5 paces. Although after the first 300 yards I couldn't see more than 50 yards each side of me, owing to the smoke, and vision obscured by the smoke helmet smothering my voice, so shut up, confining myself to watching if any of the boys went down so as to replace them by carrying men whom we had for that purpose. I don't wish to give the impression by the above that I was absolute coolness itself; I wasn't by any means, but in a horrible state of funk, as men were falling all around me and the MG fire and shrapnel from enfilade was terrible. I was expecting every moment that what seemed inevitable would happen, and that I should get a smash—where would be a matter of luck. Just before we reached there I felt a smash on the head and one over the ear and dimly realised I had been hit by something. Just previously I had pushed up my helmet to see what was happening more clearly and this action probably saved me from worse than I did get as the left goggle was smashed by a piece of shrapnel, but the glass was driven into my head. Blood was running down my face and neck when we eventually reached their second line, but got patched up and hung on as the trip back wasn't all that inviting owing to enemy fire and as I had negotiated it safely one was in no mood to try again until things quieted down. After a time I began to get very groggy and was advised to be satisfied and get back, which I did.

Coming back was no joy-ride as shells of all sorts and sizes were coming over now almost as thickly as when we were going but were more of the heavy order. It was during the journey back that I realised how heavily the poor old BATT must have paid for the name we made; all the way back were those who had fallen—some I recognised and others were men who had not been with us long.

Private A.R. Read

HQ, 141ST INFANTRY BRIGADE [BATTLE OF LOOS]

A and C Companies went over first and six minutes later it was reported that they had captured the first line of trenches. Shortly afterwards the rest of the 18th went over followed by the 19th and 20th and captured the second line. The 18th had orders to hold this line while the others pushed forward to a village. The 18th (London Irish) had taken a football over with them and dribbled it into the German trench and they kept advancing. The 17th soon followed up. By this time we were having a rare old hammering (in our trench) from the enemy artillery and chaps were being knocked down wholesale. Wounded and gassed soon began to arrive; also prisoners (whom we made into stretcher bearers). They reported that our brigade together with the 15th (Scottish) Division on our left were hand-to-hand fighting in the village of Loos. The Jocks were going mad and not troubling about prisoners. Their 'battle-cry' was: '9th of May, You Bastards.' This was for the way their countrymen had been slaughtered at Richbourg, and it was all bayonet with them.

Acting Lieutenant Colonel John Trefusis

1ST BATTALION, IRISH GUARDS

I then concocted a little plan for a bomb raid on the German trench. Owing to the gap which had been caused by our last bomb of the previous night, some of the enemy could be seen passing it to go on with their work at the end of the trench. So I had all my sharpshooters warned to be on the lookout. The first bomb fired bolted four Germans who got it hot from the sharpshooters as they passed the gap. The second burst too high, but made three more run back, the third hit the trench in front of them, and a lot of them were seen to fly up in the air and they doubled back. The forth also fell in the trench, and caused damage to it, so on the whole the raid was successful chiefly owing to Keating who aimed the mortar, and Straker who observed from a house and directed the fire by semaphore.

Private B.W. Page
C COMPANY, LONDON IRISH RIFLES

Took up position under a hedge for concealment. Lay freezing for an hour trying to sleep. Heavy bombardment from our guns commenced at 4.30 and continues at time of writing 7 a.m. Adjutant brings news. The French had captured three lines of trenches and that we had broken through in 7 places. Final attack to made on La Bassie. LIR are in reserve for 1st Army Corps, i.e. 5th London Brigade. Hear that the French are using turpentine shells for the first time. Further news that attack unsuccessful in one place and being renewed at 2.30 after bombardment which recommenced at 12 noon. Shifted to barn later but were turned out in full marching order. Moved off in direction of firing line at 11 p.m. Road thick with motor ambulances. After several tedious waits during a progress of about 3 mls, we marched to bivouac which we reached at 1 a.m. Awake at three a.m. frozen. Having nothing but waterproof cape and there being a very cold wind, walked up and down with about fifty others till thawed. Breakfast at 6 a.m. Wash in pond. At 6 p.m. marched one mile in the direction of the firing line and billeted in barn. Heard details of attack on Festubert Richburg line. Two brigades badly cut up, partly due to bad shooting of our own artillery and the fact that the Germans had many machine guns, one for each traverse in fact.

Acting Lieutenant Colonel John Trefusis
1ST BATTALION, IRISH GUARDS

The attack was arranged as follows: Ten minutes heavy bombarding followed by an attack by 50 Coldstream supported by 30 Irish Guardsmen to build up barricade when captured. At 10.50 am the fiercest bombardment I have ever seen began, and lasted for ten minutes. Then the attack began, but it was stuck just after it had passed a barricade held by Innes and 14 men. The reason for this I think was that some of our shrapnel was falling short, the barricade to be captured being only about 40 yards ahead. Innes and his 14 men were then ordered to charge, which they did most gallantly and took the attack with them. One man, Corporal O'Leary, Irish

Guards, rushed forward up the railway embankment and calmly shot down Germans behind the first barricade, five in all, then rushed on to another barricade and shot three more, and took two prisoners by himself. I hope he will be suitably rewarded. Thus a second barricade was taken besides a machine gun and about 50 prisoners, and our line was extended about 60 yards at this point. This was immediately entrenched by Eric Greer's company who worked like slaves at it.

Private B.W. Page
C COMPANY, LONDON IRISH RIFLES

Ordered to pack up suddenly, then to proceed to fire trenches without pack, which we reached at 4 o'clock. 'A' COY ordered to prepare to charge. Charged washed out and 'A' COY returned. At about 7.30 Germans exploded mine about 50 yards from my traverse making a devil of a noise and blowing the earth up about 50 ft. Opened rapid fire; machine guns and artillery following for about 10 minutes but no attack made by enemy. Mine fortunately 10 yards in front of trench and no one was much hurt. Stood by all rest of night in drizzling rain without capes.

Captain Gerald Burgoyne, C Company
C COMPANY, 4TH BATTALION, ROYAL IRISH RIFLES

My poor careless boys! One lad, one of Kitcheners (a number of K's Army have been transferred from the service battalions to the S.R.) only 19, killed at 8 a.m. He was right on the left of H2 a very bad trench; in a spot I would not have left by daylight for any money. He rushes out to get water and gets a bullet through the heart, and now my servant whom I had sent back on a message has just tumbled into my dug-out, shot through the forearm and bleeding like a pig. It's quite dark; he was carrying his rifle at full cock, with the safety catch forward. Falls into a shell hole, and blows a hole in his arm. But a brave lad, for instead of stopping at the dug-outs to get his arm bound up, he comes on another 200 or 300 yards (and 300 yards in the dark out here is as bad as half a mile by day) to tell me he had failed to deliver the message. Bandaged him up, but he bled all over my boots and puttees and is in some pain. But Boyd is a lucky man; only this afternoon he showed me with pride the photograph of his wife and child, and now he'll get home to both of them.

Private A.R. Read
HQ, 141ST INFANTRY BRIGADE

A little later the Engineers explored a mine under the German trenches (opposite our front); the 18th went over and captured the crater. Unfortunately NO 1 platoon were nearly wiped out, while NO 2 platoon (my platoon) also had a bad time. The reason for this was, they charged too soon and were caught by machine guns, while a number were buried alive. One chap was found with only his head sticking out of the ground, and his hair turned snow white. Soon after our boys made a bombing attack, and managed to dig in and consolidate their position.

Sergeant F. de Margry
2ND BATTALION, ROYAL IRISH REGIMENT

The Germans also experimented on us with liquid fire sprayed on to our forward positions, dropping of deadly darts from low-flying aircraft, gas and chemical shells, delayed action explosives, dum-dum or explosive bullets, various explosive devices to destroy our wire defences, flooding of our trenches from their usually higher positions, wholesale stripping of our freshly sandbagged parapets with machine-gun fire, concentrated fire on field cookers in operation, ration and other parties concentrated at assembly points, and even on our latrines at times.

Captain Gerald Burgoyne
C COMPANY, 4TH BATTALION, ROYAL IRISH RIFLES

We have buried all the dead in the vicinity, but a few little heaps of blue/red and khaki in front tell the pitiful tale. The last brigade here must indeed have been the limit. The lines immediately at the back of our rear parapet are a mass of indescribable filth amongst which rise three small crosses. Evidence that some Battalion had no care as to where they laid their dead. Indeed, it is quite possible they never even trouble to bury their dead, as one cross is marked 'A British soldier lies here, name unknown.' I put a working party on this morning to clean up this horrible plague spot, and a sharp-eyed sniper catching sight of a head, fired and killed one of my poor lads, quite a boy. Shot him through the back of the head and made a horrible mess. He lived for six hours in spite of it but never spoke a word and was unconscious all the time. We could do nothing but put some sandbags under his poor head.

Sergeant F. de Margry
2ND BATTALION, ROYAL IRISH REGIMENT

Being one of the first to jump into the enemy trench, I was violently butted on the head with a rifle the next moment by some fellow, about to jump in his turn, mistaking me for a German, and I suffered from a pretty sore head and stiff neck for several days in consequence. There's little doubt that my steel helmet saved me from being killed on the spot on this occasion—and that my height could also be a handicap at times. Fortunately, I recovered from the shock and heavy impact pretty quickly for the next moment, as I straightened up, I almost bumped into a fairly hefty German officer armed with a Mauser automatic which he was using like a machine gun to spray us with bullets. Maddened by the sight of our men being mowed down under such a murderous fire, I let him have it (with my whole weight behind it) before he had a chance to realise what had hit him. Shortly after this brief encounter we heard the sound of Germans rushing towards the front line through a nearby communication trench, so we hurriedly took up positions on either side of its junction with the front line and dispatched quite a few of them as they emerged, till we could hardly move for the bodies lying around us, after which we fired a few rounds at the oncoming few still left and then charged up the communication trench which we cleared of stragglers in a matter of minutes, with hardly any loss on our side.

Captain Gerald Burgoyne
C COMPANY, 4TH BATTALION, ROYAL IRISH RIFLES

At 11 p.m. tonight, a counter attack was made by the Germans. It started with a few shells and then a rattle of musketry broke out such as I have never heard before, while the guns of both sides thundered until the air even around us, three quarters of a mile away, was vibrating, and the dust was shaking from the roof of my dug-out. A star-lit night but very dark, yet away to our left, beyond a slight bend and hidden by trees, was the mound over and around which flares were lighting up the night; a red glare betokened something on fire, and a huge volume of smoke rolling slowly across the fields in the still night was, presumably, the explosions of heavy shells which must have been raining around. It is rather horrid listening to it, knowing men are being hurt, and badly.

Sergeant F. de Margry
2ND BATTALION, ROYAL IRISH REGIMENT

One night in particular stands out in my memory for we carried out several raids into the enemy trenches before we could capture one prisoner we had been ordered to bring back—a practice often resorted to when we wanted to 'pump' some information or other out of Jerry. Unfortunately, the prisoner we caught as last created such a disturbance as we dragged him willy-nilly across the narrow strip separating the two trenches that we soon came under heavy rifle and machine-gun fire and we had to leave him for dead half-way across as we dived for shelter in the nearest shell-hole—to crawl into our trench at the first opportunity. For several nights in succession after this exciting misadventure we raided the German trenches at various points, but failed to contact the Germans who had withdrawn some distance back probably as a precautionary or foiling measure. However, we made up for this in some measure by collecting a variety of souvenirs and piles of 'bunff' and private mail left by them in their dug-outs. The souvenirs we kept for ourselves, but the various papers and letters we handed over for subsequent examination by Intelligence Officers at their HQ.

Captain Gerald Burgoyne
C COMPANY, 4TH BATTALION, ROYAL IRISH RIFLES

Certainly the German officer has so blackened his reputation that no bravery in the field can ever brighten it again. The world admires brave men, but has no use for savage beasts, and though one gladly records instances of their decent behaviour the stories of their atrocities are too common and too easily authenticated to any way whitewash them.

Chapter 3

1916

1916 saw some of the most costly fighting of the war, as in the Battle for Verdun where the German and French armies locked in a deadly struggle as Field Marshal Von Falkenhayn sought to destroy the French Army in an attritional battle which would cost over 300,000 lives. The other key German attempt to force an end to the war led to the Battle of Jutland which, while a tactical draw, gave the Royal Navy a strategic victory.

For all the Irish regiments, the defining event of 1916 was to be the 'Battle of the Somme', which was in fact a series of battles lasting from July to November. Here the Irish regiments were to experience great losses, yet the 16th (Irish) Division and the 36th (Ulster) Division, fighting side by side, were to prove the worth of Ireland's volunteer soldiers. The 36th (Ulster) Division captured the Schwaben Redoubt at the battle of Thiepval Ridge (26–28 September), while the 16th (Irish) Division took part in successful attacks during the Battle of Guillemont (3–6 September) and the Battle of Ginchy (9 September). The Irish Guards also fought at the Somme, sustaining heavy casualties during the Battle of Flers-Courcelette (15–22 September). Indeed most of the regular battalions, such as the 1st Royal Irish Rifles, the 1st Royal Dublin Fusiliers, the 1st Royal Irish Fusiliers, and the 1st Royal Inniskilling Fusiliers were all in action during the Somme offensive. Despite the heavy losses, the Somme offensive was in many ways the turning point of the war. The German Army was shattered by the events of Verdun and the Somme, Kitchener's New Armies began to learn their trade, and the British Army adapted and refined its tactics. The Irish regiments were to take a full part in this learning curve as well and play a crucial role in the following years.

Lieutenant Edwin Godson
9TH BATTALION, ROYAL IRISH FUSILIERS

Never have I been so conscious of living in and for the actual moment, that any act done will bring an immediate result, that any want of action however trivial, brings lethargy and boredom, which quickly falls like a cloud on the men when it pervades the officer. I make this note because I had noticed it present in this BN and as far as my influence goes I am doing my utmost to combat these. It may arise from a long spell of trench holding or from a feeling that the German must not be provoked because he lets out if he is and it is best policy to leave him alone, and then he may annoy you, but it will be less than if you start annoying him. I am sorry to have to note it, but from different sources I am inclined to think the feeling exists up and down the line.

Cadet Henry Crowe
ROYAL MILITARY COLLEGE, SANDHURST

Back at Trinity I found that several friends had left to join the Royal Flying Corps and owing to my age the best way to follow them was to enter the Army via Sandhurst. And so after passing examinations written, viva voce and medical I joined the Royal Military College, Sandhurst in November 1915.

The Old and New buildings at the RMC then looked as they do today and the organisation into companies was the same. The officers and NCOs instructing us had all had war experience in France and we Gentlemen Cadets were so keen that our only fear was that the war would be over before we had seen anything of it!

Second Lieutenant T.H. Witherow
17TH BATTALION, ROYAL IRISH RIFLES

Alick joined the 8th RI Rifles and it was saying much for him that he was the only officer among the new arrivals who was chosen to go over the top with the 8th BATT on the famous 1st July. The Battalion was in Theipval Wood and Alick was shot in the abdomen while advancing to the attack from the wood only a few minutes after zero hour. He was taken to Puchvillers and died in the casualty clearing station. He was buried in the British cemetery there. Few fellows were more popular either at College or in the Army and to me his death was the greatest personal loss of the war.

Lieutenant Percy McElwaine
B COMPANY, 14TH BATTALION, ROYAL IRISH RIFLES

I crossed from Southampton to Le Harve in the old ss *Connaught* of the City of Dublin Steam Packet coy. Evelyn [his wife] saw me off in London. After a couple of days at the Base Camp at Le Harve I went with other new officers to join the 14th Royal Irish Rifles (Young Citizens Volunteers) in the 36th (Ulster) Division. This division was comprised of the volunteers raised by Sir Edward Carson to oppose any attempt to force Home Rule on Ulster. The YCVS was one of the battalions in the 109th Brigade; the other battalions being the 9th, 10th and 11th Royal Inniskilling Fusiliers.

Private A.R. Brennan
2ND BATTALION, ROYAL IRISH REGIMENT

[On rest from front line duties] The first village we billeted at was Terramesnil. No British troops had been there before. I made my bed that night of woolly coats, and very warm and cosy it was. Terramesnil was a quiet little village. In its tree-bordered lanes and byeways one could for a while forget the War. We were kept busy on numerous 'fatigues'. The settling of a thousand men into billets and their provisioning calls for a considerable expenditure of energy, and I was not sorry to rejoin my Platoon when the Battalion arrived the next day. We spent only two nights at Terramesnil. From there we moved to other villages. Evidently it was intended to give us a view of the country and some marching exercises at the same time. At any rate it was all very pleasant. The weather was delightful, and one got quite a thrill in discovering new places of interest each day. Beauval was the first fair sized town we stayed in. It had a very imposing church, fronted by a broad, wide flight of steps. The streets too were very wide and there were many fine public buildings. Here we stayed five days, sleeping in billets of the 'hen-coop' variety designed to accommodate the largest number in the smallest space. They were happy days.

Second Lieutenant Henry Crowe
ROYAL IRISH REGIMENT

I was commissioned as Second Lieutenant in the Royal Irish Regiment: (18th Foot—the senior Irish REGT) on 19 July 1916 and joined the Reserve Battalion in Dublin. The morning I reported for duty I went from Carahor by horse drawn cab with the driver complete with his bowler hat and received the correct salute from the armed sentry at the Richmond Barracks gate. I reported to the adjutant (Percy Martin, an old friend of the family) and the Commanding Officer. Martin was taken aback as he had not had an officer report wearing a sword before. We had been told at Sandhurst that it was unusual for an officer to be under close arrest. Imagine my surprise therefore to find no less than six officers under close arrest at the Reserve Battalion! They were all wartime temporary officers, and 'bounced' cheques and drink spelt their undoing.

Sergeant T.D. McCarthy
1ST BATTALION, IRISH GUARDS

Arrived here about mid-day; proceeded to the rest camp. Calais is a fine town and it is quite a change to get in touch with civilisation once more. A great many Belgians are in Calais. We arrived at the camp and found the 1st Battalion who we are to take over from. We heard that Major Lord Fitzgerald had been killed the previous day, 3 other officers and the priest wounded. It was caused by an accident with a bomb.

Private David Starrett
9TH BATTALION, ROYAL IRISH RIFLES

The colonel warned me of the procedure [Leave in London], one drink free, gay talk, a car ride, a nice house, friendly folk, a stunning girl, then, doped drink—and finding oneself on some common with nothing in pocket save the green pass. Funny they should leave that! Maybe that's the pleading of the girl, for even they keep some humanity. It's those devils who live on them, those dirty rotten bloodsuckers who prey on girls and soldiers alike that I would like to bayonet through their rotten guts.

Second Lieutenant Henry Crowe
6TH BATTALION, ROYAL IRISH REGIMENT

I was 19 and was very thrilled and excited at the prospect of seeing
something of 'the real thing' when I was posted to the 6th Battalion.
I took a small draft of reinforcements from Dublin to Dover where
we embarked in a convoy of old cross-channel steamers, some
'paddlers', and were escorted by destroyers and a small airship to
Boulogne. It was my first visit to France so everything was of great
interest. On disembarking we entrained in very dilapidated old
carriages and goods wagons for the Base Depot at Étaples. All the
windows in the carriages were broken so we propped up our valises
to keep out the weather.

We paused a few days at Base Depot and received our steel
helmets and gas respirators. Lectures, intense bayonet fighting
training and exercises in the gas chamber to give us confidence in
our respirators. We could hear the artillery barrages (called 'drum
fire' because it sounded like rolling drums) on the Somme where
the Battle was still raging.

Eventually we entrained for Bailleul, then railhead for part of
Northern France. The train hurtled along at a good 15 mph, towed
by an ancient locomotive 'fearfully and wonderfully made' as were
all French engines. From railhead by old London buses to where the
remnants of the 6th Battalion were billeted in farm houses. There
were very ancient and extremely crude latrine arrangements and
each farm had a large square pond which we called the 'rectangular
smell'. That part of France had not yet been overrun by the enemy
and the farmers and their wives worked hard in the fields.

Private A.R. Read
HQ, 141ST INFANTRY BRIGADE

Souchez [a village] was only a board with the name painted on;
nothing else remained, except human skulls and bones, which were
lying about in what had been streets.

Lieutenant Edwin Godson
9TH BATTALION, ROYAL IRISH FUSILIERS

High overhead, above the ruined and desolate streets of Albert the great gilded figure of the Virgin, with the Infant Christ still hanging from the Tower of Notre Dame de Brebieres. For over a year she has hung there, at an angle of some 15° below the horizontal, face towards the street below, holding the Infant above her head. In local French belief the day when the holy figure falls will see the end of the war. The German shell which throws down the Blessed Virgin of Brebieres will shatter the throne of the Hohenzollerns.

Lieutenant C.A. Brett
6TH BATTALION, CONNAUGHT RANGERS

I got to Locre, a quite small village, behind Kemmel Hill, which in that flat country seemed very large, and after a bit of a search found the Battalion, then out of the line and in tents. To my great joy I was sent to A Company of which my good friend Major Harden was in command, so I had fallen among friends and knew several officers, NCOs and men. There was very little 'new boy' feeling about it, as the Battalion had just suffered very heavy casualties and nearly everyone, from the Commanding Officer (Colonel R.C. Fielding) downwards were new also, some (like me) to France, all to the locality, and most to the particular form of trench warfare found there.

Lieutenant Edwin Godson
9TH BATTALION, ROYAL IRISH FUSILIERS

Fine day for 'taking over' again. Looked round the gardens and found some good rhubarb, some cabbages (young): we ate them for dinner and they were very good. In afternoon had a rifle and ammn. inspection of platoon and then ordered them to put on their gas helmets, at the word of command 'Gas'. This was done and the whole had their helmets fixed in one minute. Walked to Martinsart to buy tobacco and heard that 50,000 Germans had been captured at Verdun. Probably only a rumour. At 8.40 came down to Hamel.

'A' Co taking over the village and marsh posts as before. Earlier in the day I had got some fishing tackle, to set a couple of night lines.

Sergeant T.D. McCarthy
1ST BATTALION, IRISH GUARDS

This morning the ground is covered 4 inches in snow. We had a snow fight in the afternoon. The BN attended mass in the morning and received the ashes.

Private A.R. Read
HQ, 141ST INFANTRY BRIGADE

We rode into the town of Ypres. The streets were all shell holes while the houses were in ruins, and although some of the cellars had troops in them a good many were buried, probably with bodies underneath. Two large buildings, the Cavalry and Infantry barracks, were smashed up, also a church. Coming into the main square, the famous Cloth Hall came into view, also Ypres Cathedral. Both of these places had been wonderful buildings, but were now in an awful state.

Private David Starrett
9TH BATTALION, ROYAL IRISH RIFLES

I liked to lie on my ground sheet and read love-yarns or cowboy stories, when there was time and books. A bit of candle near my head, a book in my hand, and a free hour, made me forget the war.

Sergeant T.D. McCarthy
1ST BATTALION, IRISH GUARDS

Owing to the BDE moving, the BN celebrated St Patrick's day today. The BN paraded at 8.30 am and after receiving the shamrock from BDE GEN Ponsoby marched to the Church at Calais. Inter-COY Gaelic Football took place in the afternoon; after an exciting game NO 2 COY beat NO 3 in the final. A log fire concert took place in the evening, singing, jigs, etc.

Lieutenant Henry Crowe
6TH BATTALION, ROYAL IRISH REGIMENT

Autumn turned into winter with long nights, rain, wind, and snow. During one's patrols and after months of in and out of the line it became almost impossible to believe that at that moment people were dancing and dining in comfort in Britain. Mail of course was a great joy. We had to censor the men's letters but for good conduct a reward of one green envelope a month was given. This allowed the man to send an uncensored letter but a proportion were censored at Base and if any vital information was given away in it a Court Martial resulted. Leave home to as many as possible was given that winter and how welcome it was. I had many men who seemed to have a premonition that they would not survive the next engagement. Often they were right.

Sergeant T.D. McCarthy
1ST BATTALION, IRISH GUARDS

Our BN played the 1st Grenadier Guards at football in the morning on the aviation ground. I played right half. We scored the first two goals but at the end of the game the score was 2–2. After extra time we lost 4–2. The Grenadiers had 7 professionals playing. We were praised for our good display.

Private David Starrett
9TH BATTALION, ROYAL IRISH RIFLES

I took an egg in one night for supper, and like a fool put it on the ground by my side. When I looked for it it was gone. And my companions pointed to three out-size rats passing the egg from one to another on their way to their hole. Too astonished to do anything I sat and watched it disappear.

Lieutenant Edwin Godson
9TH BATTALION, ROYAL IRISH FUSILIERS

This morning I am writing up my diary with any items I can think of as Ozzard is going on leave and I intend to get him to post it home with a few other souvenirs, amongst these a German cigarette tin I got out of the River Ancre at their lines. Our food is as follows: Breakfast 8 am: Porridge, Egg and Bacon, Marmalade. Lunch: Stew, Pickles, Potatoes, Tea (sometimes Cheese). Tea: Bread and Butter, Cake (if anyone has any come from England). Dinner: Stew (fresh meat), Boston Beans, Preserved Tin Fruit, Tea. This Mess costs 2 francs a day.

Second Lieutenant T.H. Witherow
8TH BATTALION, ROYAL IRISH RIFLES

We were only about four or five miles from the French town of Bailleul where I was destined to spend many a pleasant evening. Two or three of us would set out after three o'clock and if lucky jump into a motor lorry and proceed to the town. Purchases would be made from a well stocked 'Expeditionary Force Canteen' and tea obtained in the 'Officers Club'. Both these institutions were beyond praise and added more than anything else to the comfort of the officer. Then if a 'Show' was on we would proceed thither and end up a cheerful day with dinner at the Club or at one of the several 'Officers Cafes'. The shows were given by the concert troops of the various divisions who happened to be stationed in the neighbourhood and in the vast majority of cases the programme was exceedingly good and very much appreciated by the soldiers just out of the line. The greatest amusement was caused by the 'lady' of the troupe who was often very cleverly got up and acted 'her' part exceedingly well. Divisions like the London Div had of course an exceptionally good party as it was composed of professional performers.

Private David Starrett
9TH BATTALION, ROYAL IRISH RIFLES

'Hi, Mates: would you believe it? Look: They've sent us some girls from home!' And it did look like it. Some of the men began brushing their hair with their grimy hands, and some of the young officers were nearly as bad. Even Hine winked at the performers, though only just married. By Jove, they could sing and dance, lifting legs so high that the front rows got sunburnt, and each time the curtain went down the cheers nearly wrecked the hall. But the girls were boys; for the last call there they were all standing with their wigs in their hands.

'What are you laughing at, Soapy? Didn't you get off with the fat legged one?'

'Fat legs, my arse! I knew it was a man.'

'You did like hell! Sure I could hardly keep you at peace in your seat.'

I confess I thought myself they were girls. But such evenings kept us from thinking too much about the war.

Lieutenant Edwin Godson
9TH BATTALION, ROYAL IRISH FUSILIERS

Football match at Martinsart against Scottish rifles. Drawn game. The Quartermaster, Lieut Ferguson, runs the football team and if a man is a good footballer he gets him a job in the W.M. Stores so that he can train and he does not come into the trenches. Ferguson is a 'Ranker' and has great power in this BN.

Lieutenant C.A. Brett
6TH BATTALION, CONNAUGHT RANGERS

I needed a bath badly (not having one for nearly three weeks) and was advised to go to the Convent for one, where I met the most extraordinary establishment. There was a large hall with a concrete floor, and a platform at one end (where the entertainments had been held before the war). The hall itself was completely full of British type baths, about two feet apart, and the floor was swimming with water. The place was full of completely naked males, officers and men, while on the platform were three or four nuns in full uniform boiling water in three large boilers. One undressed completely in an adjoining room, paid one franc to a man at the door who handed you a bucket. This you (stark naked) took through the hall to the platform where the ladies were where you dipped it full of very hot water, which you carried to the first unoccupied bath you could find and tipped it in, cold water was laid on and free, you made the temperature of the bath to suit yourself, and when you had had your bath you pulled the plug, the water ran on to the floor, and you retired wet to the next room where your clothes and towel were. But it was very nice, and I greatly admired the complete unconcern of the nuns.

Lieutenant Edwin Godson
9TH BATTALION, ROYAL IRISH FUSILIERS

Dull day. At Mesnil in same billets as before. Went by motor bus to Valheureux near Candas to see trench mortar demonstration. Met Gamble, now in 12th RIR. Got there to find an accident had occurred a bit before and 1 officer was killed and 9 wounded and 25 men. There was an accident 2 days before with 5 killed and 5 wounded.

Second Lieutenant T.H. Witherow
8TH BATTALION, ROYAL IRISH RIFLES

At the top of the Montes de Cats, and a conspicuous object for many miles around, was a Trappist Monastery with a very beautiful church. When the Germans captured this hill in the early days of the war they perpetrated a typical hunnish act of cruelty on one of the inhabitants of this monastery. Anxious to obtain the gold in the possession of the monastery and not meeting with much success they actually cut off the hands of one of the monks in order to force him to reveal the place of concealment of the treasure and even by such means they did not succeed.

Lieutenant Edwin Godson
9TH BATTALION, ROYAL IRISH FUSILIERS

Wet morning. Really the weather is abominable for June, so cold too, but perhaps it will spoil the German harvest. Also the last 10 days aeroplanes have hardly been seen, so the Huns cannot have noticed the large amount of new guns, especially heavy howitzers we have been bringing up. Went to the Manoeuvre Area, went through the attack. Then BDE watched a Stokes mortar gun demonstration. The demonstration was to get us to know and like the light trench mortar which will come up in attacks in the same way as Lewis guns. Really they are a great adjunct, a handy gun, light, can put about 4 mortars in the air at the same moment, and they have a very high trajectory so that they can drop projectiles down into trenches, but today they seemed to have more moral effect than damage done.

Lieutenant T.H. Witherow
8TH BATTALION, ROYAL IRISH RIFLES

One bright afternoon Patterson and I were proceeding for a walk from Hyde Park Corner to Ploegstreet Village along the stone-paved Belgian road. Overhead the Germans were firing at one of our aeroplanes and I stopped for a few seconds to watch the shells burst near the machine. Just as I did so we both heard a whirling noise that we knew was caused by a 'dud' shell dropping from a great height. The noise got louder and louder until it dropped in the middle of the road about 25 yards ahead of us, and on reaching the hard road it exploded with terrible effect. By some miracle neither Patterson nor myself were struck by any of the splinters although we were nearly knocked down by the concussion. Six men were wounded and two killed, one of the latter being in the YMCA hut which was at the side of the road.

Lieutenant Edwin Godson
9TH BATTALION, ROYAL IRISH FUSILIERS

Fine day. Marched to Manoeuvre Area and the form of attack was changed. Company fronts of 100 yards. Companies in 4 waves. 1st and 2nd, the men wear steel helmets and skeleton equipment with gas helmets, bayonets fixed and rifles slung on the left shoulder, 10 rounds in the magazine. A Lewis gun team on the right of the first wave, a bombing team on the left of the 2nd, 2 ammunition carriers in each wave and 1 runner. Every man carries 2 Mills grenades and a tool, either shovel or pick; 2 men for carrying Mills grenades. The 3rd wave are my Platoon and where I am are the Company supports. I will keep them in Artillery formation choosing my ground to come up by. The 4th wave are the Consolidation wave and carry wire and stakes to wire round the point selected to make a strong point—in our case Beaumont Station. There are no battalion supports. [15th] Parade 9 o'clock (by the way the clocks have now been put on 1 hour in France and in the BEF). About 1½ hour I gave my Platoon bayonet fighting (the new method). Then we had some sports, making all go in. This was for physical exercises. I did not think much of the idea. We had a 3-legged race, wheelbarrow and pig a back race; these were the best form for the purpose. I subscribed 11 francs for the prizes. In the afternoon took my platoon to the earth model of the trenches. It was Montgomery's idea and a very good one. He made a wooden box about 4½ ft x 4½ ft, filled it with soft earth and made a relief of the ground. I helped him put in the trenches. This I did mainly from the air photograph and also from the map. Trees, water, roads and railway lines were added. I gave my platoon a talk on the ground and objects they would meet with and a general talk. 5 pm for shooting field practice arranged by Major Pratt including firing with gas helmets on.

Private David Starrett
9TH BATTALION, ROYAL IRISH RIFLES

A chap who had been missing some time was picked up by the red-caps near Amiens, and returned under arrest. We'd thought the Germans had him. Then an officer ran from the line under fire and in sight of his men. The colonel was off the deep end for days about both, and few could get anywhere near him. Both were tried by field general court martial and the man was shot and the officer got off. That gave me a bit of thought about King's Regulations, but not very clear thought.

If the officer did not know what he was doing, did the man? We did not think so, and Bell actually chanced his three stripes and was placed under arrest himself by taking the handcuffs off the chap. I went over to the clink myself and then funked seeing him. But I had to, the day he was shot. The colonel was more upset than I'd ever seen him. 'To have to shoot one of my own men,' he kept saying, 'a lad who joined voluntarily; had the courage to join up: refused to hide under any excuse to keep out.'

'But the officer got a free pardon,' I said, and the colonel repeated the words as if he did not quite understand them. And in the snow, just after dawn, our man was filled up with rum before being filled with lead. That evening the boys did not play housy-housy or any other games. They sat about silent or loud in argument, steadily lowering the drink. The colonel buried himself in plans and maps of the line.

Lieutenant Edwin Godson
9TH BATTALION, ROYAL IRISH FUSILIERS

Very fine day. 'Stand-to' 2.15 am and 8.30 pm as usual. Went round the Guards in the village. Censored the Company letters. I got 11 fish with 2 bombs, something between roach and perch, which we ate fried for dinner and which were very good. I fished for 1 hr with worms and bread but caught nothing. Capt Menant and Sgt Palmer went on patrol and were waylaid by the Germans with bombs and were fortunate to get back safely. A German aeroplane was brought down beyond Thiepval.

Lieutenant T.H. Witherow
8TH BATTALION, ROYAL IRISH RIFLES

The next day being Sunday I walked the five miles to Meteren passing through Ballieul on the way. How strange it is to see the French people, dressed in their Sunday clothes taking their afternoon walk and only six miles away are the opposing fighting forces. Only the previous morning I had passed through a nerve-wracking experience and here back again in ordinary civilised life with everything going on as usual.

Lieutenant Edwin Godson
9TH BATTALION, ROYAL IRISH FUSILIERS

Whole morning spent on platoon drill of various sorts, mainly bayonet fighting and extended order work with the gas helmets on. Afternoon took the platoon to the sacks for bayonet practice and was very pleased to see how well they had got on with the new method, also their general keenness on their work and their handiness at handling their rifles. I finished up with a small charge paying special attention to the 'cheer' at the end which I consider of great value and very difficult to get from Ulstermen soldiers. They are very silent, hardly ever singing or whistling on the march and sometimes we will go along for a couple of miles on the road without anyone uttering a word.

Lieutenant T.H. Witherow
8TH BATTALION, ROYAL IRISH RIFLES

We remained here [Zudausques] for a fortnight and a very pleasant time it was. The only indication of the war was an occasional visit high up in the sky of an enemy aeroplane. The time was spent mostly in training for the coming offensive. On the training ground a plan was made up of the enemy's trenches and position at the spot where we would eventually attack and so day after day we were able to rehearse our part of the programme and hope that everything would work out as smoothly on the great day.

Jack Witherow's battalion was billeted in the neighbouring village and so I was able to visit him occasionally and also Tom McCay. One Sunday we were visited by Bishop Gwynne, the Chaplin General, who gave an exceedingly fine and practical address, although there was much grousing at having to attend on the part of the men who had been up since two o'clock that morning and had been wet through in the rain.

On the 30th we started on our march back to the war. The route was the same as that followed previously. During the march we met a battalion of the Irish Brigade marching in the opposite direction with their band playing 'She's the most distressful country' which produced on our part loud ironical cheering. At the end of a long march when our men were tired out and footsore the adjutant who was a RC used to order the band to strike up 'The Boyne Water' or the 'Orange Lily' and the effect was magical. Immediately the men livened up and became cheerful once again.

Chaplain Denis Doyle
2ND BATTALION, THE LEINSTER REGIMENT

Dear Mrs Sheehan, My heart breaks to tell you the bad news this letter must bring you. God will give you the strength to bear the blow. Your good husband was badly wounded early yesterday morning, and died at 7.45 a.m. the same day March 15th. We have had some cruel days lately, and lost four splendid sergeants. I was with your husband from 6 a.m. till the time he died. I gave him absolution and anointed him today; will lay him to rest with eleven of his comrades. May God rest their souls. I am sure He will, for they were all brave boys, and have laid down their lives in sacrifice as the Son of Mary laid down His life to go to the foot of the Cross with our good Mother. He will bring you and your child comfort which no human being can bring. I shall remember his soul before God. God bless you. Yours sincerely,

Denis Doyle

Lieutenant Edwin Godson
9TH BATTALION, ROYAL IRISH FUSILIERS

Busy looking into the defence of PTE Edgar who is charged with 'desertion' and looks as if he will suffer the extreme penalty. This is a stigma for the BATTN and if possible to be avoided. On looking into the case it strikes me as being very pathetic as he gave a false age on enlistment in order to be able to join up and is now only 18½ years and has been in the Army 2 years. He got a dose of gonorrhoea in Ireland and it weakened him physically and morally. On the night before he fell out of the ranks on the way up to the trenches he undoubtedly was done up and did not realise what his action would bring in for him. If he were 12 years older his action would be unpardonable but I think it will be hard for the youngster to be shot.

[Private Edgar got six months in prison.]

Lieutenant C.A. Brett
6TH BATTALION, CONNAUGHT RANGERS

When you came out of the front line (if you were lucky at the end of your four days there) you went to the support line, which could be 300 to 500 yards behind. Here you were not on the alert to the same extent, but suffered much more from shell fire, mostly 88mm

'Whizz-Bangs' or 5.9 howitzer shells and also from long-range mortar fire. Also from here you had to find working and carrying parties most nights, mending broken trenches, digging new ones, carrying up stores, laying out barbed wire, etc. After four days there you went to Reserve, half a mile back, just in front of our own field guns; you got shelled a lot and had lots of working parties by day and night, but no mortar fire.

Captain Noel Holmes
ROYAL IRISH REGIMENT

General Hickey [sic] knew my people and he wanted to give me experience at the higher staff work of a GSO2. I did a lot of work in the 16th Division as a Brigade Major for Ferrera [sic] who was a Guardsman. [We were] walking round the line one day. It was very peaceful and suddenly the Germans started to shell the front line oh about 299 or 399 yards away from us, but Ferrera said 'Look and see what they were doing here.' He was a devil to go out with because he was always in the front line and always when there was shelling he would go and have a look and I remember so vividly this day that the defences were knocked in by the shell fire and Ferrera said to the first Irishman that we saw with a shovel 'Why isn't the trench cleared? Clear it.' And he said 'Get on with it.' I remember that so well.

Lieutenant Edwin Godson
9TH BATTALION, ROYAL IRISH FUSILIERS

I am Battalion Intelligence Officer, a term which covers a wide variety of activities. It can be a sinecure, but one can be very useful and I credit myself that my services are not without use, but I grope for a position in which I would have greater scope and greater opportunity for making what talent I have of greater use in the furtherance of our one object, the winning of the war. Roughly as Intelligence Officer I am the 'eye' of the Battalion Commander and through him of the Staff on the piece of the front opposed to us. Every movement of the enemy there I try to discern and report in the Daily Intelligence Summary which I write (a) from the

Company Intelligence Reports, (b) from my sniper's observations, (c) from what I observe myself and hear from gossip with the men in the line. I am also in command of the Battalion snipers, 8 in number, and I use them for the observation of the enemy front in addition to their duties hunting for targets. I am also in command of the patrols. I have a panel of 12 per company and I go with the parties of them out between the lines at night. It is a dangerous and nerve-wracking duty, also very uncomfortable as it mainly consists of creeping and crawling in long wet grass. But it has the essence of sport and, in so far as that is so, relieves the monotonous routine of trench life.

Lieutenant C.A. Brett
6TH BATTALION, CONNAUGHT RANGERS

The normal method of making tea was to have a two gallon petrol tin (then standard and universal) with the top cut off sitting all day bubbling on a red hot brazier; the tea and sugar came up daily mixed together in a sand bag (and consequently somewhat hairy) and tins of condensed milk. A quantity of the mixture was put into the petrol tin, and all dipped their mugs into the scalding mixture (so strong that the mugs could almost stand in it), and when the petrol tin got low more water, tea and sugar and milk were put in and it boiled up again.

Private A.R. Brennan
2ND BATTALION, ROYAL IRISH REGIMENT

We were taken one day for firing practice by the Battalion machine-gun officer. He was very young and inexperienced, otherwise he would no doubt have picked a more suitable site than a disused railway siding for the purpose. Anyway, two of the sections were firing across the tracks at a target, when, probably through an unconscious lowering of the gun-sights the bullets ricocheted off one of the steel tracks and one or two of the fellows were hit. Fortunately, the injuries were not serious, but it gave the young officer a fright. He was wounded a few weeks later when the Battalion went over the top at Guinchy [sic]. Young officers were always a doubtful quantity to the men until they proved their mettle. Naturally, as our Army took the initiative casualties became more numerous, and the toll of officers increasingly heavier. The veterans who remained were at a premium, of course, and gradually one got accustomed to the ever-changing stream of new officers, and as long, at least, as we were attacking it became the normal state of affairs.

Lieutenant Edwin Godson
9TH BATTALION, ROYAL IRISH FUSILIERS

Afternoon went for Staff Ride 2.15–5.30 pm with about 6 Officers. from each BN in the BDE with BDE COM, Brig Gen C.R. Griffith. He took us over the Manoeuvre Area which is a cultivated piece of land about 1½ miles by ½ miles; the crops have been brought up and will be ruined. He explained the course of the attack to be practised next day. The ground has been marked out to represent the German trenches from the Marsh–Thiepval and back to Grandcourt. Feeling bad in the evening with fever and went to bed early. Neck very painful and swollen, boil not come to a head. Fever gone in the morning. Parade 6.30–7.30. Physical exercise 9.00–2.30 pm. Practised the attack. First BN then BDE. Four lines of trenches to be taken. We are to go through at the 3rd and attack 4th in waves. Company on a Platoon front, i.e. 4 waves in a company, interval varied from 5 to 10 yards as casualties occurred and according to the strength of the Platoon at the start. Bombing team of 9 men with every other wave and ditto Lewis gun team (2 in company and under command of OC CO. Back at 2.30 pm, one heavy storm. In evening went to 36th Divisional Follies at Clairfaye, large theatre in the Chateau grounds; fair show only.

Private A.R. Brennan
2ND BATTALION, ROYAL IRISH REGIMENT

At length we arrived at a large village near the Fricourt sector. Here we spent a week or two, going up several nights to the trenches with rations for the Ulster Division. It was rather ironical, in a way, for an old National Volunteer to be thus helping to feed his late enemies, the Ulster Volunteers. Any qualms I might have had on the matter were adequately eased by occasional pilfering of the Ulstermen's 'Plum Duff'.

Lieutenant C.A. Brett
6TH BATTALION, CONNAUGHT RANGERS

We celebrated Christmas in the line, not (for me) the front line but the support line, and Mass was celebrated on Christmas morning on Shamus Farm, a group of ruins about 300 yards behind the front line but behind a slight ridge, so not quite in sight of it. It was the most impressive service I ever attended. There were perhaps 500 men there, all on our knees in the mud, and it was something not to be forgotten. During the service there was no gunfire, but the occasional shots could be heard during the day.

Private A.R. Brennan
2ND BATTALION, ROYAL IRISH REGIMENT

It was while we were stationed in one quiet little hamlet that the news came through of the Irish Rebellion. Although we were all mildly interested, nobody took the thing very seriously. Apparently, as we now know, the Army Authorities were of a different mind. Our sojourn in the country was prolonged for a few more weeks to guard against any possible sympathetic reaction to affairs in Dublin. We spent our days route-marching, drilling, firing on a small improvised range, playing football and at all kinds of sports. I vividly remember a famous tug-of-war match in which after almost half an hour of intense excitement our company ('A') stalwarts pulled Company 'C' from one end of the quiet village green to the other. The villagers must have got quite a lot of fun out of it. In the evening we had concert parties at the nearest barn available, or YMCA available when we were lucky enough to strike one. The YMCA were a great 'Godsend' to us and life would have been very dull without them. The Association has every reason to be proud of its War record. We of NO 4 Platoon were by this time living in the most delightful harmony, and the horrors of warfare seemed a long way off. Little did we know that in two short months we should be in the thick of the Somme battle.

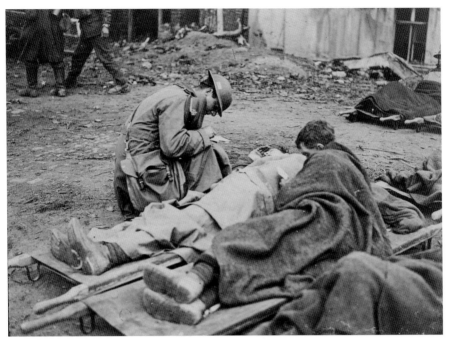

A chaplain of the 36th Division writes a letter for a wounded soldier.

A typical YMCA hall on the Western Front.

Hellfire Corner.

No-Man's Land.

The shell of Ypres.

The Irish Guards enjoy a victory.

An Army Service Corps man carves a cross.

Three Irish Guardsmen wearing captured armour examine a German Maxim gun.

A Casualty Clearing Station.

His Letter.

Soldiers from the 16th Division in a captured German trench.

A common sight from the trenches: a shell explodes.

A member of the 36th Division shares a cigarette with a wounded German.

The Somme.

Members of the Irish Guards tend a wounded German.

Freshly minted corporals of the Royal Irish Fusiliers at Holywood.

A group of newly commissioned officers containing members of all the Irish regiments (apart from the Irish Guards), at Holywood.

Officers of the Royal Irish Fusiliers enjoying a shave.

Remnant of Sergeants' Mess, 87th Royal Irish Fusiliers, after 12 Months' Campaign

Embarked 22nd August, 1914, Strength **57**.   Strength 22nd July, 1915, **9**.

BORLEY

C.-Q.-M. S. G. Reeve   S.-S.-A. R. Elliott   C.-S.-M. R. Neville   C.-S.-M. F. Rooley

C.-S.-M J. Anderson   C.-S.-M. D. Wilson

C.-Q.-M.-S. T. Reed   R.-Q.-M.-S. S. Wolsey   C.-Q.-M.-S H. Lynn

The surviving nine sergeants of the Royal Irish Fusiliers, 1915.

Officers of the 9th Battalion, Royal Irish Fusiliers.

'The Sandbags', the in-house entertainers of the Royal Irish Fusiliers.

Lieutenant William Carden Roe.

Private A.R. Brennan
2ND BATTALION, ROYAL IRISH REGIMENT

One incident stands out in my memory of this period. One of our old soldiers, a real tough but very likeable fellow, had sent off some 'lonely soldier' letters and was hopefully awaiting a response to them. Some of our practical jokers knew of this and a parcel containing a dead rat was made up, stamped with old stamps and post-marked. The post corporal was intercepted on his rounds and agreed to deliver the goods. I can still vividly recall our 'lonely soldier's' language when he opened the parcel. As far as I can recall he had no other response to his letter. Probably the game had worn a little thin by the winter of 1916.

Private A.R. Brennan
2ND BATTALION, ROYAL IRISH REGIMENT

We moved again and this time to Ploegstreert Wood. It was lovely autumn weather, and the woods behind the front line were pleasant places in which to dally. We lived in Nissan huts. Boys selling the Paris edition of the *Daily Mail* used to come up to the outskirts of the woods, which made the nearness of the front line seem a little unreal. It was real enough, however, as one would have soon found out if one were so foolish as to expose oneself to the sight of the enemy. The German snipers were deadly here, as we were soon to realize. One of our most popular officers, Captain Considine, was fatally wounded through the head when standing on the firestep early one morning. After that we were careful to make good use of the trench periscopes. We had a 'dummy' head on a pole which we occasionally revealed to the unsuspecting 'Jerry'. It was riddled with bullet marks and a very lively reminder that death was out in front for the unwary.

Lieutenant J.L. Stewart Moore
107TH TRENCH MORTAR BATTERY, 107TH (ULSTER) BRIGADE

An unexpected phenomenon: On two occasions when I was at the front line at night I saw a small occurrence which I could not explain. In the front line it was common to hear now and again the crack of a bullet passing overhead either from our machine guns firing from the rear or else from the German rifles firing from the other side of No-Man's Land. On each of the occasions to which I refer the crack of the bullet was accompanied by a small explosion and a flash some twenty feet above my head. The explosion and the flash were of the sort of magnitude that might have come from a Christmas cracker but there were no Christmas crackers about. Could the Germans have fired explosive bullets in defiance of the Geneva Convention and if they did so why should the explosive bullet go off mid-air? The only other explanation I could think of was that a British bullet and a German bullet had met head on and sent sparks flying. The first time I witnessed this phenomenon I did not quite trust my senses but the second time I had another man with me and I asked him whether he had seen it and he said he had so that there were two witnesses.

Private A.R. Brennan
2ND BATTALION, ROYAL IRISH REGIMENT

I was accosted by the Padre one day and asked if I would like to go on leave at once or wait till Christmas. Naturally I said I would prefer to go at once. This was a happy indication to me of the imminence of my leave, and from that time until my departure a week or so later I was hourly expecting it. It had a ludicrous effect on me in other ways. I remember being on duty in the trenches one sultry afternoon. A few shells were coming over, but remote enough not to worry one unduly in the normal way of things. Now and again a stray piece of shrapnel would drop in my vicinity, but normally I would probably have taken no notice of such an occurrence. On this particular afternoon it was very much otherwise. I kept thinking it would be just my luck to get hit on the very eve of my furlough, and hugged the breastworks each time I heard the peculiar whining sound of the shells passing overhead.

Lieutenant Henry Crowe
6TH BATTALION, ROYAL IRISH REGIMENT

The change over in units in the front line was carried out by night.

As I wanted to see what conditions were like by day I got the job of going into the trenches in daylight to take over stores, orders, and information about the opposing enemy, from the outgoing battalion. It was a quiet afternoon with only the occasional trench mortars being lobbed over at us. One could see the projectiles tumbling over in the air and could judge where they might fall. They exploded like a small thunder clap.

It was always said that you never heard the bullet that hit you! That when you heard the loud crack the bullet had already passed by. With shell fire it was different. The smaller field gun shells we called 'whiz bangs' because you heard the gun fire, then seconds later a noise like a violent escape of steam followed at once by an explosion in the air. A shower of shrapnel bullets and bits of shell then spattered down.

Second Lieutenant T.H. Witherow
8TH BATTALION, ROYAL IRISH RIFLES

The usual tour was six days in and six out. The six days in were in most cases divided into three days in the front line and three in the support line. Very little work was done during the day in the front line, the men mostly sleeping, but there was always supposed to be an officer on duty both by day and night. During the day this rule was not too rigorously enforced, the officer concerned often resting in his dug-out after a walk round but at night this rule was strictly enforced. This meant that if there were few officers in the line with the company the work was very strenuous, as the same officer would be forced to do two separate periods of duty the same night, each lasting two hours. As regards the men, each post consisted of six men and if the sector was quiet the work was divided as follows: During the day only a few men were employed as sentries at long intervals in the line, the remainder sleeping, but at night when the posts were fully manned two men were on sentry duty for two hours, two asleep on the firestep and two in the dug-out. One hour before sunset the whole line stood to and continued doing so for an hour or until it was dark. Similarly one hour before dawn the line also stood to. When for example you had just completed a two or three hours tour at 4 a.m. and had turned in for a little sleep, very tired and sleepy, you had no kind intentions towards the individual who rudely awakened you with the words 'Stand to' at 6 a.m.

This time the line which we were occupying was a long drawn out one and very thinly held. In fact one would walk for several hundred yards without meeting a soul and I remembered how nervous I was when I set out on my very first tour alone that night.

Lieutenant Henry Crowe
6TH BATTALION, ROYAL IRISH REGIMENT

Routine was normally about 4 days in the front line, 4 in support line (a little further back) and 8 in reserve. In reserve we were in tents or Nissen huts and could get baths in Lorce Convent, thanks to the kindness of the nuns. Clothing could be deloused at a special unit equipped with steam compartments. A travelling cinema run by the YMCA visited the reserve units. We could not undress during the eight days in the line but if things were quiet during the day we were able to take boots off and massage our feet. Whale oil was issued for rubbing our feet.

But being in reserve was not all 'beer and skittles' for we had duties each night with the Royal Engineers. We had to take engineer stores of all kinds up to the front on trucks which we pushed on narrow gauge railways. Frequent derailments which involved unloading, rerailing and catching up on lost time together with enemy shelling causing delays meant that we seldom got back before dawn.

Second Lieutenant T.H. Witherow
8TH BATTALION, ROYAL IRISH RIFLES

One morning when I was on duty I was wandering lazily round the front line when without the slightest warning there was a terrific roar and three shells exploded within about 25 yards of me. It happened so suddenly that I felt absolutely dazed for a moment, and for quite a long time afterwards felt considerably shaken. It was my first experience at close range of artillery fire and it is an experience that one never forgets. As such experiences become common they naturally affected one much less and were passed over with a joke.

Sergeant T.D. McCarthy
1ST BATTALION, IRISH GUARDS

A lovely day. A few German aeroplanes came over Popeinghe in the afternoon, flying very high. Our anti-aircraft guns made good shooting and they did not stay long.

Lieutenant C.A. Brett
6TH BATTALION, CONNAUGHT RANGERS

Of course, we, the company officers, were that much better off than the men; we sometimes did have food reasonably prepared. They fed mostly on bully beef stew made in horse-drawn carts by not very expert cooks, and tea made in larges dixies, no plates but Mess tins and perhaps a tin mug for everything.

Sergeant T.D. McCarthy
1ST BATTALION, IRISH GUARDS

BATT relieved 1st BN Coldstream Guards in front line. Relief completed at 2 pm. The trenches were in good order with long communication trenches beginning outside Mailly–Maillet. The dug-outs were very deep, the chalky ground facilitating the digging of trenches and dug-outs. Beaumont–Hemel can be seen from support trenches just behind the Hun's line. The ground behind the enemy's front line is strewn with dead bodies, mostly our fellows who fell in the attack; on 21 July they reached Beaumont–Hemel but were forced to withdraw.

Second Lieutenant T.H. Witherow
8TH BATTALION, ROYAL IRISH RIFLES

An officer and say 50 men would be reported to meet an officer of the Royal Engineers at an arranged spot. This was done and on arrival your work was detailed and the men would split up into parties if necessary. The work usually consisted in revetting the trenches, laying duckboards, carrying up materials for building dug-outs and shelters, etc. During these periods one was of course exposed to the ordinary dangers of the front line. In most cases these parties were only sent up at night so as not to arouse the suspicion of Fritz. During one of the daylight parties of which I had command a rather amusing incident occurred. While my men were working I wandered round the front line and got beyond our own sector and found myself in the sector of the neighbouring division, the 16th Irish. I was challenged by a sentry and thinking that I was suspicious he put me under arrest and marched me straightaway to his Company Commander who when I explained the circumstances offered many apologies and was exceeding nice. This man was no other than the famous Stephen Gwynn the MP for Galway.

Sergeant T.D. McCarthy
1ST BATTALION, IRISH GUARDS

In the evening in a high wind an observation balloon tethered near our bivouac broke loose while it was being pulled down. It rose very quickly and drifted towards the German line. I saw maps being thrown out, then at about 1,500 ft a man jumped with a parachute which opened after about 100 feet and the man landed safely. Soon after something black detached itself and fell some 3,000 feet. We heard afterwards that it was Capt Radford (Basil Hallam the actor). His parachute apparently caught in the rigging; in some way he slipped out of it. It was a very exciting incident to watch.

Second Lieutenant T.H. Witherow
8TH BATTALION, ROYAL IRISH RIFLES

We had quite a good little dug-out in this sector and the enemy on our immediate front was very quiet and we on our part had orders not to irritate him.

This was a tremendous contrast to the sector on our right which was occupied by the Australians where each side tried to make it as hot as possible for their opponents. All day long there was the continual noise of firing either rifles or trench mortars. These latter were truly terrifying, especially if they are of the heavy variety. The explosion is terrific and the concussion can be felt over a wide area. These mortars shells can usually be seen when travelling in the air towards you and this adds to the terror inspired. If your sector is being mortared you have to continually run up and down the trench trying to avoid the spot where you think that it is going to fall. Different people make different calculations and consequently there are many violent collisions. It would be intensely humorous if it were not so dangerous.

Lieutenant Edwin Godson
9TH BATTALION, ROYAL IRISH FUSILIERS

Very hot day. Burns marched until he dropped on the road, his pack was not well balanced and he is not a good marcher, being very small. He soon recovered. Tried to hire a room for our Mess, but did not succeed. Capt Trousdell now out with the 1st BN came over from Acheux where his COY is. Inspection by CO Blacker, of kits with special attention to hair, gas masks and emergency rations and identity discs. Inspection of arms and equipment by 2nd in Command. Took a list of all deficiencies of my Platoon and same handed in to OC COY Commander. 2.00 pm medical inspection, general and feet after march. Went with Seggie down to Acheux and had tea. Dinner with Capt Trousdell and Lt Quittrough. Learnt that in case of attack bombardment they double sentries and go into dug-outs and then line firing step and hold fire. Met CPL Davies who was of my party when I took the recruits from Royal Barracks, Dublin, the Irish Cavalry Depot to 3rd R Irish Fusiliers at Bruncrana, County Donegal. Also CPL Gaffney, both have been out with 1st BN since June last.

Second Lieutenant T.H. Witherow
8TH BATTALION, ROYAL IRISH RIFLES

We had many quiet afternoons and I well remember one very calm and peaceful Sunday evening. In Flanders the trenches are not deep in the earth but simply parapets thrown up. The result is that the back of the parapet is often neglected and you get a good view of the country in the rear of the line. In the Somme country the trenches are deep and you never see anything but the two sides of the trench which tends to become very monotonous. Well this evening I sat watching the sun set and looking towards the rear. How peaceful it all was with the birds singing their merry tune. It was a time when one's thoughts naturally turned to home and kindred. And there only a few yards away were the Germans with all that fact meant.

Lieutenant Edwin Godson
9TH BATTALION, ROYAL IRISH FUSILIERS

I was then looking at the post as the smoke cleared. Crack! A shot clean out of the middle of the smoke and struck our parapet 4 inches below my face, a dead aim at 450 yards, a doughty sniper. The nearest I have had for a long time. A hardy customer to be sure! But the next shell got a direct hit on his post and I think must have outed him. Buckley had his rifle hit by this man the night before.

Lieutenant T.H. Witherow
8TH BATTALION, ROYAL IRISH RIFLES

On the 19th [March] the battalion proceeded into the line, our company being in support. My platoon was in a strong point, a ruined farm house about 300 yards behind the front line but in full view of the enemy on the ridge. These strong points were usually to be found about 800 to 1,000 yards behind the front line. The idea was that if the front line was pierced by the enemy these positions would be able to hold out by themselves until reinforcements could arrive. Consequently they were complete in themselves and were circular in shape and entrenched and wired all round so that they could present a front to the enemy no matter from what direction he came.

My platoon were inside this strong point while Patterson and I shared a dirty, damp, smelly little dug-out which we named 'Stink Villa'.

Lieutenant Edwin Godson
9TH BATTALION, ROYAL IRISH FUSILIERS

Rifles inspected by Armourer Sgt. I told him off for coming to my Platoon in the wrong order, so he found some fault with my rifle. Out with working party in the front of line at Hamel, our new jumping off trench that is being dug on evenings front of our wire, with 50 men from 'A' COY, ditto 'B' and 50 men wiring and a screen of 20 in front. The men were a bit jumpy at first, 'B' COY went in first and I suddenly got the order down, 'About turn, quick,' as if the Germans were in the trench or it was mined so I passed it on down. By the time it reached the end of 'A' COY it was 'Double back as fast as you can,' which they did. I only checked a 'helter skelter run' by getting up on the top of the parapet and running along to the rear. I later found 'B' COY Officer had sent no order of the sort down at all. This shows what confusions arise by 'passing down' orders. 2nd Lt Ozzard on strolling out found the 'screen' huddled together in one place only (20 men) and spread them out singly (doubly would have been more advisable) and on going round later we found 2 asleep (they were of the 12th RI Rifles) and most of them had their ears covered up with scarves.

Lieutenant C.A. Brett
6TH BATTALION, THE CONNAUGHT RANGERS

The normal period in the trenches at that time was 16 days in and 16 days out, but in the days out you had to go up to the line quite often, particularly at night, to carry out repairs to trenches, to repair barbed wire entanglements, or to carry up ammunition, bombs, or supplies. During the days in, you usually did four days and nights in the actual front line, during which one got very little sleep, being perpetually on the alert. Where we were, the Messines Ridge rose before us, with Wyschaete a ruined village on top of the ridge (about two-thirds of a mile away) but overlooking all we did. We were in a swampy valley at the foot of the ridge where the trenches could not really be dug, as they filled with water immediately so we had sand bag breastworks which were pretty bullet proof (though not shell proof) but pretty fragile otherwise, and required constant repair.

Lieutenant T.H. Witherow
8TH BATTALION, ROYAL IRISH RIFLES

The morning of the 24th [March] was one which I shall never forget. I had completed my tour of duty in the front line and had come down to our Hdqrs in the bowels of the earth at 4 a.m. to snatch a little sleep before 'Stand to.' About 5.30 a.m. I was awakened by a terrible noise and we were all ordered on 'deck'. So terrible was the bombardment of our position that we were unable to come out of the dug-out. That the Germans were making a raid on our front line was evident, although so violent was the artillery fire that no messages could be sent to or from our front. Patterson who had relieved me on duty had immediately put up the sos signal and now our guns were adding to the roar. The Germans were concentrating their fire on our position for two reasons. First to prevent us from reinforcing the front line and secondly to knock in the two entrances to the mine shaft and thus imprison us who were in it and damage the mine itself. Perhaps one might think that we were funking in our den but that was not the case. Capt Regan gave me orders that I was to remain with my platoon on the stairs which led upwards and to be ready for instant action when the bombardment stopped. I stood at the head of my men at the top entrance to the mine and waited every minute for the shell which would fall at the door. It was a perfectly miraculous escape for shells were falling three or four at a time unceasingly and exploding on all sides and splinters flying about everywhere while the noise was simply deafening. Then we had no news from the front line. Had the Germans captured it? Perhaps they had and were already advancing on our position. Were Patterson and his brave fellows still alive? This is what we thought as we waited in that Inferno.

At last the fire slackened and we were able to proceed to the front line to see what had happened and if necessary to render help. What a sight it was. Our position had been battered in many places and the communication trench was also knocked about. When we arrived at the front line there was Patterson sitting on the firestep, like ourselves badly shaken but otherwise none the worse for the bad time he had come through.

What actually happened was this. The Germans knew of the existence of our mine shaft and had made up his mind if possible to put a stop to our working it. So this raid was planned and the prisoners who were captured had in their possession dynamite with which to wreck the shaft when they arrived at the entrance. This of course they never succeeded in doing as Patterson's Lewis gunners caught them as they debouched from their front line and broke them up in No-Man's Land. The strange thing about the whole affair was that there were so few casualties, only a few men being slightly wounded. It was a subdued and thankful little band of officers that gathered for breakfast in the dug-out that morning.

Lieutenant Edwin Godson
9TH BATTALION, ROYAL IRISH FUSILIERS

Fine day, nothing eventful in the line, not much sleep now because of gas alert. Located a sniper, find we have the xxth Prussians and a Saxon Corps in front of us and a Jaeger BATTN, i.e. special riflemen. I located a sniper in the hedge in front of us and will strafe him somehow. In afternoon crept out in long grass in front of our listening posts with Lt Dunwoody. Ticklish job. Found that the stories of the Northumberland Fusiliers were absolutely unfounded. There are no posts within 120 yds of our own wire, none too bad; there are gaps for going out; got stung a lot with nettles.

Lieutenant C.A. Brett
6TH BATTALION, CONNAUGHT RANGERS

Major Harden gave me a platoon, and we all went up to the line to horrible shallow rickety so-called trenches, but in a (then) fairly quiet sector. We started off in support, and the first night there was a raid taking place, somewhere on our right, and we were asked to create a diversion. We were told that an artillery and trench mortar barrage would be concentrated on a short sector of the German line opposite the part we were holding, just before the raid was due to start, and I was ordered to take a dozen men to a very sodden and thinly occupied trench when the barrage started (just over our heads), and when the German flares and rockets started to go up we were to hoist dummies (which we took with us) up and down over the low parapet to draw enemy fire and to create a distraction, while the real raid was taking place some distance away. We did this as we had been told, and the enemy responded by puncturing a number of dummies with the machine gun fire. There was quite a lot of enemy shelling also, but quite a way behind us, as we were too close to the German trench.

Lieutenant Edwin Godson
9TH BATTALION, ROYAL IRISH FUSILIERS

Noticed that our neighbourhood does not look as if it had been shelled recently. Machine gun fire is said to be the great disturber of the peace. Took a walk up to Wulverghem Messines road and had a look at the line on the north and returned. Farm held by the Germans opposite. All our line here is overlooked by the Germans whose trenches run along the slope of Messines Ridge. Took a walk to the front line held by the 12th R Ir Rifles and our front too. Went by Medicine Hat Trail Trench, King Edward Trench and through line held by the Northumberland Fusiliers who are in the 50th Division. Our line is very low lying and mostly breastwork and therefore quite different to the Kemmel sector and is enfiladed from both sides, and the German trenches are about 250 yards off. We are at Ration Farm about 1500 yards from the front line, and it is pretty quiet. I am Mess President now of the joint Mess of A, B and C companies.

Lieutenant C.A. Brett
6TH BATTALION, CONNAUGHT RANGERS

Just before we went up to the line that time an order had come down from above to say that ammunition, especially gun and mortar ammunition, was in short supply and must be conserved. I think there was a first class row going on at home and in Parliament about it at the time and that Lloyd George was about to be made Minister of Munitions to put things right. Anyhow, so far as we were concerned, it meant that the guns and trench mortars behind us were forbidden to fire more than three rounds a day each. The Germans had no such restriction and plastered us heavily, by day and night, with shell and mortar fire which did damage and caused casualties.

Lieutenant Edwin Godson
9TH BATTALION, ROYAL IRISH FUSILIERS

We had orders that our artillery would open fire at 11.45 pm and strafe for ½ hour, lift for 2 minutes and continuing 3 raids being made tonight, one by us. At 11.5 I was sitting in the Mess dug-out and 3 trench mortar shots fell near and then was hell popping all round. I ran to my dug-out and got equipped with revolver and ammunition (forgot my Field Service Dressing, wire nippers, and Verey pistol in my hurry). I then ran up to my section of the trench and on the way met 2nd Lt Boyd, rather agitated because the Verey pistol was jammed. I waited 2 mins trying to open it and took it on with me. 4 bays up I found my trench blown in for 2 bays by trench mortars and Lewis gun buried, and Stringer and another gunner. I turned and they came up with me and we started pulling the gun out. I then went on (the stuff was bursting very fast at this time) and ran over the blown-in part which was pretty level with the parapet. I got the Platoon 'standing-to' in their sections on the firing step with heads down and orders *not to fire* till the Germans were in our wire. I went to each man individually and told him to sight at 200 and fire just above the bottom of the wire. I then distributed extra ammunition and bombs and set a man digging where the trench was in (2nd Lt Ozzard had set a big flying traverse which had further gone to making a block). On going down there Sgt Whitsitt, my Platoon Sgt said he had just shot a man he believed to be German who was crawling up the blown-in part. I said get him in and we found it was Sgt Major Cross. I had him laid out on a firing step and tried to dress the wound, but each time I wanted to turn him to get at the wound he showed such signs of pain that I desisted. I finally found a Field Service Dressing somewhere on the place and sent for the stretcher bearers. We could not move him because of the traverse, the corners were so sharply turned. Soon the Germans lifted their fire onto the support trenches and I was hoping they would send on a raiding party and I still held my Platoon's fire but soon got word from Capt Allen to open rapid, so I did. The Germans did not come on.

Private David Starrett
9TH BATTALION, ROYAL IRISH RIFLES

The field ambulance being close to our dug-out we saw a good deal of the wounded from White City, and one day amongst them was my chum, Davy Mulholland. He had stopped a hand grenade. As I went to him he opened his eyes. He was all in. He put out a weak hand and I held it, wanting to grip it and afraid too lest I hurt him more. 'Hard luck, Davie,' I managed to say, and he whispered 'Thanks, Davie.' Then he smiled, and they took him away, and I'm not ashamed to say I blundered back to the dug-out without seeing where I was going.

Lieutenant J.L. Stewart Moore
107TH TRENCH MORTAR BATTERY, 107TH (ULSTER) BRIGADE

The miniwerfers were not the only mortar bombs the Germans fired, though I may have seemed to have given that impression. The miniwerfer were much the most common and by far the most devastating but sometimes they sent over small pipsqueaks weighting as I judge not more than one of two pounds. Some went off in the air above the trench and some on impact. Oddly no miniwerfers ever came uncomfortably close to me but three pipsqueaks did. My first pipsqueak was the one which started me off on my excursion to Hazelbrouck [to treat a wound]. The second fell in a mortar emplacement where I was standing with three or four of my men, and wounded one of them; he was the only man to be wounded when close to me during the twelve months I was in France. The wound was painful but not severe. He was able to walk down to the casualty clearing station with an escort. I offered him morphia from my wallet but he refused it. I always carried a wallet of medicines likely to be of use on active service, specially made up by Savoys the Bond Street chemists. The medicines or drugs were contained in gelatine sheets marked off in squares, one square to a dose. My third pipsqueak was the one which on the 3rd of October sent me off not just to a casualty clearing station but back to 'Blighty', putting paid to my service in France.

Lieutenant Percy McElwaine
B COMPANY, 14TH BATTALION, ROYAL IRISH RIFLES

Later that winter we were moved a little to the other side of Wulverghem to Red Lodge and Hill 63 near 'Play Street'. There we held Winter Trench and strongpoints on Hill 63. At night there was a very hard frost and we did a lot of wiring and trenchdigging. The ground was like iron and putting in screw stakes and digging was no easy task. We were expecting the Germans to attack over the frozen ground which was usually in a swampy condition. As a matter of fact the Germans expected us to attack and they too were busy wiring.

Private A.R. Brennan
2ND BATTALION, ROYAL IRISH REGIMENT

One of our chaps had a lucky escape. While sleeping in a shell-hole a shell burst some distance from him. A stray piece of shrapnel hit his pocket and cracked the mills bomb which he was carrying there in accordance with regulations governing battle order. Fortunately for him, it did not touch the detonator, but that the latter did not explode of itself was little short of miraculous, since detonators must ordinarily react forcibly to concussion. He was a lucky man. His name was Tom Tobin, a native of Callan, County Kilkenny, and a tough little chap. He was about five foot nothing, and could have hardly weighed more than eight stone, but he could hold his own with the best of us, and few cared to cross swords with him, verbally or physically. Withal, he was a good soldier, the kind Kipling would have admired, and he had in fact spent many years in India. I don't know what happened to him eventually. I think he survived the War. I hope he did, anyway, although he has probably drunk himself to death since.

Lieutenant Edwin Godson
9TH BATTALION, ROYAL IRISH FUSILIERS

I got the Lewis gun firing on their roads last night. Result: 4 trench mortars next morning, the first time they had been fired from that emplacement for 6 weeks. I had this continued and also from another road and found my trench got more whizz bangs than the rest. I also kept a sharp look out at 'Stand-to' in the morning and fired on parties at work with rifles; also I got the sniper busy and 2 Divl cyclist snipers. I found an Observation Post and one put a bullet into it; the result was that the slit was shut and soon two rifle grenades came over. Also when the Germans strafed us on the Saturday my trench got it much the heaviest as my diary shows. The conclusion to be drawn is that it is very hard on individuals who act in this way unless the same is done by all.

Lieutenant Edwin Godson
9TH BATTALION, ROYAL IRISH FUSILIERS

The Huns shelled the battery behind the station all day with heavies. The shells passed over our Mess and gave a good show bursting. There were no duds and the shots seemed very accurate. However, I hear one gun shelter only was hit and the gun not damaged. About the fiercest fighting there has been at Verdun this weekend. Fort Ducamont and Quarries of Hardannort captured and recaptured, also strong German attacks west of the Meuse.

Lieutenant J.L. Stewart Moore
107TH TRENCH MORTAR BATTERY, 107TH (ULSTER) BRIGADE

There was a sort of tacit understanding with the enemy that no firing should take place before lunch, though of course this understanding was somewhat precarious. The close season came to an end after lunch. At any time after 2 p.m. either side might open up with mortar bombs fired at close range from the trenches and with whiz bangs from the artillery at the rear. The Germans lobbed over miniwerfers and we replied with our Stokes mortar bombs. The miniwerfers were big things like five or ten gallon oil drums. You could see them high in the sky coming towards you, turning over and over and wobbling this and that way until finally they fell with a crash and a loud explosion. Mostly the Germans overestimated the range so their bombs went over our heads and fell harmlessly behind us, but when they did get a direct hit into the trench it made a nasty mess. Our Stokes bombs were a good deal smaller so I used to tell my men to fire five Stokes for every mini that the Germans sent over. It was all rather like a game of tennis lobbing backwards and forwards over No-Man's Land, the mortars serving from the middle of the court and the Artillery taking a hand from the backline. There were one or two strict rules: no game was to start before 2 p.m. and no game was to continue for more than an hour, play to be finished by 4.30 at the latest; when the game was over we went and had tea. The question of who would fire first was always a delicate one. Sometimes it would be us, sometimes the Germans and sometimes neither would fire and we would have a blank afternoon.

Lieutenant Edwin Godson
9TH BATTALION, ROYAL IRISH FUSILIERS

Our artillery has been very busy yesterday and today. Firing all day everywhere. We expect an attack on this line. I suppose that may have something to do with it. The wind veered to east today so I am expecting gas if it is coming at all as it is the first day for some time it has been east, so I am putting an officer on duty till 2 am and I have seen to Gas NCO's Vermorel Sprayer and have told the men that a revolver will be shot off in their dug-out door, if gas is coming, by the officer on duty. I think that will alert them. I know how difficult it is to rouse men from sleep.

Lieutenant Edwin Godson
9TH BATTALION, ROYAL IRISH FUSILIERS

Everybody is very pleased with the show [a fighting patrol] and undoubtedly it did a lot of good to the men of the Battalion. PTE Craven is to be recommended for the Military Medal. Boches were rather rattled about it and gave our right Company a fair amount of shelling. They also shouted over from Petit Douve 'Irish no good', I suppose referring to us.

Lieutenant Percy McElwaine
B COMPANY, 14TH BATTALION, ROYAL IRISH RIFLES

In the trenches we of course wore steel helmets. These would afford protection against a good deal in the way of splinters and I found mine a useful article when I crashed my head into a flying transverse across a communications trench. On one occasion when we were on the line there was a heavy bombardment at night on a section of trench near us. I was off duty and asleep in a dug-out. Of course the whole company stood to. I was missed and when found a man who wakened me said he thought I must be dead.

One day as I was returning with a working party from near the front line the gas alarm went so we all donned our gas masks. When I reached the company at the farm I found them wearing their box respirators too. In fact there was no gas; it was an alarm that started near the Swiss Frontier and travelled along the whole front to the sea.

Lieutenant J.L. Stewart Moore
107TH TRENCH MORTAR BATTERY, 107TH (ULSTER) BRIGADE

Returning to Varennes at the end of the course [Stokes Mortar Course] I was transferred to the newly formed 107th Trench Mortar Battery under the command of Captain Paddy Mulley. The battery consisted of seven officers and two or three dozen other ranks all transferred from the four rifle battalions which comprised the 107th Brigade. After the transfer we were no longer Irish Rifles but went under the nondescript description of General List and our badge was the Royal Arms. The badge of the Royal Irish Rifles was an Irish harp and I was sorry to give it up.

Private A.R. Brennan
2ND BATTALION, ROYAL IRISH REGIMENT

All kinds of fancy 'gadgets' were being issued to the troops. I myself received a formidable-looking wire cutting instrument for attachment to my rifle, and one night about a week before the offensive I had to go out on a wire-cutting expedition between our front and support lines. We were made to sew squares of pink flannel on the backs of our haversacks. The haversacks were to be worn on the back (we were not taking our packs into action) and the pink flannel was to be by way of guide to our airmen as we moved forward. I do not know whether in practice this scheme was any great help. Later on we abandoned the flannel for a coating of pink paint, but neither forms of pink were entirely successful in preventing those unfortunate 'incidents' when our men were shelled by our own artillery.

Second Lieutenant T.H. Witherow
8TH BATTALION, ROYAL IRISH RIFLES

A rather memorable incident occurred during this tour. I was ordered to take a patrol of six men out to reconnoitre a German machine gun position. It was situated just where a road, which ran across both our lines, joined the German front line. I made a special arrangement with Ireland that at 9 p.m. when I reckoned that I would have worked my way as near as possible to enemy position he would send up a large parachute flare so that I could see the position and report on it. It was a dangerous job but most jobs are in war. A parachute flare is a Verey light with a parachute attached to it so that when it is shot up into the air the parachute opens out and the light remains almost stationary in the air for a couple of minutes. Everything went according to plan and we had reached our position where we could hear the Germans at the post. We were all lying up on the ground waiting for Ireland to put up the flare. Sure enough up went the flare at the appointed time but unfortunately the parachute failed to open, the result being that the light simply came straight down almost on top of one of the men lying on the ground and continued burning for about two minutes. And there we were lying in full view of the Germans in what seemed like pure daylight. The slightest move by any of us and we would have been riddled by machine gun bullets. Fortunately the Germans did not spot us but our feelings during that two minutes can be easily imagined. We were all more than relieved when we dropped from No-Man's Land into the friendly shelter of the trench.

Lieutenant Edwin Godson
9TH BATTALION, ROYAL IRISH FUSILIERS

50 go out on patrol tonight. Felt a bit squeamish sometimes during the day as it was my first night patrol. Attended CO's conference at 2 pm. Had a look at some patrol reports by Australians who had patrolled the Wulverghem–Messines road very thoroughly and looked at 'C' COY Log Book, but found no reports of anything there. Looked thoroughly at ground over parapet and on map. No daily 'hate' today. For the first time in days. Found scouts very scared about the show and one said he had twice twisted his ankle on the way down, so went out with three, but did not get more than 70 yards from our wire as they were so scared and jumpy and reported seeing Germans on every hand and bolts of rifles clicking, etc. Came back without incident at 11pm.

Lieutenant William Carden Roe
1ST BATTALION, ROYAL IRISH FUSILIERS [SOMME]

Nominal rolls had to be prepared of men to be detailed for Brigade carrying parties, water parties, and other essential tasks, of men to be left behind at the Transport lines to form what was known as the '10% party' (As these had to be chosen so that they could form the nucleus of a new Battalion in the event of the remainder of us becoming casualties, the qualifications of every individual officer, NCO and man had to be weighed in the balance); equipment had to be inspected and checked, bombs and ammunition issued, maps minutely inspected and bearings worked out and explained to officers and NCOs—who would be responsible for maintaining direction, the plan of action to be repeated as far as was necessary to NCOs, signallers, runners and so on, with particular emphasis on their individual tasks, the times of the 'lifts' of the Artillery barrage and the meaning of the various Verey light and rocket signals to be committed to memory or written on scraps of paper in such weird hieroglyphics as would be impossible for the enemy to decipher, and last of all the final letter home, to be written in such a way as to convey to the recipients the fact that it might be some time before an opportunity to write again would arise, without contravening the censorship regulations by any actual reference to the impending offensive. By the time that such a day's work was finished, as far as I was personally concerned it would have taken far more troubles and fears than I possessed to prevent me from sleeping as only a tired man can sleep.

Lieutenant J.L. Stewart Moore
107TH TRENCH MORTAR BATTERY, 107TH (ULSTER) BRIGADE [SOMME]

The Battle of the Somme is generally regarded as having started at dawn on the 1st of July 1916, but before that our artillery shelled the German trenches continuously day and night for a whole week. During that week we remained passive in Avelay Wood while the shells passed over our heads. When we had nothing better to do we watched our shells exploding on the German trenches up on Thiepval Ridge, so intensive was the bombardment and so continuous that one felt that no German could survive. Every now and again an extra big shell would send up a column of smoke thirty feet high. We called this Charlie's ghost because we knew that Charles Hezlet who weighted eighteen stone was with one of the batteries behind us. Of course we found other diversions. Harry Brown a Dublin solicitor was one of our officers—with his aid, as a pastime as much as anything else, I made a will leaving my worldly possessions to my nephew James Andrew Stewart-Moore, then almost six years of age. My balance of pay in Cox's bank was about all I had to leave.

Private A.R. Brennan
2ND BATTALION, ROYAL IRISH REGIMENT

We were early on the move. It was a beautifully sunny morning as we made our way towards the front line. As far as I can remember there was very little gun-fire once our fellows had gone-over, and I cannot recall that there was much rifle-fire either. Nearing the front we began to meet the first casualties. They were mostly light arm wounds, and all of them seemed cheerful, probably at the prospect of an early trip to England. I should mention that my Battalion was in the 'support' line on the opening day of the Somme offensive. We were not called upon during the whole of that day. But the Gordons, who were in our Brigade, went into action in the early afternoon in support of the Devons. After an hour or two spent in a deep trench awaiting a possible order to advance, some of our fellows ventured out on top, and their example was soon followed by the rest of the Battalion. Here we lounged about, lazily watching line after line of khaki-clad figures moving towards the sky-line in front. Their pace was so leisurely, and the regularity of spacing so well maintained that one was reminded of the 'skirmishing-order' drill of field training days, and found it difficult to appreciate that this was the real thing.

Lieutenant Edwin Godson
9TH BATTALION, ROYAL IRISH FUSILIERS [SOMME]

Detrained at Watteu and walked to BATTN at Eperlecque. Great changes, general opinion that the men had faced the music grandly, but it was a sacrifice from start to finish. The course of the attack on July 1st was that at 7.30 am the waves left the front line. The 1st and 2nd got to the ravine in front of the Hamel sector without much loss, but were severely punished on trying to go on. The 3rd and 4th got it the whole way from our front line. Shrapnel barrage and machine guns from half right and half left. Our artillery bombardment seemed to have effected nothing. A man or two may have got into the Hun's front line and were instantly killed. About 1 man in 10 got back unscathed and none out of the 16 officers. All were killed, or wounded. Killed: Major Atkinson, Lt Cather, 2nd Lt Hollywood (A co), 2nd Lt Montgomery (A co), Capt Johnson, Lt Townshend, 2nd Lt Seggie, 2nd Lt Stewart. Wounded: Capt Ensor (A), Capt Bren, 2nd Lt Barcroft (A), 2nd Lt Andrews, 2nd Lt Shillington, 2nd Lt Jackson, 2nd Lt Gibson, Lt Smith. My Platoon: killed 5, missing 3, wounded 17. Strength of company for duty 39. A Company officers now Capt Allen, self, 2nd Lt Ozzard, 2nd Lt Boyd, 2nd Lt Dunwoody.

Lieutenant William Carden Roe

1ST BATTALION, ROYAL IRISH FUSILIERS [SOMME]

Our spirits were raised considerably on the final day of waiting when we rose in the morning to see the sky dotted with a long succession of British observation balloons stretching away as far as the eye could see. Groups of men assembled together to see this unexpected sight, for in the past the infantry soldier had perforce compared the British and Bosch Balloon Services as far as numbers represented efficiency very much in favour of the latter. Surely such a surprise predicted success! 'Did ye say there was twenty-two of them?' exclaimed one man; 'Shure I can only see twenty. Wait a moment though, is that wee feller a Jerry or one of our bhoys?' 'Shure ye can bet your boots that anything ye can see today is no Hun at all' was the reply. 'Them Germans is all stopped in the canteen today.'

Rifleman William Lynas

15TH BATTALION, ROYAL IRISH RIFLES [SOMME]

They did not disgrace the name of Ulster or their forefathers. Little did you think as you sat writing that letter on the first day of July that our boys had mounted the tops and made a name for Ulster that will never die in the annals of history. No doubt Belfast and the rest of Ulster is in deep mourning for the dear ones that have given their lives, so many. May the Lord comfort all of those who have lost a beloved husband, a brother or a son. Lastly may the Lord watch over those dear orphans.

Lieutenant J.L. Stewart Moore

107TH TRENCH MORTAR BATTERY, 107TH (ULSTER) BRIGADE [SOMME]

From our camp in the wood Paddy Mulley and I could see none of this [the Battle of the Somme]. Had we been free to go to the vantage point from which we had watched the bombardment during the previous week we might have seen something. As it was Paddy had to remain at the camp ready to receive messages and issue orders if necessary. Our guns were silent for they did not know how far the infantry had advanced but in the afternoon Paddy sent me to join our reserve party just behind what had been the front line trench. As I made my way there along the path through the wood I met a deserter coming in the opposite direction. I reasoned with him and tried to persuade him to return to his duty but he was obdurate. Even if I had persuaded him to go back there was no likelihood that he could find his unit or rejoin it. I suppose that by the strict letter of military law I should have placed him under arrest and brought him before a Court Martial. In the circumstances that was quite impossible. We were just two men in a wood and he was probably the more powerful of the two so reluctantly I let him go and said nothing—wonder what happened to him. When I joined our other reserve officers near the front line trench I found that they were equally ignorant of what was going on and of course equally anxious for news. There was however nothing to be done except wait. The trenches were all empty; the troops which had occupied them had all gone over the top. Peeping over the parapet of the front trench across No-Man's Land there was nothing to be seen.

Private A.R. Brennan
2ND BATTALION, ROYAL IRISH REGIMENT

Any idea we may have had that the affair was just a 'picnic' was quickly dispelled before evening, when the Gordons began collecting their dead comrades. I remember walking along a line of kilted corpses, most of them, alas, in their early twenties. I had been enjoying the day but this ghastly sight brought me up with a jerk. It was evident that if victory were to reward our efforts it was not to be a bloodless one. When darkness came we went up to do some digging in our newly captured front-line. On the way we passed some more of the fallen and a number of wounded who had not yet been picked up by our stretch bearers. It was exciting to tread one's way along what had so recently been the Boche trenches.

Lieutenant Edwin Godson
9TH BATTALION, ROYAL IRISH FUSILIERS [SOMME]

> 2,000 Hun prisoners arrived in rear of our camp of 109th, 111th, and 62nd REGTS. Mont Auban, Fricourt, La Boiselle, Sarne and Gommecourt taken. French took places and made 6,000 prisoners. Officers and men treated these prisoners without any feeling of malice whatsoever and when a Hun officer said 'It is a hard thing for a German officer to be taken prisoner,' someone patted him on the back condescendingly and said 'Fortune of war you know. Buck up old chap'. (The officer was educated at London University 1906–07). Hear a rumour that Thiepval and Beaumont Hamel are taken; puts much better complexion on the push if so.

Lieutenant J.L. Stewart Moore
107TH TRENCH MORTAR BATTERY, 107TH (ULSTER) BRIGADE [SOMME]

> For the most of the time everything was dead quiet but as the afternoon wore on we heard heavy gunfire to our front somewhere beyond No-Man's Land. There was probably a counter attack which the Germans lodged to recapture some of their reserve trenches. About midnight an infantry officer came into our dug-out completely exhausted. 'We have been fighting all day,' he said, 'and we got nowhere.' He was just at the end of his tether. It had been a blazing hot day and everyone was thirsty. He had even seen a machine gunner drinking cooling water from his gun. Next morning as I was walking about the front trench with a brother officer named Orr, a big howitzer shell arrived, one of the kind we called a crump because it made a noise like that. I was just far enough away to suffer no harm, but all were shell-shocked though not wounded. I got back into the dug-out and while we were there orders came for us to return to our camp in Avelay Wood and so I escorted Orr back. Shell-shock has a funny effect. For a little while he would walk quite ordinarily and normally. Then suddenly he would become all weak and shaky and have to rest until he recovered himself. As we made our way back through the trenches I found they were no longer empty. Another Division had been sent up to relieve the 36th Ulster Division or what was left of them and the men waiting in reserve trenches for the order to go forward.

Lieutenant William Carden Roe
1ST BATTALION, ROYAL IRISH FUSILIERS [SOMME]

Although the Zero Hour was not to be until 7.20 a.m. on the morning of the 1st of July, and the actual advance of the Irish Fusiliers was timed to commence at Zero + 2½ hours, it was wisely ordained that we should be clear of our billets by 8.30 p.m. on the evening of the 30th June. Wise indeed, because at 9 p.m. precise, passing over our heads with a dull hum, fully fifty enemy shells of heavy calibre fell with a crash on the village we had just vacated. This bombardment continued for a brief two minutes, then after a perceptible pause the same performance was repeated at the expense of the village just ahead of us. To our relief the dim twilight permitted us to see faintly that the Battalion which had lately been in occupation were drawn up in mass in a field clear of the village, preparatory to moving off. The enemy guns then switched on to another village lately full of British troops and then another, and knowing full well that many of these villages had never been shelled before, we were rather inclined to turn to one another in the ranks and say: 'There, I told you so. Is there anything else they don't know about this confounded attack?' Yet to say we were depressed would be untrue; the shells had missed us—that is all one really cares about in war.

Private A.R. Brennan
2ND BATTALION, ROYAL IRISH REGIMENT [SOMME]

On a piece of shelving bank near the entrance to a communications trench we saw lying a badly wounded German. He was a man of splendid physique, and evidently in great pain. He kept calling out in his own tongue, probably like all wounded, for water, and few of us would refuse such a request if left to our own initiative. We had strict orders not to fall out, even for one of our own comrades. In the course of the night I had occasion to pass him several times, and finally on the return journey when we found that the poor fellow had died.

Lieutenant J.L. Stewart Moore

107TH TRENCH MORTAR BATTERY, 107TH (ULSTER) BRIGADE [SOMME]

I will not dwell on the other casualties but I will relate the tale told to me by Charlie Orr when I met him at home a year later. He had served with me in 'C' Company of the 15th Rifles and was brother to the Orr who was shell shocked. He told me that he and some of his men got right through 'D' Line, the last German line of defence. There he received a shot right through his chest and out his back. For a while he lay waiting to be picked up, confident that the battle had been won. Then when no stretcher party arrived he decided to start his way back himself after assuring the wounded men who were lying around him that they would not have long to wait before the stretchers arrived to fetch them. Despite his wound he managed to crawl back through the torn tangle of barbed wire, shell holes and trenches, until he reached the safety of British lines. It is sad to reflect that it must have been quite impossible for the stretcher bearers to reach the wounded whom he left lying in front of 'D' Line —the enemy machine gunners saw to that. The most that could be hoped for was that perhaps the Germans came out of their trench and picked them up—a slender hope.

Lieutenant William Carden Roe

1ST BATTALION, ROYAL IRISH FUSILIERS [SOMME]

The exact situation to our immediate front was obscure, but from a few messages from Brigade Headquarters and the reports of walking wounded it was evident that the leading battalion of the attack had crossed No-Man's Land, the enemy front line and second line, encountering little opposition and had pushed on to the enemy third line which was their final objective. Unhappily the enemy front and second lines were not sufficiently 'mopped up' and hundreds of Germans with arms and machine guns remained unhurt in the deep mined dug-outs. As soon as the British bombardment and leading battalion had passed beyond them, these brave fellows, for they can be described in no other terms, emerged from their refuge and manning the parapet met the succeeding British waves with an annihilating machine gun fire. Try as they could and did, our men could make no further progress and lines and lines of khaki-clad bodies marked each stage of the boldest endeavour ever undertaken in the annals of the Nation. The leading battalion, surrounded on all sides, fought to a finish.

Private A.R. Brennan
2ND BATTALION, ROYAL IRISH REGIMENT [SOMME]

I went with a few of my comrades to look over one of the newly captured German trenches. It was in the nature of a revelation to us. The solidity and comfort of the dug-outs was a striking contrast to our own. Each one had been sunk to a depth of ten or fifteen feet; had two entrances, and was capable of accommodating twelve of sixteen men in comfortable wire-netting bunks. I should imagine it would be shell-proof, except against the big stuff. No doubt, it was this which brought about the failure of the Somme offensive later on. After weeks of intensive bombardment from our guns, the enemy, immune, comparatively speaking, in his dug-outs during actual bombardments, was able to emerge to defend—and so valiantly—his almost obliterated line. In one of the dug-outs we found the day's unopened mail. As the offensive had begun in the early hours of July 1st, the Germans had to make a quick evacuation, leaving mail, rations, etc, behind.

Lieutenant William Carden Roe
1ST BATTALION, ROYAL IRISH FUSILIERS [SOMME]

July the 2nd was such a day of contrast to that which had gone before as a sunny morning in June is to a winter's blizzard. At eleven in the morning we sat outside in the sun and enjoyed peace, real peace. The twittering of birds took the place of the thundering of guns, and if it had not been for unpleasantly new shell holes all about us, still fresh with the black char of the burst, one could scarcely believe that such a terrible action had been fought on the previous day. God! It was good to have come through it all unscathed.

Lieutenant Edwin Godson
9TH BATTALION, ROYAL IRISH FUSILIERS [SOMME]

Read in the papers that my Division (36th Ulster) fought very bravely and suffered very heavily. The Inniskillings seem to have got further than us. They went through Thiepval and took trenches beyond the Crucifix, but the Germans came up from dug-outs in ground taken and shot them in the rear. They had to go back. Likewise my BATTN on the north of Ancre.

Private A.R. Brennan
2ND BATTALION, ROYAL IRISH REGIMENT [SOMME]

All through the day batches of prisoners were coming in. It was pathetic to watch them showing pictures of their wives and children to our 'Tommies', who responded in the main by giving them tins of 'bully' and biscuits. I'm afraid that many of the poor devils lost such valuables as wrist-watches, cigarette cases, etc, at the hands of own self-appointed searchers. I heard grim stories of prisoners who lost more than their possessions. I hope they were just 'stories'.

Lieutenant William Carden Roe
1ST BATTALION, ROYAL IRISH FUSILIERS [SOMME]

On July 5th I was witness of a wonderful sight. Ever since the opening day of the Somme offensive, stretcher parties from the Field Ambulance as well as Regimental bearers had continually searched No-Man's Land for our wounded who lay there in their hundreds, sheltering for the most part in shell holes. By day this rescue work was a most hazardous undertaking as it was done in full view of the enemy who did not hesitate to fire whenever a favourable target presented itself. By night, though the danger was less, the darkness brought difficulties in proportion, and thus those who were too feeble or too close to the enemy's lines to cry out, were only discovered by pure chance. So it became known that No-Man's Land was still dotted with living men.

A bold scheme was the only one likely to succeed. Accordingly a large Red Cross flag was brought up to the front line trench and then slowly elevated above the parapet, its bearers still remaining under cover. When, after a few minutes, no shots had been fired, two Medical Officers scrambled on to the parapet on either side of the flag. Still the enemy held their fire, and so after a short pause the two officers advanced across No-Man's Land, with the bearers of the flag moving between them. By this time a mass of curious heads appeared above the parapet of the German trench and a German officer wearing the Red Cross brassard and carrying a white handkerchief tied on to a walking stick, hastily sprang out of their lines and advanced across No-Man's Land to meet the British party. He was followed closely by several others all presumably of the Medical Corps. It was an impressive sight. He waited until our party had come as far as he considered fit, then raised his hand signalling to them to halt. The parties of both sides stiffened to a ceremonious salute, following which he commenced to point out all the British wounded lying close to our lines. A signal from our two MOS brought forward several stretcher parties, who at once set about their task. At the same time, German parties carried wounded who had been lying close to the parapet of the German trench as far as the middle of No-Man's Land, where they were carried off by the British bearers. And so the great work of humanity went on until all who could be found were carried back to their new chance of life. It was an impressive sight. Throughout the afternoon, not a word was exchanged between the two great enemy Nations. At last it all came to an end. The German officers gravely saluted and turned about; the British officers returned the salute with a feeling of gratitude. Would that our enemies had conducted the whole campaign in an equally sportsmanlike fashion.

Private A.R. Brennan
2ND BATTALION, ROYAL IRISH REGIMENT [SOMME]

On all sides one beheld the wreckage, human and otherwise, of the battle. It was again evident that we had not won a cheap victory. We assumed, of course, that it was a victory. A great victory! The beginning of the end for the enemy, we said, and believed. Our objective this night was to drive the Boche out of Mametz Wood, but of course, we did not know this at the time, nor that we were destined to fail in the attempt. In the event, the Germans extracted a heavy price for the Wood before they yielded to superior numbers, and a big percentage of the new Welsh Division just out from home left their bones amongst the shattered trees.

Lieutenant William Carden Roe
1ST BATTALION, ROYAL IRISH FUSILIERS [SOMME]

At about 4 o'clock, 'D' Company of the Royal Irish Fusiliers, under Captain Barefoot, was ordered to move forward to the Quadrilateral and on arrival to place itself under the orders of Lt Col Hopkinson. Captain Barefoot, proceeding in advance of his Company to make a reconnaissance of the position, found a sunken road running from our original front line straight into the Quadrilateral. Along this road he led his Company and succeeded in reaching the Quadrilateral with but light casualties, that fact alone a sufficient tribute to his leadership. There 'D' Company remained all day and, with the help of this reinforcement, not a single inch of ground was lost. In fact after some abortive attacks by the enemy, our own men in turn took the initiative and following the retreating enemy down the communication trenches established several advanced 'bombing blocks' and captured a few prisoners.

Throughout the day the remaining three companies of my Regiment were never seriously engaged, and though they suffered a certain number of casualties from shell fire, had undoubtedly the easiest time of any troops in the Division. But though few of us desire unnecessarily to thrust our heads into the jaws of danger, there comes a time when it is monotonous in the extreme to remain immobile and in comparative safety whilst friends in other regiments are engaged in a life-and-death struggle in the Great Unknown, which lies at the far side of No-Man's Land.

Lieutenant Edwin Godson
9TH BATTALION, ROYAL IRISH FUSILIERS

I still have the feeling that it is beyond the sphere of human possibilities for me to survive the war, but I must die fighting and try to make myself of value until the day is over when I must lay down my life. And yet I seem to have a stand-by of luck when I get to grips. Perhaps it is to recompense me for what I look on as want of luck in other departments, foremost the pecuniary one.

Private A.R. Brennan
2ND BATTALION, ROYAL IRISH REGIMENT [SOMME]

Our bombing company were on the point of retiring from the Battalion's opening attack on the Wood. Several of them were wounded, including two from my old Platoon, Flynn and Heenan. Tom Dowling, a Kilkenny boy, was wounded also at this stage. The enemy had a trench fronting the Wood, and some of our bombers got there just as a trench relief was taking place. The incoming troops were said to be Prussian Guards. That would account for the stiff resistance we encountered, and naturally they were in a strong position. After a little wait, my Platoon, with, I think, the rest of the Company, was led away to the right flank. The frontal attack of our bombing company having failed, we were to attempt a flanking movement. With this object we were proceeding down a communication trench when an order was passed on from our rear that we were to turn back and retrace our steps. After a few minutes walking we were back on the road where we had first halted. Someone had just told me that Albert Harris had been killed, when a machine gun opened fire on us. It was an enfilading fire down the road, and Captain O'Reilly received a bullet in the wrist. He had been trying to find out who gave the order for our retirement, and his language was lurid in the extreme. He was a very popular officer, as he was a great sportsman and always looked after the comfort of his men. In moments of stress, however, he was always very excitable, and for this reason was not an ideal leader in battle.

Private A.R. Brennan
2ND BATTALION, ROYAL IRISH REGIMENT

Our march back was in the nature of a triumphal march, as although we had not seen much success in our particular sector, the belief was generally held that we had won a great victory on the Somme, and that there would soon be a return to open warfare.

How little we knew of what Fate had in store for us. On our way down we passed the Welsh Division moving up to spend itself in valiant efforts which culminated in the taking of Mametz. When we passed through the Wood a week later, their dead bodies were a silent, ghastly tribute to the bitterness of the fighting. We were sorry for the Welsh but glad that the task was done.

Sergeant F. de Margry
2ND BATTALION, ROYAL IRISH REGIMENT

I made sure before going into action that my 'armour' (consisting of as many letters as could be packed into my breast pockets) and other essentials were in proper order for the fray. The only extras I carried were a small revolver (tucked inside my respirator and secured by a short length of string) and a small tin of some French cooked meat and vegetables. I suppose I might add at this stage that after all I had been through already without mishap, I felt a certain measure of quiet confidence in my usual know-how and good luck, especially as besides being a marksman I knew quite a few 'tricks of the trade' I might aptly put it, learned partly from combat courses and partly from actual experiences of hand-to-hand fighting. For instance, I soon found out that however hard pressed one might be it was fatal to panic or admit oneself beaten—and that one could often get out of a nasty and dangerous situation by sheer bluff and 'surprise' tactics. One particular instance occurs to me in this connection. It was when I had just succeeded in parrying a bayonet thrust and, instead of backing to lunge at the German with my own rifle and bayonet (as he probably expected), I had stepped hard on his foot and simultaneously brought the butt end of my rifle upwards in a fast and semi-circular blow on to his jaw which I must have broken judging by the 'crack' I heard and the way he instantly crumpled up.

Private A.R. Brennan
2ND BATTALION, ROYAL IRISH REGIMENT [BAZENTIN LE PETIT]

As we stood in the skirmishing order awaiting 'zero' hour, the Battalion's scouts, led by Lieutenant Harrison (Parnell's old private secretary), moved across our front line and took to the sunken road. Dear old George Buckley—a scout and a Kilkenny man—called out to Frank and me as they passed, wishing us in his characteristically hearty fashion the best of luck. As they passed from our sight around the left of the incline, we saw a big black cloud of smoke just above where they had been. When we arrived at Basentin cemetery, our objective, an hour or so later and the scouts rejoined us, poor George was missing. He had been killed by the shell of which we had seen the smoke, a few seconds after he left us. After Frank Waldron he was my best pal in the Battalion, and it was a bad beginning to a day that was to prove disastrous to my friendships. We moved up the incline to the shrill command of the whistle, and met with no opposition from the enemy. We moved in short rushes of from twenty to thirty yards. At the end of a rush we would throw ourselves down; scan the position in front of us, and then rise to go forward again. Soon we attained to the level ground above, and could now clearly see our objective about half a mile away. In one of our breathing spaces an officer's servant, named Sturdee, threw himself down beside me and offered me a drink of rum from his water-bottle. I was glad to accept it and had a good long swill before we moved on again. Ere the day was over I had the melancholy duty of digging the poor fellow's grave. In what seemed a very short space of time—the excitement and action probably dimmed one's impression of the passage of the hours—we reached Bazentin cemetery. I was on the extreme right of the line, and the limit of which was marked by an old ruined windmill situated about fifty yards to the right of the valley in which the cemetery lay. As we moved forward to occupy the lip of this valley, or perhaps crater is a more truly descriptive word, I remember looking at the windmill and speculating with myself as to whether I should enter the ruins and investigate more fully. That I did not do so was probably due to a natural disinclination to exert myself more that strictly necessary, or possibly the too well disciplined soldier's disinclination to break formation or show any undue initiative. Whatever the reason, I certainly have to thank my dilatoriness for my survival. But of this more anon. Such was the speed and ease of our advance that by noon we were in complete occupation of the Cemetery, whilst the other Companies of the Battalion had taken possession of the village of Bazentin le Petit on our left. We had had few, if indeed any, casualties in the process, and had not seen a single German. Around the lip of the Cemetery crater there was a shallow trench. I do not remember our fellows digging it so presumably it must have been there when we arrived. The apparent disappearance of the enemy and the absence of gun or rifle fire had bred a careless contempt of danger in most of us, and in fact we were walking about outside our trenches, enjoying the exhilaration of our sense of victory and the camaraderie and good fellowship peculiar to men who have shared some dangerous and exciting adventure. As I remember it we were standing about in groups, conversing and joking together when quite without warning a machine-gun opened fire on us—and what an easy target we must have been— from the old windmill of which I have already spoken. There were sounds like the 'swishes' of a thousand giant canes and then the anguished screams of the victims of the daring enemy machine-gunners. I saw the legs of an old veteran, Tom Shea, completely covered in blood, and I remember thinking 'Poor old Tom has got it at last.' My own escape was little short of miraculous, as men were howling and groaning all round me, and yet I had not been hit. The general effect was most unnerving, but the instinct to survive made everyone dive headlong for the trench. At this stage it must have been—I can only speak here from hearsay—that Lieutenant Dean took a handful of men, including, alas, Frank Waldron, and tried to rush the windmill. Dean and Frank Waldron and most of them were killed before the machine-gun was finally silenced, if indeed it was silenced. At any rate it ceased to trouble my sector of the trench, which was just as well, as we soon had trouble from another quarter. We had scarcely settled down again in the trench when the order was passed along, 'Enemy advancing on the left front'. And sure enough there they were. About six hundred yards or more half-left of us we could see small groups advancing by short rushes towards the village on our left flank. They were using the old skirmishing tactics of a short rush of a few yards then a flop, and apparently their counter-attack was meeting with success. We blazed away in volley after volley of rapid fire, but I doubt very much if my own particular marksmanship was contributing to any degree to the fortunes of the battle. Despite the excitement of the fray I remember noticing that a poor little youngster on my right hand had been a mark for an enemy bullet. I tried to do what I could for him, but when I saw the blood pouring from his mouth I knew that it was 'finis' for him. He died soon afterwards. In the meanwhile the Germans had gained quite a footing in the village and had forced our people to retire. This left us isolated in the Cemetery and subject to the enemy's enfilading fire, so the Captain, a very cool and capable officer named Hegarty, gave the order to withdraw also, and we retired down the road to Mametz. We halted a little way down the road and waited. In the meantime things had begun to happen again over in the village. Our Adjutant had been proceeding from Battalion Headquarters towards Bazentin le Petit, doubtless to ascertain for the Colonel what the true position might be, when he observed our fellows being driven from the village. He rallied them and, collecting every available man in the vicinity, regardless of regiment (his force even included some old veterans of a pioneer battalion who had been gravedigging in the vicinity of Mametz), he led them in a brilliant and successful counter-attack which sent the enemy flying back from whence he had come. As soon as we became aware of the changed situation we moved up to the Cemetery again, and continued to occupy it until we were relieved at nightfall by the Gordons. There were no more counter-attacks, and if the machine-gunners in the windmill had not been silenced, they must have taken advantage of our temporary retirement to rejoin the main body. At least, they did not trouble us again. Neither did the enemy in front. I had not seen Frank Waldron since the beginning of the battle, and my first action after we regained our position was to traverse the trench in front in frantic search of him. Nobody seemed to be able to say where he was, or what had happened to him. I was very perturbed, and if my duties had permitted, would have gone out to seek for him amongst those who had fallen. In the Army, however, one is far from being a law unto one's self, and if it had not been that I heard Captain Hegarty call for volunteers for a burial party I might not have been able to do so. In company with five others I searched for poor Frank long and anxiously, but though we collected the bodies of several other poor fellows, including the officer's servant who had given me a drink of rum earlier in the day, and a boy named Booth from Castlecomer, my search was fruitless. I remember digging the grave with the tears pouring down my cheeks.

Lieutenant Edwin Godson
9TH BATTALION, ROYAL IRISH FUSILIERS

At 10.35 pm a German patrol was shown up by a flare at our wire, seen by 2nd Lt Grundy. They were fired on by Lewis gun and thought to have gone, but in 20 minutes they were seen again and strafed with Lewis gun and bombs; none were hit. This place was the thinnest in our wire and was where the Brown party were strafed. I think the Huns were trying a silent raid on our trenches. They would not have been seen half up unless they were attempting something. Night dark, rough and raining. Our sniper Goodfellow smashed a periscope and made the sentry keep bobbing his head up to look out. Water was being pumped by the Huns from their minehead at the rate of 40–60 gallons a minute for an hour and then it was dark. Reported same to our Mining Corporal (RE Tunnelling COY. Gas was to be let off on our left but it was cancelled, wind being the wrong way. I have had the new Rifle Battery firing most days which I have fixed in a German trench tramway (indirect fire). As Sniping Officer I usually go round the posts in the morning to evening 'Stand-to'. I took Buckley for some sniping. First we knocked up a German loophole in a building, then an instrument (rifle I think) fixed to a sand bag on the parapet. Then put one through their machine gun loophole. I went to search ground for bodies of Germans killed the night before but found none.

Private A.R. Brennan
2ND BATTALION, ROYAL IRISH REGIMENT [BAZENTIN LE PETIT]

After the grave-digging there was not much doing until about an hour before daylight ended, when we were treated to the stirring sight of a squadron of cavalry going forward on our right. It was, I believe, the first time that cavalry were used on the Western Front since 1914, and I do not think they were in action again as cavalry until two years later when the Germans were in full retreat. Anyhow their use on this occasion was somewhat premature, and they paid dearly for somebody's blunder. We gave them a cheer as they passed, for we really believed that it was a sign that the 'break-through' had come at last. I heard afterwards that most of them left their bones and their horses on the enemy's barbed wire.

Sergeant F. de Margry
2ND BATTALION, ROYAL IRISH REGIMENT

Some time later, my remaining companion had to clean his Lewis gun which had just jammed, and while he was thus occupied I kept a good watch on our immediate front. It was just then, and as dusk was falling, that disaster suddenly struck us both with a bang as a shell exploded on top of us and buried us alive. Although completely buried myself and unable to see or move, I soon realised that I was still able to breathe in partial fashion, due mostly to the wide brim of my steel helmet and to my stature (6 feet), and perhaps also to the cushionary nature of my 'breast-plates' as provided by my fiancée's bulky letters. While realising that I was in a hell of a hole and that my chances of survival were practically nil I began to think of a variety of trivial things in quick succession with, I'm afraid, food, drink, and a smoke predominating. As I considered these tempting prospects, and the thought suddenly struck me that I had been deprived of these essentials for some nineteen hours, the hungrier and thirstier I became. Unable to judge the time while thus imprisoned and engaged, I soon felt as though I had already spent hours in my tightly wedged position, while at the time vaguely aware of the shelling still going on around me. I probably dropped off to sleep from time to time but, fortunately for me, I was sufficiently awake about dawn the next morning to hear a voice fairly close to me calling out 'Any of the Royal Irish about here?' I shouted back 'Yes, I'm here,' which the chap must have heard somehow for he then enquired 'And where are you, Chum?' I shouted back 'Buried alive right here and I'll try and move my head a shade to show you exactly where.' I gladly heard him say then 'Right, I've spotted your position and I'll now see about getting you out of there as fast as I can, so hold on, Chum!' This last made me smile wryly, but true to his promise my would-be rescuer, and a couple more men from the Royal Warwickshire Regiment, returned armed with picks and shovels to start on the work of digging me out. It took longer than I had anticipated, due to their anxiety to avoid injuring me in the process, but eventually I was helped out of my hole, and not satisfied with literally saving my life, one of them delighted me beyond measure by graciously offering me a cigarette from his own 'Crayon' packet. Although not a cigarette smoker I certainly enjoyed that smoke and then I suddenly remembered my buried companion for whom I held little hope but whose body I wanted recovered. As I had surmised, we found he had died from suffocation almost at my feet.

Private A.R. Brennan
2ND BATTALION, ROYAL IRISH REGIMENT [BAZENTIN LE PETIT]

The dead bodies of Welsh soldiers killed in the various assaults on the wood were so numerous, and the men available to bury them so few, that large numbers of them remained lying about all around us throughout the time we were there. *Rigor mortis* had set in and the intense heat served to expedite the ghastly process. Anyone who had to witness the gruesome sight of decomposing bodies lying neglected and uncared for and who realised that each body represented all that was left of someone's loved one could have little illusion left as to the romance of war.

Private A.R. Read
HQ, 141ST INFANTRY BRIGADE

I came upon one of these mystery tanks, which had broken down. It was a huge armoured car, with caterpillar wheels. Its job had been tearing up barbed wire entanglements and flattening machine gun emplacements (and Germans) which happened to be in the way. The inside was all machinery (petrol driven) and also a couple of machine guns, beside pom-poms, a gun which fired 3 pounder shells. The crew all wore leather crash helmets, and were made up as follows, the driver ASC machine gunners from the MGC, while the pom-pom gunners [were] from the RGA.

Sergeant F. de Margry
2ND BATTALION, ROYAL IRISH REGIMENT

Handicapped myself by a rifle badly clogged up with dirt, and which at the time I was hurriedly endeavouring to render serviceable again, I was suddenly attacked by a German with his saw-like bayonet pointed straight at my stomach. Fortunately for me, I instantly remembered an unarmed combat trick for dealing with just such a situation so that having deflected the threatening bayonet slightly to one side with one hand, I quickly and firmly gripped his own hands holding the rifle in such a way as to overlap them in a firm grip and at the same time exert a powerful twisting motion, resulting in my taking easy possession of his rifle and quickly turning it round in self defence, causing him to impale himself on his own bayonet as he lost his balance on the slippery edge of the trench which partly gave way under him. After ascertaining that he was dead, we disposed of the body which soon joined some of our own dead comrades lying near-by.

Lieutenant Edwin Godson
9TH BATTALION, ROYAL IRISH FUSILIERS

No matter what befalls or who dies, a prisoner must be got. The 2nd Army very impatient; we shall have to make use of rifles at 2 yards and no bombs. At 9.30 we sent out a scout with B COY and 'D', Davidson with 'C' and myself with 'A' in front, 40 yards interval between Companies. Total party 16 NCOs and men and Lt Wingfield and myself. Arrive at end of willow trees and get into arranged formation by 10 pm without incident. Vigil begins and plenty of shells pass overhead in the next ¾ hour. Some bursting shrapnel clean over our heads (shorts). No harm done but a scout Jeffries comes to me and says that he wants to go home, he 'has a bad throat' (He was the one who tried to make me turn home 2 days before by coughing and trying to make out he could not stop it.) I told him he could go back if he liked but it would be alone. He lay down in the ditch. I took up my position with Lutton on my left very close, Butler on right and CPL Clements and Erwin in ditch facing German line. At 11pm I see, I see, what do I see, a little black mark in grass 40 yards in front that was not there when I looked before. Oh, yes it was. I look about. The moon is very full. Out now on our right front, what a nice night and so quiet, not a sound from the German lines. I look to the front again. I'm getting fed up with this. I am wet from head to foot crawling in the wet grass and I have had diarrhoea all day. If it would not have been that the regiment said I had funked it I would not have come out at all tonight and still there are 2½ hours to go and nothing will happen. At best we shall get back alright but maybe some stray shell or machine gun bullets will knock off half a dozen. This is not a job for one man to be at day after day. Everybody ought to take his share at this. The discomfort is beastly. It is alright till I move and then I have to warm a new piece of the dank wet grass. Hullo, by Jove, I've forgotten that black spot, the only thing in sight that I had made a mental note to look at again. How one's thoughts do wander. Hullo black spot, black spot! It's bigger, its growing bigger, what the devil is it? There's more of them behind it, another. They're coming! I have heard of hearts leaping into the mouth; it meant nothing to me, but by Jove that's what mine did. It nearly made me dizzy just for 2 seconds. I collected myself, 25 yards off and coming, oh so slowly and cautiously, moving down a little ditch in the open that I had not noticed. The long grass had hidden it, no man could have trodden it since it sprouted out from little spring blades. Heads bent down, legs hidden in ditch. I tap Butter on the boot and CPL Clements, he taps Erwin, I sign to the sick scout (Jeffries) to stop his poise and lie close to the ground. I level my revolver. They're coming and coming and some of the other men (unaware) cough. I cannot sign them oh, to heaven. I hope they will lie still this 5 minutes, yet now I see the first distinctly. He is 10 yards, 9,8,7,6,5,4,3. He sees something, he whips round, all turn behind him as far as I can see, one, two, three, four, five, six, seven, how many? Bang, bang, bang rings out the rattle of rifles. I let off 5 with my revolver and they have disappeared as if by magic. 'Come on, boys'. I'm up and out. I see a figure on his back at bay, I leap on his throat, knees on his chest. 'Kamerard, Kamerard!' I shout. He waves his hands. Clements whips by me and Erwin and Breen. Bang, a bomb burst by me, bang bang, shots. The damned fools behind are going on shooting. No matter, here is my man and I drag him up and off. Everybody is up now. I bundle through them. All back now. I shout and off we go; 250 yards I ran. I stumbled over craters and wire. He did the same. The emergency party call to us the way through the wire, and safe at our parapet with my man, hurrah!

Sergeant F. de Margry
2ND BATTALION, ROYAL IRISH REGIMENT

After two months of heavy fighting during which we had progressed at great cost and with almost super-human effort from Fricourt to the Deville Wood area, we once again found ourselves faced with a tremendous task, namely an attack on the German stronghold of Ginchy (finally taken by the Guards a few days later after the most bitter fighting). As usual we were briefed in a few words about this action, stress being laid on the weakness of the enemy opposition and the strength of the support we would receive from flanking and rear units close by, not to mention aerial co-operation by the RFC. The briefing seemed to us a minor echo of the one we received prior to our attack on Mametz Wood where we had been badly beaten back on failing to overcome a whole German Division.

Sergeant T.D. McCarthy
1ST BATTALION, IRISH GUARDS [GINCHY]

At 6.20 am (Zero) the whole Guards Division attacked in waves of battalions. Our Battalion was the 6th wave. By 9 am the BN had advanced about a mile, captured 4 lines of trenches and held them. The Huns were slightly disorganised and did not show fight at close quarters. Some of our patrols entered the village of Les Boeufs. Owing to the 6th Div being held up on our right we could not advance our line further. The tank assigned to us unfortunately broke down and did not go over before the attack. On our left, however, one did good work and succeeded in getting into the village of Flers.

Sergeant F. de Margry
2ND BATTALION, ROYAL IRISH REGIMENT

It was becoming increasingly obvious to the few of us who survived such repeated heavy losses, that surely our turn could not fail to come in the very near future—and that one's outstanding good luck up till then could not last much longer, specially handicapped as we then were by battle-weariness, under-manning of units, and lastly but not least, the loss of so many of our better trained and more experienced leaders and men. I suppose that much the same applied to the enemy forces confronting us, although we noticed no encouraging signs of any such adverse changes on their part.

Private A.R. Brennan
2ND BATTALION, ROYAL IRISH REGIMENT

For the next few days, after rejoining my company I had to listen to all sorts of tales—some true and some exaggerated, about the battle of Guinchy [sic]. It had been a massacre, I was told, and the Manchesters who went over with us had suffered even heavier losses than ours. Apparently, the Boche knew all about the impending attack and greeted our chaps with a withering blast of machine-gun and rifle file. Captain Hegarty was killed early in the fray, and Sergeant-Major Jock Dempsey was mortally wounded. We were in Gough's fifth Army and the staff work was very bad. After holding the line for 48 hours or so Major Considine retired with the remnants of our Battalion which, despite the little or no progress made in the attack, was left without rations of any kind. The Major ultimately raided an ASC depot and commandeered food for his men despite the protests of the depot quartermaster. Most of our officers had been casualties and it was clear that we should require considerable time refitting and bringing up to strength before venturing towards the front line again.

Sergeant T.D. McCarthy

1ST BATTALION, IRISH GUARDS

The DIV held the trenches all day and repulsed three counter-attacks with heavy losses. Some of our patrols penetrated in the village of Les Boeuf. Every BATT was mixed up on account of the attack. Afterwards the men were reformed and at night the whole DIV was relieved by the 20th DIV.

Lieutenant J.L. Stewart Moore

107TH TRENCH MORTAR BATTERY, 107TH (ULSTER) BRIGADE

Our way to the front line was up Durham Trench. I have already described how it had been allowed to grow wide and shallow and how it had a special attraction for German shells and bombs. I was about halfway up when something happened that made me glance down and I saw my right arm broken above the wrist. I also had some shrapnel in the base of my right drum and I narrowly escaped losing my left thumb, but I did not find out about that till later. A small pipsqueak mortar bomb had landed close beside me, not in the trenches but near the edge. Perhaps it was just as well that the trench was shallow. Had it been any deeper my wounds might have been head wounds instead of at wrist level. I heard no noise that I can remember but to this day my right ear sings gently, that is when I think about it which is not often. When I realised what had happened I turned and started back down the trench again. I had not gone far before I met one of my men coming up. I must have looked a nasty sight, for had I been carrying my head under my shoulder, he could not have looked more aghast. He himself poor fellow was killed the following night by a direct hit from a miniwerfer. With his aid I walked down the trench to the dug-out just beyond its entrance where they dosed me with whiskey, put me on a stretcher and sent me down to the first aid post. At the first aid post they gave me an injection which knocked me out and save one small incident I remember no more until I came to be in the casualty clearing station at Bailleul. The small incident was as follows. I was in an ambulance which had stopped somewhere, the rear door was opened and I heard somebody saying in a solicitous voice, 'Stewart-Moore, you'll be all right, won't you. You'll be all right.' I did not reply. Although I could hear clearly I was very comfortably asleep and did not want to wake up. I have often wondered who my unknown friend was.

The Bailleul casualty clearing station was a unit of the Regular Army and had come out to France as part of the British Expeditionary Force in August 1914. They were established in a building that had formerly been a boy's boarding school. The nurses were first-class. I remember in particular a sergeant who was an excellent male nurse and gave me a lovely blanket bath. The first thing they did after my arrival was to amputate my right arm at the elbow. They also bandaged my left arm so much that I was unable to feed myself or to use it for anything. It was a great relief when after some days they altered the bandage so that I could hold a piece of bread and butter.

Sergeant F. de Margry
2ND BATTALION, ROYAL IRISH REGIMENT

The opening phase of our dawn attack at Ginchy one morning in early September, 1916, could not have been more simple or common-place. We just formed up in two ranks just below a sheltering ridge, with 'A' Company (to which I belonged) on the right. At this stage one of my friends in the front rank turned round towards me and calmly remarked 'I'll say Goodbye to you now as I know I shan't come out of this alive.' Such words coming from one of the longest serving members of the Battalion naturally shook me, but before I could think of a few suitable words of encouragement to cheer him up, the order to attack was given and we were soon advancing in extended order towards the enemy's front line. No sooner were we exposed to view than we came under murderous enemy fire. The air about us was literally buzzing with the peculiar whine of flying bullets from rifle and machine gun fire, and one of the very first to fall was our Company Captain (Capt H.J. O'Reilly) and as I hurriedly helped his batman (PTE Tatam) to carry him to a nearby shell-hole we soon realised that he had been shot right through the chest, from side to side. When I asked him if I could be of any further help he murmured, 'No, thank you,—my batman will attend me—you're more badly needed with the others.' Obeying a sudden impulse I gave his batman my field dressing to help staunch the double flow of blood from his wounds and I then re-joined the fight in earnest. By then the German field guns and mortars were harassing us with increasing effect and exacting a heavy toll in our already thinning ranks. As one chap gaspingly expressed it as I approached him "Tis a b..... death trap, Chum, and it sure looks like the b...... end for us.' In the meantime quite a few of our walking casualties had passed by on their way to the nearest field dressing station cheerfully calling out 'I've got a blighty, Chum, so cheerio, ting-ting, as they say.' Unfortunately, most of them including our wounded Captain and his batman, were either blown to bits or shot down before they could reach the comparative safety of the dressing station, and I could not say at this stage that I was making for any safer spot myself as the few of us still standing approached the enemy trench with its dreaded and vicious barbed wire defences still to be penetrated. Quite a few of us, in fact, were riddled with bullets while trying to get through this almost impenetrable obstacle. Those who finally succeeded in doing so were soon engaged in bitter hand-to-hand fighting with the enemy armed, as we soon realised, with short saw-like bayonets and, strangely enough, wearing red shoulder badges bearing the one name 'Gibraltar' in capital letters. I must admit that I have not as yet puzzled that one out, but I believe the German Field Service Engineers did carry this particular type of bayonet as part of their equipment, and presumably for a dual purpose. In the meantime, a few of us who had become detached from the main body then converging towards the centre of the main attack had reached a point where a wide fan-shaped clearing in the barbed wire seemed to offer us easy access to the enemy trench near-by, but somehow sensing a trap of some sort I motioned to the others to wait. Only a few seconds later a German machine gun opened fire from its well-hidden position nearby, practically at ground level and sited in front of their main trench. Realising our opportunity and lucky escape, we then crawled towards the rear of this machine gun post and once there quickly created an opening by jointly levering the roofing off the top of the machine gun post with our rifles and bayonets and then promptly throwing a couple of hand grenades right inside—which minor operation silenced the machine gun and its crew of two. Making sure the machine gun was sufficiently damaged to be of no further immediate use we then wormed our way, as it were, towards our hard-pressed centre. Our bitter and deadly struggle with the enemy seemed to last a long time, and with rapidly changing fortunes, before we finally gained the ascendancy and could spare the breath to lick our wounds, so to speak, and prepare ourselves for further action as and when the need arose. Alas! our moment of triumph was short-lived as the enemy soon launched a strong counter-attack and practically slaughtered us where we stood. Everything happened so quickly and there was such a confused mix-up at the time that I have no clear recollection of what followed except that some hours later I found myself slowly recovering consciousness as I lay stretched face down between two freshly made shell-holes—from which I presumed that I had suffered some form of shell-shock or double concussion from the double explosion of the shells. My first impulse was to ascertain if I had been wounded and as I could find no sign of injury I decided to make my way to our front trench and therefore proceeded to rise in readiness. However, I then discovered that I had lost the use of my legs and was unable to even stand up. I then did my best to crawl towards the nearest point of our badly battered trench. Once there I found that I had partly recovered the use of my legs and after a while I even ventured to explore the trench in both directions in the hope of finding some sign of life in this apparently deserted part of our line.

Private A.R. Brennan
2ND BATTALION, ROYAL IRISH REGIMENT

Just then the Battalion Lewis gun Sergeant came up and ordered O'Brien, myself and the Company Lewis gun Sergeant to advance with him to give the Battalion protective covering fire. Accordingly we picked up the gun, and I loaded myself with several panniers of ammunition—which should have been carried by the missing members of our section—and made our way forward cautiously towards the enemy lines. O'Brien was very reluctant to advance but did so, however, after the Sergeant had threatened to shoot him. A short distance out we came to an enemy battery of horses and ammunition carriers which had been put out of action by our artillery when trying to get back to their own lines. Some of the horses were still alive although badly wounded. The Sergeant with his revolver put paid to the poor animals' suffering. I could not help thinking what a beastly thing war is when poor dumb animals have to suffer the consequences of human folly. Our gallant Battalion Sergeant was evidently after a medal because he insisted on our penetrating still deeper towards the German lines. Eventually we ran into an artillery barrage and had to seek shelter in a fairly deep shell hole. The Boche peppered us with shells for about an hour but none of us were hit. O'Brien seized on a chance remark about the paucity of our ammunition and eagerly—too eagerly—volunteered to go back and fetch some. Oddly enough, the Sergeant agreed, and this was the last we saw of him until we returned to our lines. We made some tea from emergency rations and ate some bully-beef and biscuits. After another hour or so the shelling abated, and our gallant commander decided that by now the Battalion had had all the protective cover it needed. We had not seen a sign of a German all this time, and as the shelling had abated we returned to our lines. On the return journey I carried back the Lewis gun, and the spare parts and about four panniers of ammunition. We got a great cheer from our lads when we rejoined them, and the two Sergeants were subsequently awarded Divisional honours. I think the Battalion Sergeant got a military medal, but am not sure about this. I got nothing.

Lieutenant J.L. Stewart Moore

107TH TRENCH MORTAR BATTERY, 107TH (ULSTER) BRIGADE

Early on the second morning I was transferred to a hospital ship and I was in London before noon. My family were staying at the Charing Cross Hotel. I was able to send them a telegram from Dover so they were waiting for me when I arrived at Charing Cross Station in a hospital train. The hospital train was not so posh as the one in France. It had not been built specially but rather seemed to have consisted of guard's vans in which bunks had been erected.

There was nothing to complain of and plenty of space. My family were not allowed on to the platform but were given a privileged position outside the barrier where I saw them standing as the ambulance drove out. I waved to them and that was the first time they knew that I had my left hand left at all. The War Office telegram had said 'Right arm amputated, Left hand' and they naturally feared the worst. As we drove across the courtyard outside the station the flower sellers there threw flowers into the ambulance. I was lying prone on my back on the stretcher but there were two others who were mobile and they gathered up the flowers and spread them over me from head to foot which gave my arrival at Lady Mountgarret's Hospital for Officers an appearance which suggested a funeral, not that I had any intention of being the central figure of such a ceremony. I had arrived and was looking forward to meeting my family. I was in the best of spirits.

Chapter 4 ∾

| 1917

1917 saw some of the most dramatic events of the First World War. Germany recommenced unrestricted submarine war, and ensured the entry of the United States of America into the conflict. Yet while a new ally entered, an old one departed; the Russian Revolution removed that Empire from the war—a move which would in time allow the full weight of the Imperial German Army to be brought to bear on the Western Front. Prior to these reinforcements, the Germans in an attempt to secure their position from any further deterioration retreated behind the formidable Hindenburg Line. Yet as they did so, large sections of the French Army, disillusioned after the failure of the Neville Offensive, mutinied. So for a time, the British Army held the Western Front.

Irish soldiers were to fight their way through the Battle of Messines (7–14 June), and through the disaster of the Passchendaele Offensive (July–November), while some of the regular battalions saw action at Cambrai (20 November–7 December). Irish losses were replaced by a steady but dwindling stream of volunteers, and by assigning some recruits from England, Scotland and Wales to the Irish battalions.

By the end of the year, the situation on the Western Front remained similar to that of the previous years. While there was a sense of anxiety among some of the troops about German reinforcements to the Western Front, there was also a feeling with American entry that the tide had turned, and that the Battles of Messines and Cambrai had shown the way to future victory.

Lieutenant Edwin Godson

9TH BATTALION, ROYAL IRISH FUSILIERS

New Year's Day. I wonder what this year is to bring forth. As far as last year was concerned I hope this will be as good. Last year for me personally was very successful. I suppose this year will bring the reverse tide. At any rate I am always expecting to 'go to glory' so it won't come exactly as a surprise. Looking at it broadly too I think the course of the war turned definitely in favour of the Allies. Verdun proved the breaking point of the enemy offensive and the Somme showed him that we were preparing something to set him thinking. It was a victory, though an expensive one for the Allies. However, experience once bought ought not to have to be repurchased.

Lance Corporal Thomas Healy

ROYAL DUBLIN FUSILIERS AND 2ND BATTALION, ROYAL IRISH REGIMENT

In 1917 I was called to serve with the colours, and after some months of training, we embarked at Dover and eventually arrived at the Base Depot at Calais after a stormy crossing. From the Dublin Fusiliers, we were transferred to the 2nd Royal Irish Regiment, and left for the line the next day. We embarked in our first class compartment 'Cattle Trucks' at Pontefert Station, and after passing through Boulogne and Etaples, arrived at Doulennes about midnight. Alighting, we shouldered our packs, which I might say weighed about 80 lbs, and after the usual standing about, we marched four kilometres to a place of which I have forgotten the name, in which we were to spend the night. What a sight! arriving in such a straggling fashion that an onlooker might have called us 'the forlorn hope'. However, we were shown into a large building, and were told to make ourselves comfortable on the wooden floors for the remainder of the night.

We took off our equipment and lay down with empty stomach, as bully beef and biscuits, which we had partaken of in the train, are not very appetising. Still everyone was in the best of spirits, although this night might have been our last sleep under a roof for some time to come. Next morning we awoke feeling rather tired and stiff, and found what I might call a thimble full of water in which about one hundred of us tried to wash. Luckily I was one of the first; the last man, I suppose, tried to wash in the water that had been used and spilled about by the others. They then gave us our rations for the day, biscuits, bully and pozzy (jam) and some were fortunate enough to get some dry tea and sugar, which they drummed up, or boiled.

Private A.R. Read
HQ, 141ST INFANTRY BRIGADE

I reported to Victoria Station. Returning was a job which none of us liked very much, especially when we thought of what we had to go back to, and Christmas so near. Anyhow it had to be done. Arriving at Folkestone, on the boat, then Boulogne. Same old rest camp. Here we had to stand on parade while orders were read out. Suddenly a very brave Sgt Major started to make himself known, by swearing and bullying. Of course he had a safe job (at the base) with a nice private billet and would be very sorry to see this war come to an end. Anyhow, what with Australians, Canadians, New Zealanders, South Africans, Newfoundlands, Jocks, Irish, and Tommies, he soon got some back chat. One Aussie told him to go up the line and play his funny stuff. I was one to volunteer for cookhouse orderly, because we could not leave the camp and it saved moping. There was plenty of grub, but nobody seemed to want any, so finding a pal we both filled a couple of sandbags with tins of butter, jam, cheese, bread, tea, sugar, also lumps of bacon (cooked). The most disgusting thing was that the food was thrown about and even burned, while the people in charge were living in private houses in the town and flogging rations to the civilians. These merchants (Base Wallahs) were supposed to be unfit. No doubt a good many were, but the Sgt Major was A1 in health and the bullying was only done to make us chaps glad to clear out, which we preferred. Up the line was the 'real soldiers'.

Captain C.A. Brett
6TH BATTALION, CONNAUGHT RANGERS

After our first tour in the line (sixteen day as heretofore) we came out to a very newly constructed hutted camp, again Ervillers. The Nissan huts were completely empty and very cold at night. Seeing lots of bricks in the ruined village [Bullecourt] I thought it to be cold so with the help of a couple of men I took an end section of our (officers) hut, and with my own hands built with bricks and clay a fireplace and chimney to fill the gap. There was lots of wood from ruined houses and we soon had a fine fire, though my workmanship was highly unskilled and not very good. We had lots of visitors to admire and envy, and several bricklayers and builders forthwith made themselves known among the troops and within twenty-four hours every hut had its fireplace and fire, much better designed and made than mine, but even so it was better than nothing.

Lieutenant William Carden Roe
1ST BATTALION, ROYAL IRISH FUSILIERS

The state of the front line was even worse than that of the communication trenches. By the month of December lateral movement was impossible except over the top at night, and the Garrison of the line were obliged to live in a series of wooden cages, constructed at intervals along the front by the Royal Engineers. The dug-outs, which had seemed to us so magnificent during the autumn, in many cases collapsed owing to the weight of the water-sodden chalk overhead cover. It was therefore no uncommon sight when visiting the line at night to find thirty or forty men crowded into one dug-out and there being insufficient room for them to lie down, sleeping as they stood, each man propping himself against the comrade beside him. Truly a pitiful sight!

Yet in spite of it all, the men remained as cheery as ever, and a casual onlooker seeing them playing football during a tour out of the line might well have thought that not one of them had a care or trouble in the world. Christmas Day, which happened to coincide with a spell in billets, was a particularly happy day, and the whole

Regiment sat down together to a generous feast of turkey, plum-pudding, oranges and all the usual Christmas fare. Many officers of the Regiment, now removed to Staff appointments or the Command of other Battalions, returned to spend that particular day in their real home, and loud were the cheers of welcome which greeted them as they visited the men at their dinners.

Lieutenant T.H. Witherow
8TH BATTALION, ROYAL IRISH RIFLES

The battalion removed to Dranoutre, about three miles behind the line, on the 14th where we were billeted in tents. From now until near the offensive our work consisted in furnishing working parties for the conveyance of artillery ammunition from the dumps to the battery which would fire them on the great day. If the battery position was well concealed from the enemy the work could be carried out by day, but as the enemy observation was of the best the work had of necessity to be carried out under cover of darkness. Railways had been built at a marvellous speed behind the whole line of the offensive. A line would suddenly spring up in a night and the next thing that you would see was a big L&NWR Railway engine outside your billet. One night one of these huge engines became derailed in a position behind the line which in daylight was in full view of the enemy. The consternation was great as in an hour or two the sun was due and then the Germans would start shelling the engine and the battery position to pieces. Everybody worked with feverish activity and we succeeded in getting the engine on the rails just as the first streaks of daylight were beginning to make their appearance.

Captain C.A. Brett
6TH BATTALION, CONNAUGHT RANGERS

We got a group of villages round Bollenzeele where Battalion Headquarters was. The village where A Company was in was called Bayinghen. I don't think British troops had ever been in the district before, and there were certain problems. One was the language. None of the inhabitants could speak French, and we had never even heard of Flemish. I remember our company Mess cook asking vainly for eggs. He eventually said 'Compris Chuck Chuck!' and was hurt when not understood. The people worked frightfully hard, and the cultivation everywhere was wonderful. I visited a farm where the farmer was scutching a very small quantity of flax on a small home-made scutch mill driven by a dog running in a big wheel. And everywhere were dogs drawing carts. The men of the country seemed to have a habit of getting very drunk every Saturday night on a foul mixture of beer and schnapps and then beating their wives. The troops did not approve.

Private A.R. Read
HQ, 141ST INFANTRY BRIGADE

Arriving at Saint Omer, detrained. This town was a very big one. Here were all the different workshops, such as guns being re-bored, lorries being repaired. Motor ambulances, motor cycles, simply thousands of them. While marching through the street, we saw the first WAACs, in other words, English girls who had volunteered to come out here to release men for the firing line. It didn't seem real. They knew where we had just come from and gave us a few laughs. This only made us feel a bit nervy. What with being dirty and ragged, we felt out of place, so didn't have much to say.

Lieutenant T.H. Witherow
8TH BATTALION, ROYAL IRISH RIFLES

Our company was billeted in a very pretty old French farmhouse which dated from the 18th century. On the 21st the joyous news was gently broken to me that I had been granted my leave. It is impossible to imagine the feeling that comes over one when such news first arrives. To think that you are about to leave that scene of death and destruction and behold once more the dear homeland and your own loved ones even if only for a short time sends one into rapture. That evening I packed my belongings and sped to the Divisional Headquarters at Winizeele where I caught the leave bus which conveyed the fortunate ones to the nearest railhead, which was in this case Poperinge. Poperinge station had once a very bad reputation as the Germans used to always shell it just as the leave train was due to start. The enemy seemed to know exactly the time that the train was due to move. Suspicion was aroused and it was discovered that the station master had been in communication with the Germans to whom he communicated each day the time of the train's departure. He was shot on the spot.

When I was leaving the regiment preparations were already being made to abolish the separate existence of our 8th battalion and amalgamate it with the 9th, the joint battalion being called the 8/9th RI Rifles. Thus I knew that there would be great changes when I returned to the fold.

I went straight to Portrush where everybody was making merry, few having as yet failed to realise the awful disaster which had befallen our Division. What a contrast Portrush presented from that awful scene of death from which I had just come. Still such is war.

Lieutenant Norman Jones
LONDON IRISH RIFLES

There were particularly strong pillboxes in a certain sector and we were very much aware of them. We knew we had to attack them. I remember as intelligence officer going to the observation post of a 6-inch battery. They were observing for a 13-inch howitzer. Naval, right back. Miles back and I can remember how it went. You heard the chap at the end of the wire say Fired Sir, and presently a sound like an express train and over came this thing and if you looked you could see it drop. The first round was a bit to the right. The second was a bit to the left and the third round, this whacking great 13-inch shell, caught this large pillbox plumb. As far as I remember the Germans came running out and our machine guns got up to them.

Private A.R. Brennan
2ND BATTALION, ROYAL IRISH REGIMENT

The mail arrived from home, and I received among other things a green flag with a harp and the words *Érin go Bráth*, put on by my mother in large Gaelic letters. On the afternoon of the 2nd August the Battalion moved up to occupy our old front line. Our Colonel (Gregory) watched us on horseback by the roadside as we marched past, and called out jokingly 'Where is the Crown?' when he saw my green flag.

Lieutenant Percy McElwaine
B COMPANY, 14TH BATTALION, ROYAL IRISH RIFLES

After I returned to my tent between Drainnoutre and Locre the mere lighting of a cigarette would recall the stench of Wyschaete. Lt Brian Boyd, a nice clean youth, and Sgt Austin of 'B' Company were among those killed in the 14th Royal Irish Rifles (YCVS). Major McKee lost a leg and won a DSO. He was subsequently secretary to the Headmaster of Campbell College Belfast. Willie Redmond MP, who was serving as an officer in the 16th (Irish) Division, was wounded and was brought into one of our Field Ambulances where he died. He was far too old for soldiering but we all respected him, political enemy though he was. I attended his funeral at Locre Convent.

Lieutenant T.H. Witherow
8TH BATTALION, ROYAL IRISH RIFLES

We stood up on the parapet of our trench far in the rear of the fighting line, but we could only see the great line of the bursting shells in the air and we knew that just behind that white line our brave men were advancing and no doubt enduring a terrible shower of machine gun bullets from those innumerable pillboxes. As we were among the batteries the noise was deafening and it went on all morning for many hours. All this time we could get no news whatsoever as to how the fight was proceeding, although soon the long string of wounded began to pour down the road to the various dressing stations. The barrage was certainly advancing but the men were also: this was the point. I soon gave up on the watching and read a novel. The whole sky was alive with one mass of aeroplanes of all sizes and descriptions.

About noon it became evident that things were not turning out as expected and later on we learned that the attack on our front had been a ghastly and costly failure. That terrible ground in front of our front line which was thick with the dead of the 55th Division was now full of brave Ulster lads who had followed their brave Lancashire comrades in a vain effort to gain a foothold in the pillbox area.

Lieutenant Percy McElwaine
B COMPANY, 14TH BATTALION, ROYAL IRISH RIFLES

On one occasion there was a slight adjustment of our front near Wulverghen. A battalion of the Dublin 16th Irish Division took over from one of our battalions, I think indeed from YCVS. As the Dublins came in, one of them remarked 'Glory be to God, will you look at Carson's Boys!'—'Get the hell out of that, you Bloody Fenians!'

Lieutenant T.H. Witherow
8/9TH BATTALION, ROYAL IRISH RIFLES

What a terrible area it was even now when the fighting line had long advanced beyond its limits. Like Ypres the whole country was one mass of shell holes and disused trenches. It was with a feeling of awe and reverence that I approached the ridge at Thiepval with its sunken road which on that fateful day was choked with the bodies of our brave and gallant Ulstermen. There was Thiepval Wood where our men had collected for the attack and in debouching from which Alick Witherow was fatally wounded. There was the ancient mill in the marshes of the river which had often been the scene of fierce conflicts. And there towering above all was the ridge which our men had captured, while the village of Thiepval itself remained in the hands of the enemy and from which he was able to pour fire into the flanks of our men, a murderous fire which eventually enforced them to retreat. It will ever remain holy ground as far as Ulster is concerned.

Lieutenant C.A. Brett
6TH BATTALION, CONNAUGHT RANGERS

About 9th January 1917, I was just finishing the morning's work and we were contemplating heading off for dinner when the Germans (who had obviously been watching us) sent over two whizz-bangs —88mm shells. One of those fell about three feet away from me, and a large clump of shell knocked the top off the head of one of my men who was about 20 or 30 feet away. The other shell fell a short distance away. The party scattered and went to some dug-out shelters nearby, while I went to the man who had been hit and lifted him up and carried him towards the dug-outs; people came out then and helped me, but he was of course quite dead, and I was covered in his blood and brains. I went off to clean myself up as best I could (remember we had no change of clothing of any sort) and then went to the company headquarters dug-out where the rest had gathered for dinner. After starting my dinner I noticed a stream of blood flowing down my right knee, which was sore—I thought I had bumped it. But on inspection there was a hole in my breeches, through which blood was flowing, and we concluded I must have been wounded by the shell. I finished my dinner, collected my few belongings and set off walking down the communications trench to the first aid post, where the doctor found a substantial piece of shell embedded in my knee, so I was sent back to the General Hospital at Wimereux near Boulogne where the piece of shell was extracted.

Private Felfus Long
25TH BATTALION, NORTHUMBERLAND FUSILIERS (TYNESIDE IRISH)

'The Post' as it was called was merely a small trench about four foot deep and four yards long, being a good half full of water and mud, this having to hold seven of us. A few nights previous to this the Germans had taken all the men prisoners off this same post. Well, we spent the night there doing an hour on at a time, and having to bob down every minute or two as the enemy's machine gun had us spotted, and the bullets were chipping the ground a bit further up. It began to break day so I told the LCE/CPL it was time to be moving, without we wanted certain death. We made our way out over the top to what was a supposed trench but it was towards the enemy and we must have been within 100 yards of the Germans when we found our mistake. We instantly turned back and made all haste to our own trench for by this time it was getting quite light and it's not very healthy on the top in broad daylight, I can assure you.

Lieutenant T.H. Witherow
8TH BATTALION, ROYAL IRISH RIFLES

On the 30th we left Dranoutre and our shell-carrying jobs and moved further back. Before we moved I witnessed a rather exciting incident. From our tents we could see that the Germans had put two observation balloons about four or five miles behind his line. Owing to the proximity of our attack this kind of thing was not to be allowed and so we wanted to see what action our aeroplanes would take in the circumstances. In a few seconds five planes whirled just over our heads going at terrific speeds and passed over the Bosche line at only a few hundred feet up, thus rendering themselves very liable to be brought down by hostile rifle fire. The reason for flying just over the enemy's head was so that the men in the balloons could not see them as they approached and have the balloons lowered before the aeroplanes could reach them. As the planes disappeared out of sight we waited anxiously to see what would happen. We had not to wait long for sure enough there were the two balloons coming down in flames. As the aeroplanes came back, flying low over our heads, they received a hearty cheer for the fine work which they performed. Alas, two of the planes never returned.

Lieutenant Percy McElwaine
B COMPANY, 14TH BATTALION, ROYAL IRISH RIFLES

Early in the spring of 1917 a return was required from GHQ of all officers, NCOS and men who spoke Chinese as they were required for the Chinese Labour Corps. We were told that nil returns were not to be sent in except after personal enquiry of the men in the companies. One morning as we stood to and I went round with the rum I asked 'Do any of you men talk Chinese?' As my men came from the factories and shipyards of Belfast where linguistic attainments are rare, my enquiry was received with silence, which I knew was highly charged with contempt, and I would fain have hidden my diminished head in a rat hole. As I passed from one fire bay to the next I heard a voice behind me say 'Holy Jesus, what more will they want for a bob a day?'

Captain C.A. Brett
6TH BATTALION, CONNAUGHT RANGERS

Our own front had by this time become quite unpleasant. The latest stunt was to dig in 500–1,000 tubes, each about six inches in diameter facing the German lines, into which gas cylinders were put, and all fired off at once, electrically, to deluge the Germans in gas. This was done once while we were not in the line, and once when we were, and the Germans did not like it one bit and retaliated with much shell fire. Also our artillery gave tunnel trench and its surrounding area a fierce pasting, which of course did not harm the concrete emplacements which were quite shell-proof.

Lieutenant William Carden Roe
1ST BATTALION, ROYAL IRISH FUSILIERS

As we proceeded, the Colonel leading the way, the trench became worse and worse. The mud was nearly three feet deep and gripped our legs so vigorously that each step became a labour and for minutes at a time we might be seen straining forward, until with a squelch a foot came loose. When we nearly reached our goal, [the Colonel] after a few minutes' perspiring leverage with the pole which he invariably carried, found that he could not budge an inch. 'Damn! I'm stuck,' he exclaimed. 'How are you getting on, William?' 'Oh, it's not too bad here, Sir,' I replied, with difficulty shifting one foot and finding a firmer foundation at the side of the trench. 'Well,' he replied, 'I can't budge an inch, and here I'll have to jolly well stick until you produce someone to dig me out.'

Twenty minutes later I had made my way back to our old Battalion Headquarters and there enlisted the services of PTE Grogan, desperate character but fine fighting soldier. He did not work at Battalion Headquarters on account of any particular merit, but merely because he happened to be carrying out a sentence of 28 days' Field Punishment NO 1 (no uncommon occurrence in his case, I regret to say) and was at the time under the tender mercies of the Provost Sergeant. Armed with a shovel he returned with me to the scene of action.

'You've been a devil of a long time,' said the Colonel as we toiled round a bend in the trench. PTE Grogan threw his service dress jacket on to the liquid mud in a way which made me squirm, spat on his hands and handled his shovel. Then he hesitated. Suddenly he made up his mind and lowered his shovel. Turning towards me he began, 'Beg your pardon, Sorr, but I'm a married man with four children. Would you be so good as to approach the Commanding Officer as to remitting my twenty-eight day FP NO 1.'

I am afraid I laughed aloud. The whole thing was tantamount to blackmail. At last I controlled myself. 'You'd better get on with the work,' I said, 'or you will find yourself doing another 28 days.' With a philosophic smile at the failure of his effort he set to work like a Trojan, and a few minutes later the Colonel, minus one gum boot, was continuing his round. Poor Private Grogan, he deserved to succeed, but the ways of authority are hard.

Captain C.A. Brett
6TH BATTALION, CONNAUGHT RANGERS

Then a subaltern who had joined me fresh from home lost his nerve, and started shouting and weeping, and tore off his gas mask. So Sergeant Major O'Neill (my company sergeant major) and I had to forcibly put it on him again and hold it on. Eventually sometime after 11 o'clock the shelling slackened and I decided to start off again, which we did, passing through the most horrible mess of bits of lorries and men, and the road was torn to pieces with shell holes. We were all completely exhausted, but eventually all got back to Poperinge shortly before dawn. After handing the subaltern over to the doctor (to be sent home quick) we all got a bit of sleep, and later next day marched back to the railhead and entrained. I had bad dysentery and was in a poor way, but thankful to be alive. It was during those sixteen days that I really got down to considering deeply my religious beliefs.

Lieutenant G. de Pass

4TH (ROYAL IRISH) DRAGOON GUARDS

I will now try and describe a night patrol. In my regiment, the Commanding Officer, who was an exceedingly brave man, was very keen on these patrols and he made up his mind that as these were winter months, there should be two patrols a night—one from 19.00 hours to 24.00 hours and the second patrol from 24.00 hours to 05.00 hours. A patrol consisted of 25 men—a fighting patrol armed with rifles, bayonets and some grenades, and with faces blackened. It must be realised that this was a fairly deep No-Man's Land and you could not survey the ground at all except from maps or an occasional look over the trench with a periscope, as it was not a health resort to have your head over the parapet!

I will now describe a patrol: You proceeded from the front-line trench through a gap in the wire in which our listening posts were. One must remember that these gaps were only where the listening post were, so that they could go backwards and forwards when relieved and patrols could go backwards and forwards, but it was vitally important that you should find the right parts of the wire when coming back, as otherwise you could not get back into your own line, and any sign of movement always brought a good deal of fire down, both from the German side and your own. It is said it is marvellous how a man's mind is concentrated before his end. I think it is equally true how you concentrate and remember when your life depends on it: I certainly found this to be the case! The patrol, having moved through the wire near the listening posts, finds itself in No-Man's Land. Obviously a great deal of fire from both sides was continually taking place and the scene was continuously lit up by star shells and when these star shells fell anywhere near the patrol they were all trained to 'freeze', that is to say, they looked down, and, if they were crawling, which they generally were, they remained absolutely still in whatever position they were in. Looking down was to avoid the faces of people being visible, even though they were blackened.

The patrol proceeded at a very slow pace, going a very few yards at a time, lying down, listening and watching, and then going another few yards until we arrived at the German wire, and, listening, we waited to hear any movements or signs which would lead us to believe an attack was imminent; this procedure went on for 5 hours and then we gradually came back.

Lieutenant T.H. Witherow
8TH BATTALION, ROYAL IRISH RIFLES

As soon as it became dark everybody became as busy as bees. The rations had to be brought in, the trenches improved, meal cooked, etc, while a very watchful eye had to be kept on the doings of the enemy. That night I was visiting my posts and as usual had a little conversation with each group. I had just finished talking to one of these posts, consisting of six men, and no sooner had I turned the corner of the parapet when down came three German whizz bangs and killed or wounded the whole lot. I had just escaped by a matter of seconds. One of those killed was a man called Maude to whom I had taken a great fancy. He was a middle-aged inhabitant of London of the clerk type who, bedecked with frock coat and silk hat, make their way every morning into the City. He ought never to have been a soldier but was conscripted along with the rest and eventually found his way into our battalion. He was so different from the ordinary type of man in the trenches. His wife wrote me a very nice letter in reply to my letter of sympathy.

Private A.R. Read
HQ, 141ST INFANTRY BRIGADE

One shell burst outside our pillbox, killing an observer, also wounding a corporal, both belonging to Headquarters. The corporal was blown against the sandbags, catching several pieces in the arm. We called the stretcher bearers, and picked him up, to find the sandbags soaked with blood. The observer was buried inside the dug-out. When we tried to dig him out, his body fell to pieces. After this I was only too thankful to get away before anything else happened. Coming back along the track, we ran across a chap who had been buried by a shell. He was trembling like a leaf, also sobbing like a baby, a clear case of shell shock. My pal and I got hold of him, to take him down to the dressing station. This was a rare job, because every time a shell burst, he would get away and run into the nearest dug-out or shell hole. Fritz now started sending some shells right on the track (very close too). Grabbing our patient, we treated him rather rough, but we had to be cruel to be kind. Anyhow on reaching the RAMC post, both of us were fed up to the teeth.

Captain Edwin Godson
9TH BATTALION, ROYAL IRISH FUSILIERS

The raid of the 9th RI FUS, in which I had quite a lot of preliminary work to do, was very successful and just missed being a roaring success. The party got in and killed a lot of the enemy, but one party who were to do the enveloping movement got hung up owing to some new wire. That was the fault of the Intelligence Officer in not reporting it. They ought to have looked over the ground very carefully on the day of the raid. I must not let this occur again.

Lieutenant Henry Crowe
6TH BATTALION, ROYAL IRISH REGIMENT

I think it was about August when the rains came. It rained and rained day and night for weeks it seemed, turning the shell-torn ground into a great slimy bog in which men drowned and guns and vehicles disappeared. Passchendaele was a shambles. The 6th was then very under strength and we were used to relieve units in the front line for a few days only and then we were brought back behind Ypres for a short rest before repeating the performance. There was no recognisable front line, just a rough line of occupied shell holes. There was nothing to be done except to crouch down in the shell holes in pouring rain, hoping for the best. The rum ration saved the day. We used to crawl round each shell hole at dawn with a couple of men and the rum jar. For food we had the bully beef and biscuits from our 'iron rations'. The biscuits were like the old dog biscuits, about 4 inches square and thick. It took a long time to eat one biscuit but that passed the time. Just to vary the treatment German low-flying aircraft machine gunned us at intervals.

Private A.R. Read

HQ, 141ST INFANTRY BRIGADE

A battalion bombing raid was made by the 18th Londons [London Irish] at the Ravine Sector. After a short bombardment, they went over the top and got to the 4th German line. Here Fritzy had massed his reserves, who offered a very stubborn resistance, so that our lads were soon having hand-to-hand fighting. They managed to bring back 18 prisoners and inflicted a large loss on Fritzy, besides doing a rare lot of damage to machine gun emplacement, dug-outs, etc., before they returned to our front line. They were relieved immediately by the 13th London (Civil Service Rifles), having a train journey back to Halifax Camp. Here they had messages of congratulations from HM The King, Sir Douglas Haig, also the Divisional Commander, Major General Gorringe. The casualties to the London Irish numbered 130 killed, wounded and missing. A very dear price to pay for a bombing raid.

Lieutenant T.H. Witherow

8/9TH BATTALION, ROYAL IRISH RIFLES

Immediately in front was the Hindenberg [sic] Line which really did look impregnable. In front of it stretched great belts of wire about a hundred yards thick. It looked one black solid mass through which, even without machine guns behind, it would be impossible to penetrate or to attempt to cut in the ordinary way. The line had been cleverly sighted so as to cover all the approaches and to command all the important ground. Our own line was poor in comparison, especially as regards wire, but compared to our line at Ypres it was magnificent. It had been constructed slowly and scientifically and as the ground in the Picardy area is ideal for trenches these were of the most approved type, deep and well revetted with wood. Then we were provided with deep dug-outs where no shell could penetrate. What we would have given for one of these at Ypres! The distance from one front line to another was about 800 yards on an average. Consequently both sides, as always happens when the distance is so long, constructs long saps or trenches running towards the enemy's line. The points of these saps often came very near each other. In our battalion area there were three of these long saps proceeding from our front line towards the enemy. At the head of these saps there were posts and there was always the fear that these would be raided, this being a favourite sport of both side.

Lieutenant T.H. Witherow
8TH BATTALION, ROYAL IRISH RIFLES [MESSINES]

On the morning of the 6th we marched back to our old camp at Drancutre where we were to remain all day and make final preparations preparatory to marching at night to the position in the front line where we were to attack at dawn. It was not and could not possibly be in the circumstances a pleasant day. Try as one would it was impossible to get away from the next day's work and what it was going to cost. So powerful was the enemy position on the famous Ridge that it was thought that our casualties would be very heavy in spite of excellent artillery preparation. The medical authorities had made preparations for dealing with over a hundred thousand cases. Knowing these facts as we did we could not be light hearted. Strange to say it is not so much of oneself that one thinks as of the fact that the happy party is about to be broken up. How many of us would be in the regiment tomorrow? It was a gloomy day and we were all glad when it came to an end.

Lieutenant Henry Crowe
6TH BATTALION, ROYAL IRISH REGIMENT [MESSINES]

Before zero hour on June 7th 1917 we ordered everyone to crawl out of the trenches into No-Man's Land because it was expected that the mines would demolish the breastworks and bury the occupants. The Germans had not expected our attack on the 7th. They thought it would be later. So all was quiet.

Precisely at zero hour about sunrise the mines were blown. What a fantastic sight it was! Like the eruption of a volcano. Great curtains of scarlet and purple flame, smoke, debris and earth, soared upwards hundreds of feet and then the artillery and machine gun barrages opened up. It was said to be the most intense artillery concentration of the whole war and that was saying something.

The 16th Irish Division went forward on schedule with the Ulster Division on our right. But we got held up by the huge mine craters with their lips 20 to 30 feet high and had to go round them. It was the first time we had seen tanks in action. It was an unforgettable sight to see them coming out of the mist and smoke with their sleeve valve engines pouring oil smoke astern and their guns spitting flame and fury.

Private A.R. Read
HQ, 141ST INFANTRY BRIGADE [MESSINES]

The explosions cannot be described. All I can say was that it seemed as if everything turned black. Then a terrific roar. I was in the door of our dug-out, when I was flung yards, finishing up in a shell hole. The next I remember was feeling dazed. Then looking around saw some of the boys lying around. Our dug-outs had collapsed while one and all were deaf. After a while I could hear myself talk. I discovered I was stuttering.

Lieutenant T.H. Witherow
8TH BATTALION, ROYAL IRISH RIFLES [MESSINES]

At 11 o'clock we marched off by platoons to take up our final positions in the front line. What a memorable night it is just before one goes into action for the first time. What feelings and emotions, absolutely indescribable, surge up in one's brain. Happy is the man who is not endowed with a vivid imagination.

It was a very hot night and, loaded as we were with all our fighting kit on our backs as well as our personal necessities for which on an occasion like this there was no obliging transport, consequently we were very hot and tired when we eventually arrived at our destination. The exact place where one is to 'jump off' is not easy to find in the dark and this time we had to search before we located it. Then the bombs and rifle grenades had to be collected from the dump and distributed, which took some time. By this time it was drawing very near to zero hour which was to be 3.10 a.m. so I began to give out a tot of rum to each of my men. This tot, about the size of a table spoon, was just enough to cheer up the men and send a thrill of warmth through their cold bodies. How easy for an armchair critic sitting before a comfortable fire at home to say that our soldiers ought to have been deprived of this comfort. It had always a wonderful and beneficial effect on the men.

Lieutenant T.H. Witherow
8TH BATTALION, ROYAL IRISH RIFLES [MESSINES]

On the first flash of the exploding mines I had given the signal to my platoon and leading the way I sprang up the scaling ladder and out into No-Man's Land. It was still very dark and as this portion of the line was one mass of craters and shell holes it was impossible to keep together or form any straight line. In fact if we had not had the German sos lights to show us our positions, in the dark it would have been as easy to go right or left as straight ahead. We floundered in and out of deep shell holes and old disused trenches in our endeavour to reach the enemy line with as little delay as possible. Then a terrible thing happened which I shall never forget and which nearly put an end to my fighting days. Going through the machine gun and artillery fire we had reached the enemy position when all of a sudden the earth seemed to open and belch forth a great mass of flame, and with a deafening noise went up in the air huge masses of earth and stone. We were all throw violently to the ground and debris began to fall around us as it descended. Luckily only soft earth fell on me but the lance corporal, one of my best section commanders, was instantly killed by a stone which fell on his head, as he lay at my side. This was one of our mines which for some reason had failed to go up earlier. Only a few more seconds and we would have gone up in it. As it was we were considerably affected [by] the gas left by the explosion.

By this time most units had become hopelessly mixed up, but the main thing was to keep advancing. The Germans gradually retired, leaving their wounded on the field but as usual their machine gunners made a brave stand until overborne by our rush.

Private A.R. Read
HQ, 141ST INFANTRY BRIGADE [MESSINES]

On reaching the German line we saw some of the damage done by our mines. Hill 60 was a hill no more, simply a huge crater. Looking down we could see what had been tunnels. Here the German reserves had been massed. It looked as if the whole German Army had been killed. This was besides those buried alive. Concussion had caused all this as the majority never had a mark on them. It was as if they had been asleep. Naturally our boys had no pity, because Fritzy had done worse when he gassed our chaps in the early days of the war, in this same district. The more German dead the better for everyone.

Private John Page
9TH BATTALION, ROYAL IRISH RIFLES [MESSINES]

On Wednesday night June 6th at about 11.30 pm we were relieved from the front line and proceeded back to the support lines to a place called Fort Victoria. On the way down we passed a tank which was going up to get into position, and it crawled across the communications trench down which we were passing. Our aeroplanes were flying backward and forward from the front line chiefly, I imagine, to deaden the noise made by the motors of the numerous tanks. Eventually we arrived at Fort Victoria where we were put into some assembly trenches for a few hours rest before the battle [Messines]. At 1.45 we had our 'dinner' after which we could sleep if we wished. After 'dinner' my chum and I went and filled our water bottles and by the time we returned it was about 2.20 a.m. Directly we got back into our portion of trench we made preparations for a few minutes sleep. Having got settled and just beginning to doze, we were suddenly aroused by the violent shaking of the ground around us and it seemed as though we were in a huge swing. It seemed like a dream at first but we soon knew different for it was followed by a huge red flash and the noise cannot be described. These were the mines that our engineers had worked on night and day without ceasing for over nine months and the whole job was finished in less than a number of seconds. The noise of the mines had barely finished when the Artillery opened out to add the grand finale of the whole outfit, and within five minutes of the Artillery commencing our first wave had already mounted the bags and were just about to meet the German if he had not already fled.

Lieutenant T.H. Witherow
8TH BATTALION, ROYAL IRISH RIFLES [MESSINES]

Our company had succeeded in reaching their objective and the 10th BATT, according to programme, had passed through them and were tackling the enemy further on. Our casualties had been very few and I was delighted to see that Patterson and Ireland were safe. Our chief duty now was to consolidate the position that we had won while the battle raged in front of us.

The tanks now began to make their appearance, advancing to attack the isolated strong points that were holding out. All day the aeroplanes had been flying overhead like great flights of birds worrying the enemy, and keeping contact with our advancing infantry and carrying back information as to how the attack was proceeding. In the height of battle it is by this means that the General gets his most reliable information. As our infantry advance they burn flares on the ground when a particular position is taken and the airmen, seeing these, send back word to headquarters. The line to which we advanced had been the old German 4th line and we proceeded to put it into a state of defence in case the Germans counter-attacked.

Lieutenant Edwin Godson
9TH BATTALION, ROYAL IRISH FUSILIERS [MESSINES]

Our mines have gone off; there were 19 of them on the front of about 9 miles attacked. Crash came the opening of our artillery of all calibres and it continued so the whole day and next night. Australians, N.Z. Brigade 25th DIVN, 36th (Ulster) DIVN, 16th (S Irish) DIV, 19th English DIV, was the order of battle south to north and the boys went over together. Multitudes of coloured flares were sent up by the Boche. It was still grey dawn and one could not see the Wyschaete Messines Ridge. After it grew light the smoke was too thick to see through. Our attack went like clockwork. Our men followed the creeping barrage and leapt on the Germans unawares. His artillery made little reply and occupied themselves in getting away. Each line was taken at its appointed time and our casualties were very small. How different from July 1st last year.

Private John Page
9TH BATTALION, ROYAL IRISH RIFLES [MESSINES]

Our new position was about 500 yards in advance of the one we'd just left and we had just about got into it when a hellish strafe started and the familiar coloured lights were going up from the front line. It was Fritz trying on a counter-attack on the ANZACS who were on our right and of course we got the order to 'Stand-to' *tout suite* and be prepared to either advance or retire which ever it might be. Fritz was putting up 'some' bombardment and we shortly got ordered to move up close to our front lines as things seemed to be looking rough and we had to be all ready for him in case he got through.

The next morning we had just finished our bit of breakfast when Fritz started again, this time with high explosive heavy shell and shrapnel and he was right on our trench every time. During the time he was shelling we lost 6 more men. Three were sergeants and three were Lewis gunners. Our platoon sergeant (Shepherd) had his eye knocked out and we were all very sorry for him because he was such a jolly good fellow.

Well, we hung to our positions until 10 p.m. June 9th when we were relieved by the York and Lancs (11th Division). As soon as all relieving was finished we made our way back to Kemmel Hill where some tents had been pitched for us. We eventually arrived there about 12.30 p.m. and when we had all found somewhere to sleep we were dished out with a dose of tea and hard biscuits after which we all settled down for a real good peaceful sleep, the first real sleep for two weeks.

Lieutenant T.H. Witherow
8TH BATTALION, ROYAL IRISH RIFLES [MESSINES]

It was a glorious victory and considering the natural strength of the German position and its strategic importance the casualties were surprisingly few. The heat during the day had been very great and consequently the water in our water bottles soon disappeared, leaving a lot of very thirsty soldiers. In the afternoon our transport officer made a very gallant and successful attempt to convey water and ammunition on the back of the transport mules. This was a very difficult operation owing to the bad state of the ground which was one mass of deep shell holes and to the fact that as soon as the mules appeared in sight the enemy opened a heavy artillery fire through which they had to pass. For this successful effort the transport officer received the MC.

Lieutenant Henry Crowe
20TH SQUADRON, ROYAL FLYING CORPS

I was very thrilled when I was posted to NO 20 Squadron in France. This was in November 1917. The Squadron was then based at St Marie Cappel near Cassel behind the front where I had served in the infantry. It was equipped with the Bristol Fighter aeroplane, a splendid new 2-seater fighter with a Rolls Royce engine. Like all aircraft at that time it was made of wood with metal fittings and undercarriage and wire bracing. Covering was of the best Irish linen sewn on and tightened with rope. All aerodromes were grass fields. No thought of runways in those days. St Marie Cappel was large enough to operate four squadrons. We lived in Nissan huts and had individual flight Messes. We were most comfortable, with linen sheets and pillow slips. Everything was kept clean by one batman per hut. The aeroplanes were housed in canvas hangers (camouflaged) beside the aerodrome and had to be man-handled on to the airfield for flight. Engine changes were carried out by the squadron but any major repairs had to be done at Aircraft Depot St Omer. Offices, Armoury, Photo Section, bomb and ammunition stores, equipment stores, and transport, were of course necessities. Leyland lorries and Crossley tenders made up the unit's transport.

During the winter of 1917 NO 20 was employed on offensive patrols at about 17,000 feet, designed to establish air superiority for the Allies in the particular air space detailed. The pilot flew the aeroplane while the observer carried out the following. Operate the rear gun or guns. Navigate by map reading. Drop bombs 112 lb and 20 lb when carried. Operate camera for vertical photos. Compile recce reports. There was a spare 'joystick' in the rear cockpit and rudder control which would enable the observer to get the aeroplane down if the pilot was wounded. The observer's flying badge, 'the flying O', was almost a decoration. Before one could wear it one had to complete so many hours war flying, have had at least two successful air combats, and pass a viva exam in memorising a map of enemy aerodromes etc in a large area. I remember a lady asking me 'Have you ever been up?' as she was examining my wing. And I was annoyed.

Private John Page
9TH BATTALION, ROYAL IRISH RIFLES [MESSINES]

The position we took up was just on the other side of the Messines –Wyschaete road just in front of Messines Village; when I say the other side of the road I mean the side nearest Fritz. The place where we stopped was like a pepper box with shell holes, so there wasn't an extra amount of digging to be done. It was just a matter of linking up the shell holes to make some sort of trench. From our new position to the German's front line the shell holes weren't more than a yard apart so one can imagine what kind of barrage our artillery must have put up. Well, I got to digging my bit of a shell hole and later found that my two chums were beside me, so knocking our heads together we decided to dig out a comfortable place for the three of us. We soon started and by the time we had finished it was almost daylight, so our thoughts turned to souvenirs and sightseeing, both of which were very risky in daylight. After a look round we managed to scrounge a few souvenirs which were one bayonet, one revolver, two pairs of field glasses, and a gas helmet which we sold for a few decent francs, sharing the money.

Lieutenant T.H. Witherow
8TH BATTALION, ROYAL IRISH RIFLES

On the morning of the 31st [July] I rode on horseback into Poperinghe the large town in a straight line behind Ypres, about 6 miles. There I saw General Gough who had charge of the operations standing outside the Corps Headquarters. It was very difficult to find out exactly what had happened or how things had gone but it was easy to see that things had not turned out as well as had been expected. What had really happened was that the enemy had practically given up his two front lines either without any fighting at all or with very little resistance, and had retired to a rear line consisting not so much of long continuous trench lines which we could bombard with impunity, but an irregular line of strong concrete pillboxes in which he took refuge during the barrage and when it had passed overhead came out and machine gunned our advancing troops. This new German tactic completely upset all our calculations and did not fit in with our barrage idea or our method of advance. Consequently our casualties on the opening day were enormous and we only succeeded in gaining the enemy third line which was on the border of his pill box zone. Any troops who advanced into this zone were driven back with great loss by the converging fire of the pillboxes which were strong and well concealed. To attack this zone on the same principle as one would attack a trench line as we did on the first day and also later on the 16th was a great mistake.

Private John Page
9TH BATTALION, ROYAL IRISH RIFLES

At about 3.30 a.m. on the morning of the 16th [August] we were ordered to leave our trench and to dig in half way across No-Man's Land in readiness for our kick-off at 6.30 a.m. Just before it got light we were given a nice tot of rum. I remember our officer (a Lt Turner) smiling and chatting with us as he issued the tots. By 7 a.m. this gentleman was dead, having got one in the head. 6.10 a.m. was the signal for our own bombardment to commence and from then until the whistle blew for us to go at 6.30 a.m. the din was awful. At the blast of our signal whistle everyone seemed to go mad and they rose as one and trotted at the high trot towards the enemy lines. Then the boys began to fall, some on the right, some on the left and some behind us (we were the first wave). The smell of powder and cry of those hit was indescribable and I remember my CPL (Barnes) getting one in the thigh and one in the arm and going down. I got down beside him and ripped his trousers to dress his wound, but he told me to go on, so I went. A little further on we had to take cover in shell holes and I shared one with another fellow. The MGs were playing hell and we had to keep low for some time. My partner of the shell hole got inquisitive and got up to have a look around and immediately fell back dead with one through his head. After that we got on the move again and I passed some of our fellows bombing a blockhouse (strong point) while others were throwing dirt through the slits to prevent the Germans from firing. Then I saw the enemy retreating through some wire at the back of their trench. I distinctly remember shooting two of them. One was very tall and he had a bandage round his head, no hat, and a long grey overcoat. I remember him falling across the wire after I hit him. Then all of a sudden egg bombs started coming over, apparently from nowhere and I got one which knocked me out. I got it on the right side, beside the right ear, under the right arm, on the right knee and right ankle.

I started crawling back to a German dug-out in our rear where I perforce had to remain until about mid-day as a machine gun was 'on' the dug-out and kept hitting the walls. Inside the dug-out was a Tommy of the Irish Rifles who was badly hit in the stomach by a ricochet. He asked me for water but as this was not advisable I gave him half of an orange I'd got with me. I remained with him nearly 6 hours and I more than once pushed back portions of his insides that were working out. He being unable to walk had had to stay there until dark as he would not be carried in daylight, but I doubt whether he lived that long. He was in a very bad way. When I left his face was an ashen grey colour. I managed to get away down to an aid post and from there to a casualty clearing station at Veamestenshe where I was dressed.

Captain C.A. Brett

6TH BATTALION, CONNAUGHT RANGERS [THIRD YPRES/PASSCHENDAELE]

As we advanced across the open country we were obviously spotted by the Germans, who laid down a fierce artillery barrage on the slight ridge a couple of hundred yards in front of us. I was leading the leading Company, and did not like the look of it a bit, as the ridge was spouting smoke and flame, and mud and dust flew in all directions. However, we were ordered to relieve the troops in front, so I told (by signs, the noise was dreadful) the Company to get into single file behind me (a most unmilitary formation actually) and I took the lead and walked (with my heart in my boots) straight up the ridge and into the barrage, with the Company like a snake twisting this way and that behind me. Straight up to, and straight through, the barrage, and to my astonishment we had one man wounded. When the other Company commanders saw what was happening they adopted the same formation and all got through with very little loss.

Private A.R. Read

HQ, 141ST INFANTRY BRIGADE [BATTLE OF CAMBRAI]

Fritzie's aeroplanes had been giving us a very lively time by swooping down and firing their machine guns. All at once a Fritzy made a dive and crashed a short distance away. His machine burst into flames; the pilot was thrown several yards away. Several of us made a rush to the German, but just then the ammunition in the burning plane started popping out, so we had to get under cover until things got a little quieter. The aeroplane was badly burned when we reached it, although some of the boys managed one or two souvenirs. We thought that the pilot was dead, until one of the chaps heard him groan. He muttered 'Vater', meaning water. I got some, but he was too bad to swallow anything. Fetching a doctor, he found that poor old Fritzy had an arm and leg broken, also several ribs. He told us (in broken English) that his observer was in the machine, so he must have been burnt to a cinder. Anyhow the stretcher bearers came up and took our old pal away, but he died before they got to the dressing station.

Captain C.A. Brett

6TH BATTALION, CONNAUGHT RANGERS [CAMBRAI]

We had about two hundred yards to go. It was still pitch dark and the noise was infernal. Gaps had been cut during the night in our wire, and white tape laid through them to guide us, so that we could at least start in the right direction. I led the right platoon of the right hand company, while French led the left hand platoon, and I endeavoured to set my pace across No-Man's Land so as to keep the shrapnel shells bursting about twenty feet in front, and about twenty feet or less above us. With me was the Royal Engineer Officer with the explosive charge, but unknown to me he was hit and killed half way across. We found (as we hoped) the German barbed wire substantially destroyed by our shell fire. It presented no serious obstacle, and we got into the German trench (which was really a foot track through shell holes) and found quite of number of Germans wearing gas masks, and very much at a disadvantage accordingly. They were a pretty poor lot and badly shaken. Only a few put up a fight and they got killed, and the rest surrendered. We then turned our attention to the concrete pillbox, which was a pretty large and immensely strong affair, which had not suffered at all from the shell fire, and whose occupants were firing at us from loopholes. One of my men got on the roof (which was flat) and lobbed a mills bomb in through one of the loopholes and this caused confusion inside, and some wounded and some unwounded men came out and were duly dealt with, the prisoners being sent back to our front line under escort.

We were complimenting ourselves that we had done pretty well (so far), not knowing that the tunnel had not been blocked; when out of the tunnel on our right emerged a considerable number of Germans and launched a fierce attack on our right flank which was a short distance to the right of the newly captured pillbox.

And these were not the miserable, shell-shocked, gas-masked Germans we had found in the trench, but fierce storm troopers who had remained below, safe and warm and comfortable, and who were fresh and had innumerable hand grenades which they threw at us in showers. One of my men distinguished himself by picking up German grenades and throwing them back again. There was also a lot of rifle and machine gun fire. We organised ourselves as best we could and as quickly as could meet this new peril, and things were extremely hot for a few minutes but we held the Germans twenty yards or so away.

All this time, five miles south of us, the Battle of Cambrai was raging. A large number of tanks attacked without artillery bombardment, and went clean through the German trenches to a depth of about four miles, into open country. There, owing to incompetent staff work by General Gough and his Fifth Army, the tanks ran out of petrol, as no arrangements had been made to supply them with more. They were therefore stranded, and the Germans counter-attacked in two days time, re-taking all the ground they had lost and more, capturing many tanks and guns, and causing us heavy casualties.

Lieutenant T.H. Witherow
8/9TH BATTALION, ROYAL IRISH RIFLES [CAMBRAI]

Sleep did not come to me on the eve of this great battle. About 2 or 3 in the morning there was the roar of many guns and I thought that perhaps the enemy had discovered our plans after all. But this firing turned out to be our own guns firing to drown the noise of the tanks as they assembled in No-Man's Land. We rose early on the morning of the 20th and as we were on parade previous to moving off for the scene of action, Zero hour arrived, and with one concentrated noise the guns burst forth and, led by the tanks, our men leapt forth to the attack of that strong and impregnable line.

The battalion marched to a position about three miles behind the line, there to wait whatever orders should arrive in case our help was required by any of the attacking brigades. I was in command of B Company and with Somerset, Boyd, and Knox as company officers, the remainder being left behind at the transport lines along with 30% of the qualified men of the company. This was a necessary rule as in case of heavy losses there was always a nucleus to start a new company. Although such a short distance behind the fighting line, we were able to get very little reliable news but we knew that things were going fairly well. A great and unforgettable sight was the action of our flame throwers which showed to what war had really come in fiendishness. Although some miles back we could see these great volumes of what looked like white smoke going high into the air and then coming down and in their descent break into a great expanse of red flame. Who could withstand such weapons?

Private A.R. Read
HQ, 141ST INFANTRY BRIGADE [CAMBRAI]

That afternoon one of the Guards Brigades went over the top. The objective was a village (which was a very important position) called Fontaine-Notre Dame. Our bombardment opened at 3.30. The Irish and Coldstreams attacked shortly after. They managed to get into the village, but were forced to retire owing to having suffered heavy losses and receiving no support. An orderly from the Irish Guards brought a message to our Headquarters and told us his brigade had nearly been wiped out.

Lieutenant T.H. Witherow
8/9TH BATTALION, ROYAL IRISH RIFLES [CAMBRAI]

I ordered Somerset to attack the Lock on the right and Boyd on the left. So we set out on our advance. I moved a little to the rear and in the centre of the two platoons with my headquarters consisting of signallers, runners, stretcher bearers, and one Lewis gun team. The ground rose to a small ridge which ran parallel to the Cambrai–Bapaume Road and by this we were covered from view and therefore from fire, but as soon as this low ridge was surmounted we came into full view of the Hindenberg [sic] positions and a tremendous machine gun fire was directed against us and the tanks that preceded us. During this advance for about 900 yards we were under this heavy fire and the bullets were falling around us like hailstones. Fortunately most of them seemed to be directed against the tanks which were what the enemy feared most. In spite of this heavy fire we got quite near to our objective without any casualties. The men that were hit simply had to be left behind while one of the stretchers tried to convey the unlucky one to cover or a dip in the ground and there bind up his wound.

When I got to within about 150 yards of the Lock I established my headquarters flag in a trench formed by a sunken road and from that position was able to witness the attack on the Lock itself by the platoons. Boyd's platoon went round to the left and became lost from view but I could see Somerset and his men most of the time. They followed at the rear of the tank which helped knock out the German machine gunners who were holding the position. This Lock was a very substantial structure. Indeed this canal was only in the process of completion and was therefore, especially its locks, a great engineering feat and not the usual type of country canal.

At this place the canal was running through a cutting and the Lock was a large hollow with four steep banks on either side and in the hollow were buildings with all kinds of machinery for working the Lock gates. The enemy had their machine gun on the top of the steep banks when our men advanced but these were put out of action and the enemy retired to his line by means of the canal bed which was dry. The main Hindenberg [sic] Line Support Trench was one of the outlying defences of that line.

Somerset's platoon, in advancing towards the Lock by the right, came under very heavy fire from the enemy's main line and they had to crawl in single file as low as possible. In spite of this I could see that he was suffering very heavy casualties as the men were forced to lie in full view of the enemy line. Some of the wounded were able to crawl back to my position but the majority had to lie where they had been hit, so heavy was the fire. Boyd's platoon had now got into the Lock by advancing up the bed of the canal and this enabled Somerset to also get in the shelter of the Lock banks, but unfortunately he was forced to leave some of his men out in that exposed position. Three of them eventually found their way into an old dug-out which was very near the enemy wire.

The enemy had now been driven out of the Lock and he had taken shelter behind the defences of the main line and its impregnable wire.

Lieutenant T.H. Witherow
8TH BATTALION, ROYAL IRISH RIFLES

That night our Brigade was ordered to relieve the few remaining survivors of the other two Brigades. My platoon proceeded right up to a position in front of our previous line which consisted of a row of six German concrete dug-outs which had been wrested from the enemy that morning. As it was in advance of our general line and was therefore practically surrounded by the enemy it was a very precarious position and it looked as if he could retake it without much difficulty. As usual we experienced great difficulty in discovering the place in the dark. While I was leading my men to the position a shell burst just behind me, killing some of my men who were bringing up the rear.

That was a very sad night. All around us lay the scarcely cold bodies of the men of the Belfast Young Citizen Volunteers, the 14th RIRs, the first battalion in which I had served. Then we expected the Germans would perhaps make a counter-attack, seeing that we were partly disorganised after our defeat, but the night passed off quietly except for the usual artillery fire.

The 16th Irish Division on our right had met with a similar fate, making practically no progress and losing very heavily. It was a sad blow to the hopes of a great victory which would eventually drive the enemy out of Belgium. Vivian Green was killed that day while advancing with the 16th Division.

Private A.R. Brennan
2ND BATTALION, ROYAL IRISH REGIMENT

I was awakened by O'Brien some time after dawn, and he told me that shells had been dropping in our vicinity for some time. He was always a bit nervous under shell fire, and he thought we should move. Only half awake I mumbled something fatalistic like 'If we're to be killed we'll be killed,' and made as if to resume my slumbers. The next shell settled the question. It was a high explosive and burst just above us. I saw my trouser knees suddenly go red and could tell from their calling for stretcher bearers that my comrades had been wounded. No doubt I did my own bit of yelling too. It must have been effective because in a few minutes I was in the gentle hands of our Company stretcher bearers, amongst whom I recognised dear old Paddy Kelly. They dressed my wounds, those that they could see, and with all kinds of cheery remarks—bless them—carried me down to a dressing station on the Menin Road. Here my wounds were looked at and re-dressed, and soon I was in an ambulance bumping its way across Ypres Square on the way to the casualty clearing station. After the shrapnel had been extracted from my wounds—of which they were many—I received the usual anti-tetanus injection and was dispatched with many other wounded to a Canadian hospital at Etaples. I believe I was four or five days at this hospital before being sent back to England. As far as the war was concerned this was the end of the road for me. Of my three comrades who had been wounded at the same time I heard later that O'Brien died of his wounds, Sullivan had both his legs broken, and McCarthy was only slightly wounded.

Lieutenant Percy McElwaine
B COMPANY, 14TH BATTALION, ROYAL IRISH RIFLES

Plumer, the commander of the Second Army, was the most successful of our commanders. I saw him several times as he was fond of taking a look round even if he was not making a formal inspection. It was said, and I can believe it, that he was better known to the rank and file and to junior commanders than most Divisional Commanders. His name was familiar to me from the days when as Col Plumer he led the Rhodesian Forces to the relief of Mafeking. One hardly expected one who had served so much in the native wars and with colonial troops to be immaculate in his attire but Plumer, with his monocle, was always faultlessly dressed with shining boots. Yet he was no fop. He was a highly efficient soldier who inspired confidence in all who served under him.

Chapter 5 ∾

1918

1918 saw the arrival of the long-awaited German divisions from the Eastern Front, and Ludendorff orchestrated one last throw of the dice for Germany, the *Kaiserschlacht*. The German Spring Offensive pushed the Allies out of the trenches and forced them back through almost all the ground they had gained since 1914. However, the Germans were held once again at the Marne (15 July–6 August). The effort exhausted the German Army, and its logistical structure could no longer cope with the demands of intensive attritional warfare. Instead it was the Allies who were to push forward to victory in a spectacular series of battles collectively entitled the 'Hundred Days'. It began at the Battle of Amiens (8–11 August), and was followed by the 2nd Battle of the Somme (21 August–2 September), the 5th Battle of Ypres (8 September–2 October) the Battle of St Quentin Canal (29 September–10 October), and the 2nd Battle of Cambrai (8–10 October).

The 16th (Irish) Division had suffered such losses it was taken back to England in early 1918 to be rebuilt, yet the 36th (Ulster) Division remained. As indeed did many of the regular battalion, though many were scattered among English New Army Divisions, such as the 2nd Royal Munster Fusiliers which served with the 31st Division, while others such as the 1st Royal Dublin Fusiliers served with the 29th Division, a regular division.

The war the Irish soldiers fought in 1918 was radically different to that in 1914. Now aeroplanes and tanks emerged to rule the battlefield, but for the infantry ground still had to be fought for, won and held. Little perhaps did Irish soldiers standing in France on 11 November 1918, relieved at the end of the most terrible war in history, imagine a homecoming to a violent and troubled land.

Private Felfus Long

25TH BATTALION, NORTHUMBERLAND FUSILIERS (TYNESIDE IRISH)

The sector we were going to hold was directly in front of the town. We started about 4 o'clock in the afternoon as the relief had to be finished by midnight. We started off a Company at a time, and my Company, being B, was the second to start. After arriving in the town we were split up into smaller parties of about 20 men, so as to avoid the shelling as much as possible, and we also got the order 'Gas helmets at the alert'. The town had been blown to atoms, but we got through to the end of the communication trench without mishap. Here, there was the usual commotion of taking the machine guns out, etc, but at last we got going down the trench in the dark, as it was pitch black by this time. I had some young lads with me straight out from England, first time in the trenches, and I can tell they had a few wettings before they got used to the duck boards, as they would try to go round corners a bit too sharp and the result was that they missed their footing and down they went up to their thighs in icy cold water. Well, after a bit of struggling we arrived at Battalion Head Quarters, only to find there was no guide for our Company. 'But we could walk it easy in a quarter of an hour' so they told us, so off we set. After walking for nearly an hour and climbing places where the trench was blown in, we came to the conclusion that we were lost, which is by no means an uncommon occurrence in the trenches, seeing I've been lost a score of time. In this state we all sat down or leaned against the trench side, absolutely done up, what with our packs, etc. After resting here for about 10 minutes one of our officers comes up and says, 'Come on, lads, it's only a quarter of an hour's walk now but whatever you do keep your heads down.'

So off we went, following him, till we came to the front line which our Company was to hold. Then we stood about in the trench for an hour till the 23rd N Fus got away, for they were the Battalion we were relieving, having finished their six days in. I along with three more was put in Gas Guard and we secured a decent little dug-out, although not shell proof but rain proof, for it was impossible to dig down owing to the watery state of the ground. It was now well turned midnight, but duty first and sleep after. That's how we passed our first night in the line.

Captain C.A. Brett
6TH BATTALION, CONNAUGHT RANGERS

R.H. French MC, an English Roman Catholic, who later became a Master of the High Court in London and who was one of my best friends, had commanded B Company at Ypres in the absence of Tuite who was its commander, but Tuite came back when we came to Ervillers and French came to me as 2nd in command. He was older than I, and very short-sighted, with thick glasses, but utterly dependable and apparently fearless. Also there came to me Fenton Cummins who was another good friend, a Cork Protestant of good family, about my own age, small, pale faced and insignificant to look at: but with the heart of a lion. He was killed on 21 March 1918, as we knew he would be sooner or later; if anyone ever deserved a decoration (and did not get it) it was Cummins. And we three were a happy party. We had served in France for more than twelve months (which was unusually long for a junior officer of infantry to survive).

Private David Starrett
HQ, 119TH BRIGADE

Father O'Floightry [sic] had been killed during our retreat whilst attending some of our boys. He was not of my faith, but he was a man, every inch of him. ... I respected all who tried to do their duty and a bit over, but the Father had a way with him that made us his friends for all time, no matter how much we differed from him in the little non-essentials of his calling.

Lieutenant G. de Pass
4TH (ROYAL IRISH) DRAGOON GUARDS

I was sent to hold a crossroads at a place called Demuin, and I had about 20 men. The Division in front of us had been very shattered, and the Germans were attacking with great force and it was important to hold the high ground in the area of the crossroads. I arrived at Demuin and selected what I thought was the best position in a ploughed field. Stragglers were coming back and we managed to re-form quite a substantial number of them, who had lost all their officers, and they fought extremely well. We were heavily attacked, but managed to hold until such a time as the Australians, who had formed up behind us, were able to counter-attack and relieve the position. The lesson I learned from this hard fight—which it was—was that the stragglers were very willing to fight, directly they found there was cohesion in their command.

Private A.R. Read
HQ, 141ST INFANTRY BRIGADE

Shuffling along the road we came across a box of sardines, also a bundle of new socks which we shared among us. Reaching a water-point we managed to fill our water bottles, after having to fight for it—the civvies in England could not picture the scene. All sorts of Tommies just going barmy fighting to get a drop of water. Sergeants and corporals as bad as anyone else. Then back on the road again.

Lieutenant Henry Crowe
20TH SQUADRON, ROYAL FLYING CORPS

On my second operational sortie we were suddenly dived on by three Albatross fighters, all painted startling colours, but they only did slight damage to our tail plane. I failed to hit any of them. German pilots were allowed to paint their fighters in this manner hoping to scare their opponents, rather like Red Indians painting their faces and bodies with their war paint. In January 1918 winter weather set in. Some of us got frost bite in the face and the guns froze. We rubbed whale oil on the face and then out on vaseline. We fired short bursts at intervals to try and keep the guns free. Even with the radiator shutters tight shut and lots of revs, it was very difficult to keep the engines warm enough when descending to give proper power. Blood coming back into the hands when descending was painful.

Lance Corporal Thomas Healy
2ND BATTALION, ROYAL IRISH REGIMENT

Our road now led through ground over which 'Jerry' forced us back last March, so there were 'umpteen' shell holes, and here and there bodies of German and British soldiers still unburied. Of course we had plenty of halts at places, where bully and biscuits had been left in haste, and to which we freely helped ourselves. About 6 p.m. footsore and weary, we arrived at our transport lines, but everywhere there was a happy smile.

We now began to dig in, making bivouacs of old pieces of cast iron, and wood lying about, and then the rations for the next day came up, with a Dixie (bucket) of hot tea. This time, we were given a loaf between five men, together with the usual active service diet, which I have previously mentioned. The proverbial showers, so common in France, now began to fall, so we turned in. I was in a 'Bivi' with five others, and though we were crushed together, yet we felt the perishing cold, which increased as the night advanced.

Captain C.A. Brett
2ND BATTALION, LEINSTER REGIMENT

One thing I saw then which I had not previously seen in France, but which was with us till the end of the war, and that was the spoiling of the dead, by night. People (I must assume they were human; we never saw them and never knew) prowled the fields the night after a battle and relieved the dead of anything valuable, a ring, a watch, money, a pair of boots, but not uniforms or military equipment. If a ring did not come off easily, the finger was cut off; if someone was lying wounded, he did not remain wounded long, but died quickly. I made a point of leaving my signet ring with the Adjutant.

Acting Captain T.H. Witherow
8/9TH BATTALION, ROYAL IRISH RIFLES

Instead of looking for a billet in the village we encamped in the outskirts. The Padre of the battalion [Father Gill] who had been with the regiment since the beginning of the war was now with us. He was a fine looking priest of middle age and very distinguished looking. He was rather inclined to look askance at the temporary officer but personally I got on very well with him. He was of great help to us as we retired because of the respect with which the French people treated him. He could get any billet he wanted in a village because the inhabitants were only too glad to have a priest in their house, both for his own sake and for the fact that his presence would be a guarantee that the property would be respected. The French I'm afraid did not trust us very far and in some cases they had good reason for not doing so. I had some very interesting arguments with his reverence, who had the DSO.

Lance Corporal Thomas Healy
2ND BATTALION, ROYAL IRISH REGIMENT

About 10 a.m. we arrived at a ridge and joined the remnants of our battalion who had been relieved that morning. They were a very miserable looking lot, some fast asleep, dirty and unshaven, and others trying to wash themselves in the rain which fell into their steel helmets. Seemingly, however, all were happy and overjoyed at being relieved and the prospect of a rest. The new arrivals made bivouacs as before, and tried to make things look as ship shape as possible under the circumstances. We stayed here resting, or supposed to be looking to be resting for three or four days, having a few rifle inspections, and receiving issues of Lewis guns etc, etc, when news came that we were to be prepared to quit and move again.

About the 30th of August, we left the ridge at 11 p.m and marched to another part of the front line in the Arras Sector, and this night march I may say has been one of the worst in my experience. After we had travelled about five kilometres, someone in the leading Company kicked a Mills hand grenade lying in the middle of the road, which accident caused seven or eight casualties. Although it was only an accident, it gave us a rather sickening and peculiar feeling in the pit of the stomach at first, but after a short time, we became hardened to these incidents of blood, and eventually I must confess, thought nothing of them.

Acting Captain T.H. Witherow

8/9TH BATTALION, ROYAL IRISH RIFLES

The attack [*Kaiserschlacht*] was delivered on a 50-mile front by an enemy vastly superior in numbers at the point of attack. The numbers of the enemy divisions attacking on this front were more than the whole of the British Army in France. As it was not definitely known where the enemy would actually attack and as the Northern portion of the British line guarding the channel ports was of vital importance, all our reserves had to be congregated there and the front of the 5th Army left bare. This in spite of the fact that the line was drawn out and therefore could only be thinly held. It was against this weak line of Gough's 5th Army that the great masses of the enemy were hurled. It was an extraordinarily foggy day and when the enemy attacked the artillery was unable to see the SOS signals thrown up by the infantry in the line. Previous to the attack the enemy artillery opened out about 5 in the morning and drenched our line both front and rear with gas. The number of enemy guns was evidently enormous.

Our battalion being in reserve had to occupy the strongpoints, and D Company were in their position before the attack. But so great was the enemy fire and so accurate that many were killed as they huddled up in this position.

Private Felfus Long

25TH BATTALION, NORTHUMBERLAND FUSILIERS (TYNESIDE IRISH)

We had just nicely got settled when the enemy started shelling very heavily, mostly gas shells, so we had to put on our respirators. This was about nine o'clock, but soon after the range altered and all the shells went further back into the reserve trenches and Armentieres. After a while we took our respirators off, but the smell was something cruel, as he was using that awful mustard gas. Still the bombardment went on but we saw no signs of attack and our artillery never replied so we didn't know what to make of it. As it grew into morning we saw that something was happening on the right about two miles away. The sky was one vivid light and we thought he must be attacking the Portuguese who were holding the line on our right. Morning came and we came out of the post, or shell hole, shall I call it, for it was nothing more, but still the bombardment went on and the air was alive with shells. Once more we returned to our little dug-out, and there got to know that our Commanding Officer and doctor along with nearly all the men of two company's [sic] had been gassed, as these two companies had been left in reserve. This was bad news but still we hung on deciding to make the best of a bad job.

Captain C.A. Brett
2ND BATTALION, LEINSTER REGIMENT

On 21 March 1918, 6th Battalion Connaught Rangers was more or less wiped out by the German Offensive. Of the eighteen company officers, seventeen including my good friend Cummins were killed and one was taken prisoner. Of the 650 odd men in the Battalion about 30 survived, mostly transport drivers and Battalion Headquarters staff, and even they had to fight hard. Most of the men were killed; very few were taken prisoner. Both French and I were much upset, especially as we knew full well that had we not been wounded at Bullecourt, we would have certainly been killed too. Happily Colonel Fielding survived, but the 6th Battalion as such ceased to exist.

Private A.R. Read
HQ, 141ST INFANTRY BRIGADE

As the Infantry were so short of men everyone who could handle a rifle was pressed into digging trenches to form a line; our party was mixed up with Scots, Irish, Welsh, Engineers, Drivers, Gunners, in fact plenty of men who had never fired a rifle since being in France. Late that night we had a wind up. The cry went out 'German cavalry advancing'. That was it, everybody starting firing and it was some time before we found out that it was our own hussars who had gone out on patrol and quite a few of them must have been hit.

Private Felfus Long
25TH BATTALION, NORTHUMBERLAND FUSILIERS (TYNESIDE IRISH)

The officer of the company said, 'Come on, lads. The Germans are nearly all the way round us and I'm afraid we'll have to fight our way out.' Every man then loaded his rifle for we decided to give a good account of ourselves if it came to a fight. We got into the town only to find the enemy were closing in and it was like a bottle neck so we had to run the gauntlet which in this case was between two factories and they had machine guns on each which were facing across open ground which we had to cross. However, we split up into twos and threes and ran for it. We were rather lucky here for I saw very few get hit, but we kept on for about 900 yards when we were stopped by a stream about five yards wide, and 4 feet deep with dirty water. However, we didn't stop to think but waded through it, holding our rifles above our heads so as not to get clogged up with dirt—it looked as we'd want them later on. Rather wet, we got going again for it was only a few hundred yards to the river Lys and we saw some of our chaps on a pontoon bridge waving their hands for us to come on, and this we did, getting across allright [sic].

Private John Page
9TH BATTALION, ROYAL IRISH RIFLES

Very soon we should be inside the circle [surrounded] so we decided between us to make a dash for it. It was a sporting chance and it was the only opening we had. Soon we would be as rats in a trap, so emptying our pockets of our letters and burying them anywhere in the trench we prepared for the dash across the road. We arranged to go across one at a time at irregular intervals. A young officer went first but as soon as he was half way over he got one right in the head and fell down dead right in our path. The second chap started off and he tried crawling on his stomach. He was almost in the other side when he caught one in the ankle. Then a young lance corporal ran across but fell headlong into the other trench with one in his head. I went next and I ran over bent right down and literally threw myself into the trench. I got a bruise or two but at least I was safe from that touch anyhow. I watched the next chap come over and bent down as I did but got 3 right through the buttocks. He yelled like fury and my God when we got his trouser off he was like a slaughterhouse. Some more of our chaps got over alright, but goodness knows what became of those we had left lying on the road.

Private Felfus Long

25TH BATTALION, NORTHUMBERLAND FUSILIERS (TYNESIDE IRISH)

There were only ten of us in this place and no officers, sergeants or anybody, and it was quite evident the others had all retired. It was just breaking dawn when a German aeroplane came over about 300 feet high and was dropping Verey lights just over our heads, so we instantly opened fire on him but that was our greatest mistake for while we were doing our best with the aeroplane the Germans came over us. The few of the 23rd N FUS that were left came running down the trench shouting 'Jerry is coming' and sure enough he was, for I just glanced round only to find we were surrounded and the enemy were pouring in, in hundreds. There was only one thing to do, that was throw down our rifles for we were all covered by the enemy, so that we did. Some of them thought they could get away and one of my pals got on the top and was going to run for it, but he never went a stride before he got a bullet clean through his stomach which laid him helpless.

Private John Page

9TH BATTALION, ROYAL IRISH RIFLES

One of our officers, Lt Henry by name, was in our trench so of course we asked him what he was going to do. He said, 'Well, chaps, you can see our position. We are surrounded and it would be madness to even attempt to rush it with thousands of those *******
not a thousand yards away and all round us. I will tie my handkerchief on my stick and we must surrender.' He waved the handkerchief a few minutes and German rifle fire fell off a bit. After a while it ceased and someone shouted and when we looked over we saw a German officer coming towards our officer, who had now climbed to the top of the trench. The German was accompanied by

two big hefty soldiers with rifle and bayonet. After making some gestures to our officers making him understand that we were to be disarmed and file out of our trench with our hands above our heads. Our officer came back to us very downhearted and said 'Well, chaps, we're finished and are prisoners. We couldn't have done any better if we had made a bid for it. There would only have been more loss of life to no beneficial purpose, so, boys, we must make the best of it.' So we all put our rifles, bayonets, ammo, bombs, etc, in the trench and filed out of the trench behind the officer, each one of us with his hands above his head. We walked towards the advancing Germans, their officer again coming towards us with about 25 German soldiers all of whom were jeering and laughing at us, but our chaps were as good as they and laughed at them too. It was the same indomitable spirit that had carried the boys through some rough times and the same spirit was prevailing even though we were beaten so to speak.

Lance Corporal Thomas Healy
2ND BATTALION, ROYAL IRISH REGIMENT

Sunday morning came, so I improvised an altar, and most of us heard Mass, and received Holy Communion, although the candles would not keep alight on account of the strong wind. In the evening we were on the move again, to take over support lines. We marched until 11 p.m. and the only incident on the way was that one of our observation balloons was shot down in flames by a 'Jerry' aeroplane. The intruder however managed to get away, but not before he got a few doses of shrapnel on his tail, from our ever watchful gunners.

We now reached a small system of trenches where we halted, and were told to make ourselves comfortable. Just imagine us crowding together for warmth in the bottom of the trench, and in the thick of the mud, ground sheets being our only covering. Soon we were ruthlessly awakened, and told to make room for a Battalion of the Munsters, who had to pass through. Although naturally enough, there were plenty of mumbled curses and grumbling, yet we had some fun with the 'Old Neighbours' or 'Dirty Shirts' as they are sometimes called. 'Are you from Cork', etc, etc. We bedded down again, but were aroused from our pleasant dreams a second time, at 5 a.m. for breakfast. We ate what we could there and then, and received our rations for the day.

Private A.R. Read
HQ, 141ST INFANTRY BRIGADE

A big attack was launched on our right, by the Canadian Corp and several British Divisions. They had advanced very rapidly, to a depth of 8 miles and from our sector we could see the bombardment and later watched observation balloons going forward on lorries. That same night all our patrols and forward posts were withdrawn from Albert and our artillery, French mortars and machine guns opened up a bombardment (also using gas) on the German machine gun and sniper posts.

Lieutenant Henry Crowe
20TH SQUADRON, ROYAL FLYING CORPS

On March 27th and after many more low flying sorties just after shooting down a Fokker triplane we were set upon by three bright red triplanes obviously part of Baron Von Richtofen's 'circus', and got badly shot up. I was short of ammunition after the low attacks but got a few bursts at them. After a stern attack two triplane pilots came up close enough for us to see their faces clearly. They must have wondered if we were both wounded! We limped back to Bruay and found the aeroplane so badly damaged that it had to be 'written off'. It said much for the Bristol that it could stand such punishment.

Lance Corporal Thomas Healy
2ND BATTALION, ROYAL IRISH REGIMENT

We marched now by companies, or rather ran through the shell-swept ground, over which the Canadians had passed in the morning. From every side groans could be heard of men in their last death agonies, but alas, we had to go on. Here the ghastly faces of dead German and British soldiers sent a shudder through us, which I am sure none of us will ever forget. Wounded were being carried down with a cheerful smile on all of their dirty and unshaven faces; they were, most of them, thinking of the swift passage to 'Blighty'.

As we advanced, we arrived in a more dangerous position, and naturally we had some narrow squeaks, but all went well. We stopped about 11 a.m. as 'Jerry's' machine bullets were becoming nasty. As I happened to be carrying the Lewis gun, I ran out into an advanced shell hole with another fellow, and opened fire at a range of about 700 yards. Although the main body of Germans had run away, they had left behind a number of machine gun nests, from which the bullets whizzed, with that queer sound which cannot be explained, but only felt, 'Zip, Zip, Zip'. They had such a splendid knack of camouflaging their pieces that we had great difficulty in locating them.

Receiving no orders to move, we stayed on, but later, seeing that this meant being cut off from the rest, we took 'French Leave' and followed. To use the words of a well-known poet, 'Someone had blundered', for by this time the Division had become a hopeless mix up. Our Platoon Officer came up just then, so we joined him. He told us that our Company's objective was about 900 yards away to the left, over the open plain, in face of those 'Blessed' machine guns. How we got across, I don't know; only God must have preserved.

We jumped from shell hole to shell hole, endeavouring to hide behind tufts of grass, and still around us the bullets came 'Ping, Ping, Ping'. People talk about men forgetting their religion in France, but I am sure I said more prayers that day than ever in my life before. About half a dozen of us reached the objective, which proved to be chalk mines, but 'Jerry' had already evacuated them: here we waited for the rest of our Company, but only about twelve more turned up; goodness knows where the others had gone.

Private A.R. Read
HQ, 141ST INFANTRY BRIGADE

German aeroplanes were reported and we were ordered to put all lights out; shortly after, bombs, and we saw our searchlights catch one of the Gothas and follow it along, which our machine opened fire on and brought down, just near the village of Bonnay. There were four occupants, including an officer; 2 were killed, while the other 2 were taken prisoner. All the next day the dead were left beside the aeroplane and several of us who went to have a look noticed that one of the dead had hands like a woman (small and smooth). The following day when they were about to be buried one of our chaps pulled the leather helmet off the head of the one with the woman's hands and found that it was a woman, dressed up in aviators' clothing. She was taking the place of a bomber, or else was a spy going to be dropped behind our lines.

Lance Corporal Thomas Healy
2ND BATTALION, ROYAL IRISH REGIMENT

After the strenuous time of the morning, we sat down on the side of the road to rest and have luncheon, but Jerry had a balloon up, which I suppose must have signalled to their gunners, because we got a most merciless shelling, right on the mark. Many were killed outright with the concussion caused by the explosions. One poor fellow in particular was sitting in the middle of the road, with a horrible grin on his face, stone dead. By this time, our own heavy artillery came up, and not knowing our exact whereabouts, we were caught between both barrages. The excitement and horror was terrible. I shall never forgot the whining of those missiles of death, which seemed to want you each time one came.

Captain C.A. Brett
2ND BATTALION, LEINSTER REGIMENT

We passed through an area where the Americans (then comparatively very rare as infantry in France, at any rate with us, rather than with the French) had been in action the day before and the fields on each side of the road (not now the main Peronne Road but a side road off it, leaving Peronne on our right) were strewn with literally hundreds of dead American soldiers, with hardly a dead German to be seen. We deplored their (very heavy) loss, but put it down to their inexperience of warfare. Nowhere through the war did I see so many dead as there.

Lance Corporal Thomas Healy
2ND BATTALION, ROYAL IRISH REGIMENT

On September the 26th, we left this desolate spot at 2 p.m. and marched to a little village, or rather a large one named Queant, about 10 kilometres away. The whole place was one mass of ruins; here were the remains of what seemed to be a kitchen, there broken pieces of furniture lay around, with scarcely any notice taken of it; we passed through to the outskirts, and there lay down in shell holes to rest. Soon we began to feel intensely cold, as the night advanced, and at 11 p.m. they gave each man a tot of rum (what a blessing!). It invariably happens that before any large attack it rains, so it did not fall on us now, but it came down in torrents. At 11.30 p.m. we fell in again and moved off. It was terrible walking, drenched through to the skin, with one's steel helmet falling over one's eyes and the rifle would persist in banging against one's legs, or slipping off the shoulder, added to which every minute some poor unfortunate would slip into a shell hole. We had just passed the artillery lines, when 'Zip, Crash', a 'Whiz Bang' dropped amongst us. These are shells which can only be described by pronouncing the name which burst upon you without the slightest warning, so giving no chance of safety. In our Platoon alone, we had 7 casualties. One fellow had his head knocked off, and it was so dark that we could only recognise him by a white cup hanging on his bayonet.

Lance Corporal Thomas Healy
2ND BATTALION, ROYAL IRISH REGIMENT

No poet has ever, or I suppose shall ever describe the feelings truly which a man going over the top, in the grey dim light of early dawn experiences, and every minute we were losing men, by the bullets and shells with which the enemy attempted, though feebly, to stop our rush. We arrived at Canal du Nord, where the opposition was expected, but the German gun teams had left, probably not able to withstand our barrage. Fortunately, the canal was dry, so we jumped into it, and crossed over to the other side. My clothes and puttees were nearly in ribbons, torn by the barbed wire, which was lying about the ground everywhere, cut down by the shelling.

The objective lay between the villages of Inchy and Molueres; prisoners were coming over by the score, with their hands above their heads crying 'Mercy Kamerand'. No escorts accompanied them, but they just ran back, reporting at the first dressing station. We now came to a chaulk [sic] trench, where we found three German Officers hiding in a dug-out. Our Company was the 'Mopping up' Company, or was in reserve to the other three of the Regiment, so we stayed here and established Headquarters. Searching in the magnificently made dug-outs, we obtained a great many enemy revolvers, and thousands of cigarettes. Some kept the small revolvers, but I did not trouble. I am sorry now that I missed the opportunity.

Lieutenant Edwin Godson
9TH BATTALION, ROYAL IRISH FUSILIERS

What desolation. The Boches left this country in the great retreat last March and laid it waste high and low before going. No houses, no crops, no civilians, just a barren waste of rank weed and grass. The roads have been made up and are good. Spent a most uncomfortable night. Our kits had not arrived. Till 3 am I lay on the floor and woke up then stone cold, borrowed a blanket and lay again till 6 am and then my kit had come and I had a better sleep. Seems bleak and windy in this country and makes one feel very far from home.

Private A.R. Read
HQ, 141ST INFANTRY BRIGADE

We were in action for 13 days during which we had detachments of American troops from the 131st REGT, who were attached to our front line Battalions for instruction. Each detachment had 48 hours in the front line. They seemed to like being in action, although several started doing a lot of bragging. This we quite understood, especially as they were new troops and also owing to the fact that things at the moment were fairly quiet. To prove to them that Jerry wasn't asleep some of our lads stuck up a tin of bully or a French periscope. Naturally the Jerry snipers soon got busy and they were all crack shot. After this the braggers all went quiet and the Sammies as we soon nicknamed them were quite ready to rejoin their units when the time came around.

Captain C.A. Brett
2ND BATTALION, LEINSTER REGIMENT

We had to advance much further than anyone else then had, and we were at the extreme point of a sharp salient, with the Germans behind us on both sides. This they soon discovered and began to shell us unmercifully, so that my company suffered a number of casualties, and the shelling continued all day! I will never forget the look of horror on the face of one of my men, as a splinter of shell disembowelled him, in the seconds or moments before he died. Another had one of his legs almost amputated just at the knee, and I with my penknife severed the few scraps of flesh and sinew which held it together before tying him up and sending him back (where I wonder) on a stretcher.

Lance Corporal Thomas Healy
2ND BATTALION, ROYAL IRISH REGIMENT

At the time, I was sitting at the bottom of the trench, half-asleep, when I woke up, by receiving a terrible heavy, hot thump on the left thigh, and another in my left hand. There were three killed, and several wounded by it, myself among them, so you can imagine what a mournful cry for the stretcher bearers was set up. I had my knocks dressed fairly quickly. I was covered with blood, and just felt like giving up the ghost at once.

There were so many casualties that day, the 27th, that there were no stretchers vacant, so I had to wait for an hour, although quite conscious the whole time. The shells were still dropping round, and I was scared of receiving another dose. Eventually, two German prisoners, carrying a stretcher, picked me up. They carried me down to the aid post where an American RAMC Officer put a few more bandages on me. Then four more Jerries took hold of the stretcher and bore me down to the Corps Dressing Station, at Queant, about four kilometres away. I do not remember now much about that journey, except that it was terribly cold, lying there without moving, but I managed to have a couple of smokes, to while away the time.

Private A.R. Read
HQ, 141ST INFANTRY BRIGADE

We passed a good many dead Germans, mostly machine gunners who had been left behind to hold up our advance. The rumour was that these Jerries were mostly sacrifice troops, who had had orders to kill as many of our Tommies as possible, before giving themselves up. They had certainly accounted for a good number of the Royal Fusiliers (58th Division). Officers and men were strewn all along the road, some simply cut to pieces, the majority being only 19 years old. Needless to mention, not many of the Jerries had been taken prisoner. Yes the bayonet had seen to that.

Captain C.A. Brett
2ND BATTALION, LEINSTER REGIMENT

We were told that the Germans were holding the last line of their prepared trenches and that we might expect to get into open country if we were lucky. There was no sleep for anyone that night, and the next morning just before dawn we got off behind a very heavy barrage, in company with four tanks. The tanks were a great help to us. They drew fire from the enemy who were so busy shooting at the tanks that they paid little attention to us (the tanks were all knocked out before we had gone very far). So we had a fairly easy job putting the Germans out of their trench and getting into open country beyond. Our first objective was a village called Serain about a mile behind the German line.

On our way there, we passed several batteries of German field guns which they had tried to get away; the horses they had brought up to pull out the guns had been caught by our shell-fire and killed or dreadfully wounded; many were screaming pitifully. Alas we could do nothing for them to put them out of their misery; I hope that some of those who followed us did. When we got to the outskirts of Serain, our guns were shelling heavily, and we were held up (as it is unpleasant to be shelled by one's own guns), but up came a reconnaissance aircraft about one hundred feet up and I was able to signal to its observer with a piece of flashy tin. He saw and understood, and waved at me; and a few minutes later the guns lengthened the range, and we were able to enter the village, which was full of terrified civilians and also several German snipers, who gave trouble till they were found and liquidated.

Acting Captain T.H. Witherow
8/9TH BATTALION, ROYAL IRISH RIFLES (1918)

Since the previous day the continual roar of the guns had never ceased and the sound seemed to be nearer. Here we were walking along a country road. It might have been in Ireland. A band practising in a neighbouring farm was playing 'The Last Rose of Summer' and only a few miles away the greatest battle in the history of the world with all its tragedies was being fought. Still we were not downhearted and were ready for whatever should happen.

Captain C.A. Brett
2ND BATTALION, LEINSTER REGIMENT

A feature of all the German hutted camps were vast wooden latrines, labelled 'Abort', always in duplicate, one for men suffering venereal disease and one for those who were not. And what really shocked me was the 'venereal' aborts were twice the size of the clean ones. And the whole area smelt of Germans, a horrid but highly distinct smell.

Private A.R. Read
HQ, 141ST INFANTRY BRIGADE

News came through that our attacking Divisions had captured 7 thousand prisoners, 100 guns, besides a large number of machine guns, stores, ammunition, transport columns, etc, and further reports stated that our cavalry were in action, meeting with only slight resistance. Patrol fighting continued on our sector, several prisoners were brought in, who stated that they had been on outpost duty for 18 days and finding there was no hope of being relieved, they gave themselves up.

Captain C.A. Brett
2ND BATTALION, LEINSTER REGIMENT

Unfortunately, several delayed action mines had gone up on the Amiens side of the train, so it had become immobile. And as quickly as the engineers mended one place, another went up. So our high command ordered German prisoners to be employed to search for mines along the railway. We foot soldiers highly disapproved, but nothing could be done about it. The Germans who laid the mines were highly skilled technicians, and those made to search for them were poor devils of ordinary soldiers who had no idea of what they were looking for or how to find it, so quite a few of them got blown up. Those who had given this most inhumane order were not the sort of people who were likely to be taken prisoner, as we were.

Private A.R. Read
HQ, 141ST INFANTRY BRIGADE

Talking to some civilians, mostly women, they told us that all the men and boys, from 15 upwards had been taken away by the Germans, who made them work. Those left behind had been nearly starved and the women's clothes were very old fashioned. Boots were mostly black canvas tops, with wooden soles. The bread was nearly black in colour and was like rubber. For coffee they had a substitute which looked like and smelt like burnt sawdust. Apart from this all they had to eat was vegetable soup and potatoes and when we showed them white bread, chocolate, sugar, bully beef and bacon, well it nearly caused a riot. Sorry to mention but many a French woman that day, offered herself for food. Naturally we gave the kiddies anything that we could get from our canteen.

Acting Captain T.H. Witherow
8/9TH BATTALION, ROYAL IRISH RIFLES

Every road was now a sad sight with the long unending stream of French peasants going they knew not where but only trying to escape the dreaded foe. Whole families with their farm carts packed with the most valuable of their possessions, and perhaps a cow, filled the roads mingled here and there with military. A look of

sadness and intense hate was on the faces of one and all, for the
Frenchman dearly loves his home. What a scene of confusion it was,
and the sadness and tragedy of the whole thing and the look of
hopelessness on the faces of these poor homeless people made an
impression on one's mind that time will not obliterate.

Captain C.A. Brett
2ND BATTALION, LEINSTER REGIMENT

As soon as the Armistice happened, the roads were full of refugees
returning home, and of many thousands of British and French
prisoners of war, hungry, ragged and tired, but overjoyed to see us,
the first British troops. There was little we could do for them, but
many were picked up and taken back by lorries to some place where
they were presumably looked after. All the cattle in these parts were
suffering from *fievre aptheuse*, foot and mouth disease; we were
forbidden to buy milk or butter or to drink or eat either if invited
to do so. Many young women in the towns and villages round about
had their heads shaved, because they had been too friendly with the
Germans, but they and the unshaven were most anxious to be
friendly and more than friendly with the British troops.

Private David Starrett
HQ, 119TH BRIGADE

Bethune, when we reached it again, had changed from a town of
laughter and song to a shambles. Women killed in their nightgowns,
men lying stark naked by bursts, children disembowelled, babes
smashed to pulp. War is certainly a beast from hell.

Private A.R. Read
HQ, 141ST INFANTRY BRIGADE

The London Irish Pipe Band took the attention of everyone. The
reason was, perhaps, that they were the first Irish pipers to have
been seen in this part of France. At 10.30 am we moved off, passing
through Loome. The civilians lined the streets and started cheering
us. In front of our brigade was the 142nd Brigade, consisting of the
22nd, 23rd, and 24th Londons, while behind us was the 140th

Brigade, 15th, 17th and 21st Londons. Reaching a pontoon bridge, we passed over the canal and entered the gates of Lille and this was when the fun really started. This was really a huge town, and it took us all by surprise when we saw the houses and streets packed with people. The Brigadier-General was on horseback just in front of us and he came in for no end of fuss, while us cyclists were greatly admired or at least our cycles were, because they had real rubber tyres while the civvie bikes we noticed only had wooden tyres. Flags were hanging everywhere and directly we were spotted coming along into the town, well the crowds just let themselves go. It was 'Vive La France', 'Anglais Soldat' and plenty of nice compliments which nobody understood. Then flowers were thrown at us. Some of the women held up their babies to be kissed. As we were marching 'to attention' we could not look round or acknowledge the cheers. Then the Pipers struck up and it was all we could do to save ourselves from being mobbed.

Captain C.A. Brett
2ND BATTALION, LEINSTER REGIMENT

I was attached to Battalion Headquarters (and learned for the first time how much more luxuriously they lived compared to us Company Officers). Several people came out to join us including French, and I tried to teach illiterate soldiers (mostly from Connemara) to read and write, and enjoyed it a lot. I discovered that what they really wanted was (1) to sign their own name and (2) to read the bookies odds in a newspaper, and I did my best to oblige.

Private David Starrett
HQ, 119TH BRIGADE

The population, especially the young, were intoxicated by the release of the oppression, and gave us all a good time. Our boys did enjoy themselves for there were enough girls to go round, fickle maids who took enjoyment as they could and were thankful. But some of the older women, standing in doorways and at the back of the crowds, wore the far-away expression we'd seen so often in what have been so well called the devastated areas. They didn't see us, or if they did they saw us wearing the faces of fathers and husbands and sons they'd never see again. Nor did they seem to see the girls changing from Tommy to Tommy like robins hopping from branch to branch. They saw in their mind's eye the daughters and sisters done to death by bestiality or within padded cells by reason of the ordeals they'd suffered. Well, we only gave what we gained—a good time, and maybe all were better for our passing.

Private A.R. Read
HQ, 141ST INFANTRY BRIGADE

Some of our Tommies who had been taken prisoners began to trickle into town. The first two were from the Welsh Guards and Machine Gun Corps. They told us of the dirty treatment dished out by the Germans. A little later thousands of men and boys who had been made to work for the Jerries were released, also hundreds of young women and girls. The prisoners included French, Russian, Italians, Belgians, and British. They were quite a pitiful sight. They had all sorts of nondescript clothing, many were with wooden clogs or rags wrapped around their feet, some had bandages (made from paper) on wounds which were maggoty, while all looked verminous. They had been half starved and knocked about. Naturally they were overjoyed to meet us. Some broke down and cried like kids. They were put on lorries and send back to Lille, where they were well looked after.

Private Felfus Long
25TH BATTALION, NORTHUMBERLAND FUSILIERS (TYNESIDE IRISH)

Rumour began flying about that they were discussing peace and also an Armistice but we never got to know anything definite till the riots started on the coast. It soon spread to the soldiers and they started raiding the railway wagons, etc, in search of bread.

After this they started wearing the red rosette and soon after we had the Red Flag flying over the camp. Our Feldwebel got a bit frightened and smashed a statue of the Kaiser, throwing it into the fire.

On November the 9th the Revolutionists all marched in a body to Soltau and disarmed all the officers they came across. At Soltau they had a meeting as to what to do with the prisoners, and on Sunday morning we had a roll call, and delegates of the revolutionists came and spoke to each nationality. One fellow could speak English very well and he told us, or rather asked us, to keep strict neutrality on the revolting question as it was a German movement only. However, they kept very decent to us so we did nothing. A few days later they asked us again to keep on working till we went away for by now the armistice had started. On November 15th, which is a day I shall not forget in a hurry, me and [my] Belgian pal received 7 parcels between us which was the most we'd ever had. I got the first parcel of white bread and didn't we have a feed after that. It was about this time the weather started to change, and it became terribly cold, freezing night and day and we were glad enough to work inside. On Sunday Nov 17th we went to the church at Soltau and I enjoyed it very much. In the sermon the parson said (for he was a German), 'We are the defeated, the vanquished, and I want you to go home without hatred in your hearts for now we are one people.' It was quite allright [sic] him saying this but we shall never forget what the Germans did to the women and children of Belgium and France and also there [sic] treatment to the prisoners.

Private David Starrett
9TH BATTALION, ROYAL IRISH RIFLES

So the curtain fell over that tortured country of unmarked graves and unburied fragments of men: murder and massacre: the innocent slaughtered for the guilty: the poor man for the sake of the greed of the already rich: the man of no authority made the victim of the man who had gathered importance and wished to keep it. Greed and lust for power, that was the secret. We were said to be fighting to stop future war, but none believed that. Nor ever will.

Lieutenant Percy McElwaine
B COMPANY, 14TH BATTALION, ROYAL IRISH RIFLES

On 10th November we got word that the Germans asked for an armistice. Next morning I got a telegram that Evelyn [his wife] was dangerously ill. I at once applied for leave but could not get it. Next day I got it and set out. When I got to 55 Primrose Mansions, Mrs Mack opened the door. She said I must be brave so I knew the worst. Evelyn was dead of influenza on the 10th. She was dead before the telegram reached me. She was in her coffin which had not yet been closed. I spent the night sleeping beside the coffin. Before it was closed I had her wedding ring put in: it had been removed and I felt she would have liked to be buried with it. She was looking forward to becoming a mother in April.

GLOSSARY OF BATTLES

The Battle of Loos
The Battle of Loos took place during September and October 1915. The key objective of the British forces was the capture of the French town of Loos-en-Gohelle. The Irish Guards were heavily involved in the fighting, and it was during this battle that Rudyard Kipling's son John was killed in action while serving with the regiment. The London Irish famously became known as the 'footballers of Loos', when members of the battalion dribbled a football across No-Man's Land as they attacked the German lines. The battle also saw two firsts: the British Army used poison gas in an attempt to weaken German resistance, and the Royal Flying Corps flew the first close air support missions. However, the battle did not break the German defences, despite considerable British casualties.

The Battle of the Somme
The Battle of the Somme, or more accurately the Somme offensive, was a series of interlinked battles which took place from July to November 1916. Both the 16th (Irish) Division and the 36th (Ulster) Division took part, suffering heavy casualties as a result. The Somme offensive is now remembered as a disastrous error on the part of the British generals, and has come to symbolise the futility of the First World War. Yet, as many of the accounts in this book show, the men who fought at the Somme saw it, despite the massive loss of life, as a victory from which they went on to win the war.

The Battle of Bazentin Ridge
This was one of the battles which formed the Somme offensive. It was fought on 14 July 1916. The goal was the capture of the village of

Bazentin-le-Petit. The area was held by the elite German 3rd Guards Division. Despite early British success, the attack was ultimately unsuccessful.

The Battle of Ginchy

Ginchy was another battle within the overall Somme campaign. It was fought in September 1916 for control of the town of Ginchy. The town was captured by the 16th (Irish) Division in one of the most successful minor battles of the whole offensive.

The Battle of Messines

This battle was fought in June 1917, and was the most successful British operation of that year. It resulted in a clear British victory, in no small part won by the 16th (Irish) Division and the 36th (Ulster) Division, who fought side by side and captured all of the objectives assigned to them. It is a battle perhaps best remembered for the mining operations associated with it. The British had tunnelled under the German positions and stored a vast amount of explosives there, which they detonated on the opening of the battle. It was the largest man-made explosion prior to the use of atomic weapons and it has been claimed that the blast was even heard in Dublin.

The Battle of Cambrai

Cambrai is one of the most famous battles of the First World War. It took place towards the end of 1917, and saw the first major deployment of tanks in battle, with over 400 being used in the assault on the German positions. Despite the use of tanks, and over 70,000 casualties, there was no real breakthrough. From an Irish perspective, one of the most interesting points is that a substantial part of the British plan was drafted by H.H. Tudor, who went on to command the Royal Irish Constabulary and the Auxiliaries during the Irish War of Independence.

The Battle of Passchendaele

Fought during the months of November and December 1917, Passchendaele has written itself into history as one of the bloodiest disasters ever experienced by the British Army. Tens of thousands of men were lost in futile and unimaginative operations which only occasionally resulted in minor tactical victories. The aim of the battle was to capture the Belgian town of Passchendaele. It was, however, a complete strategic failure, and did little to enhance the reputation of the British generals with Lloyd George and his cabinet.

Kaiserschlacht/The Spring Offensive

The collapse of Russia allowed the release of the German divisions on the Eastern Front, and they were moved to France. The German Government hoped to launch a final offensive which would end the years of stalemate on the Western Front. Like the Somme offensive, *Kaiserschlacht* was a series of battles: the Battle of the Lys, the 3rd Battle of the Aisne and the 2nd Battle of the Marne, to name a few. Ludendorff's plan was to capture Paris and force a French surrender and a British withdrawal. It almost succeeded. However, the failure of the offensive exhausted the German Army; it had used up nearly all of its resources in this final throw of the dice and, with American entry into the war, German defeat was inevitable.

The Hundred Days

This series of battles included Amiens, 2nd Somme, and the Battles of the Hindenburg Line. During these battles, the Allied Forces were able to fuse all the past lessons of trench warfare and finally break through the German lines, restoring open warfare to the Western Front. Using a new tactical model of combined arms—i.e. the integration of artillery, airpower, tanks and the infantry—the Allies crushed the German Army, forcing Germany to sue for peace and end the war.

BIOGRAPHICAL NOTES

This book has been created from the recollections, diaries and personal papers of thirty-two men who served in various Irish regiments in the First World War. They include men both from Ireland and from the Irish community in the United Kingdom, and they come from all social classes. Some did not see the end of the war. Woodroffe, Daniell, Rixon, Speed and Trefusis were all killed in action on the Western Front. Many of the others created a post-war career in the British Army. William Carden Roe served in Palestine in the 1930s and later in the Home Guard during the Second World War. Henry Crowe spent the remainder of his career in the Royal Air Force. Gerald Burgoyne served in the post-First World War British Mission to Poland, and later worked with the Red Cross in Ethiopia. Sergeant T.D. McCarthy retired from the British Army a Major; and Gerald de Pass as a Colonel.

Others left the services and pursued new careers in civil life. Percy McElwaine returned to the legal profession and practised law in Canada and Kenya, before becoming Chief Justice of the Straits Settlements. He was to spend the Second World War as a prisoner in the notorious Changi prison camp in Singapore. C.A. Brett returned to Ireland and spent the rest of his life as a solicitor in Belfast. T.H. Witherow joined the clergy.

Many of those who returned from war faded back into society, returning to live in Ireland and the United Kingdom. However, their families ensured that they would not be lost to history and gave their papers to the Imperial War Museum and the Liddle Collection at the University of Leeds Library. It is with their gracious permission we can now restore the voices of these men to Irish history.

SELECT BIBLIOGRAPHIES

The following lists are not intended to be comprehensive; rather they are suggested reading for those who wish to continue to learn about the First World War in general and the Irish experience in particular. These are books which I have found both compelling and engaging.

Select Bibliography of General Works

Holmes, Richard, *Tommy: The British Soldier on the Western Front* (London, 2005)

Keegan, John, *The First World War* (London, 1999)

Sheffield, Gary, *Forgotten Victory: The First World War: Myths and Realities* (London, 2002)

Stevenson, David, *1914–1918: The History of the First World War* (London, 2005)

Strachen, Hew, *The First World War: A New History* (London, 2006)

Select Bibliography of Irish Works

Bowman, Timothy, *Irish Regiments in the Great War: Discipline and Morale* (Manchester, 2004)

Denman, Terence, *Ireland's Unknown Soldiers: The 16th (Irish) Division in the Great War* (Dublin, 2008)

Dungan, Myles, *They Shall Grow Not Old: Irish Soldiers and the Great War* (Dublin, 1997)

Falls, Cyril, *A History of the 36th (Ulster) Division* (London, 1998)

Grayson, Richard, *Belfast Boys: How Unionists and Nationalists fought and died together in the First World War* (London, 2010)

Horne, John, *Our War* (Dublin, 2008)

Jeffery, Keith, *Ireland and the Great War* (Cambridge, 2000)

Murphy, David, *The Irish Regiments in the World Wars* (Oxford, 2005)

Orr, Philip, *The Road to the Somme* (Belfast, 2008)

Richardson, Neil, *A Coward if I Return, a Hero if I Fall: Stories of Irish Soldiers in World War I* (Dublin, 2010)

INDEX